Tokyo Rose

TOKYO ROSE

ROSE

Orphan of the Pacific

MASAYO DUUS

translated from the Japanese by Peter Duus

Introduction by Edwin O. Reischauer

KODANSHA INTERNATIONAL LTD.

Distributed in the United States by Kodansha International/USA, Ltd., through Harper & Row, Publishers, Inc., 10 East 53rd Street, New York, New York 10022; in Canada by Fitzhenry & Whiteside Limited, 150 Lesmill Road, Don Mills, Ontario; in Mexico and Central America by HARLA S.A. de C.V., Apartado 30-546, Mexico 4, D.F.; in South America by Harper & Row, International Department; in the United Kingdom by Phaidon Press Ltd., Littlegate House, St. Ebbe's Street, Oxford OX1 1SQ; in Continental Europe by Boxerbooks Inc., Limmatstrasse 111, 8031 Zurich; in Australia and New Zealand by Book Wise (Australia) Pty. Ltd., 104–8 Sussex Street, Sydney 2000; in the Far East by Toppan Company (S) Pty. Ltd., Box 22 Jurong Town Post Office, Jurong, Singapore 22.

Published by Kodansha International Ltd., 2-12-21 Otowa, Bunkyo-ku, Tokyo 112, and Kodansha International/USA, Ltd., 10 East 53rd Street, New York, N.Y. 10022 and 44 Montgomery Street, San Francisco, California 94104. Copyright © 1979 by Kodansha International Ltd. All rights reserved. Printed in the United States of America.

FIRST EDITION, 1979

Designed by Gloria Adelson

LCC 78–60968
ISBN 0–87011–354–2
JBC 0023–787185–2361

To Erik and his generation

Contents

Illustrations

Introduction

Pearl Harbor—Zeros—General Tojo—Guadalcanal—Iwo Jima—kamikazes—Tokyo Rose—Hiroshima. These are all names that bring back deep waves of emotion for any one old enough to have lived through the Pacific war. Even for their juniors, these names may still stir reactions. All conjure up places, weapons, or people significant in that terrible war—all save one, Tokyo Rose. A mere wartime myth, Tokyo Rose was to become a postwar disgrace to American justice.

The name Tokyo Rose suggests no scenes of slaughter or destruction. It was simply the name the American fighting man in the Pacific humorously pinned on the voices of English-speaking girl broadcasters who announced in disc-jockey fashion shortwave programs of popular music emanating from the Japanese side. Some of these voices may have added a modicum of war propaganda, and of course other parts of the Japanese shortwave broadcasts were full of propaganda, since that was their underlying purpose. But there was certainly no single "Tokyo Rose," nor was any person ever discovered who had traitorously engaged in propaganda activities against the United States in the fashion attributed by some to "Tokyo Rose." Most of the American listeners had actually developed a whimsical affection for the American-sounding feminine voices offering them programs of music they enjoyed hearing.

But the myth of an alluring, siren-voiced "Tokyo Rose," who undermined the morale of the American fighting man, was a powerful one. It was pursued pantingly by journalists, hungry for a scoop. It was taken up by counterintelligence officers and then by civil law officials more eager to prove themselves relentless bloodhounds on the trail of malefactors than upholders of justice and the individual human rights of which we today are so conscious. It was tolerated by politicians and other public figures who, at a time of growing witch hunts, did not wish to appear to be soft on traitors. It was egged on by a public still much under the influence of traditional racial prejudices and far from free of the anti-Japanese hatreds of the recent war.

The myth of "Tokyo Rose" settled on a helpless and hapless young Japanese American girl, Iva Toguri, who had been stranded by the war in Japan. The whole story is sad and often sordid. She herself was naïve and foolish. Some of her colleagues, as well as the newspapermen, army officers, and law enforcement officials involved, were self-serving in various ways—to protect themselves, to gain notoriety, to evade politically dangerous decisions, or simply to vent their own particular spites. There were a few semiheroes, but a host of semivillains—the common run of callous, egocentric, small-minded, or even vicious people. American justice showed up very badly indeed. Throughout, the case was pursued more for political reasons than to mete out justice. Harassment, intimidation, distortion of the truth, even falsification of evidence by so-called law enforcement officers proved all too common. There was clear judicial bias and a press seeking sensationalism rather than the truth. It is not a pretty picture, but hardly as surprising to us today as it would have been a couple of decades ago.

The tragedy of "Tokyo Rose" basically grew out of the unhappy position in which the *nisei,* Americans born of Japanese parents, had been placed. Caught between two civilizations, and more or less rejected by both, they strove bravely to find their identity. The story of how all the Japanese on the West Coast, whether they were American citizens or not, were rounded up and herded into virtual concentration camps is undoubtedly the most disgraceful incident in America's whole World War II record. Despite this outrageous treatment, the vast majority of the *nisei* opted to be 100 percent American. Through a spectacular record of loyalty and valiant combat service, they eventually won full acceptance in the United States, as attested to today by several respected and powerful Japanese American members of the Senate and Congress.

It is sad to note that Iva Toguri was harassed and then jailed for years as the mythical "Tokyo Rose" basically because she was so American. She steadfastly refused to do the easy thing in wartime Japan and accept Japanese citizenship. She remained confident of final American victory, and of American justice. She refused to abandon the United States, though her country, by playing false to its own ideals of justice, certainly abandoned her. One is reminded of the fact that the *nisei* who had the most trouble and were therefore the worst "troublemakers" in the so-called relocation centers for West Coast Japanese were precisely those who were the most confident of their Americanism—the men who had fought in American uniform.

The Tokyo Rose story is a dwindling sidelight on the history of the Pacific war. But it is a powerful reminder to Americans today of the dangers of racism and the need for true justice.

EDWIN O. REISCHAUER

Foreword

Over thirty years have passed since the defeat of Japan in World War II, yet many tales are still to be told about the wartime and postwar years in Japan. One is the story of Iva Toguri d'Aquino, a Japanese American woman falsely accused of being the infamous traitor, Tokyo Rose.

I first became interested in this story a dozen years ago when my husband and I were living in St. Louis. The nearest place to buy imported goods from Japan was North Clark Street in Chicago. The trip was long, but it was worth it. We went there every three or four months. After stocking up on Japanese canned goods, I would usually browse in the book section of the Toguri Mercantile Company, a store we particularly liked. No other place on North Clark had such a good selection of magazines and books from Japan.

The book section was usually attended by an elderly Japanese American gentleman who spoke little but exuded an air of calm. He always smiled or nodded when I took a purchase up to the counter. But one day I was waited on instead by a Japanese American woman. I remember that day very well, for the woman made an unusually strong impression on me. As she crisply wrapped my purchase, she raised her head and stared at me for a moment. I was startled. Her eyes were not those of an ordinary shop clerk trying to please a customer. They were eyes that told you not to come near, and the face behind them was expressionless, almost like a Japanese Nō mask. That evening, as we dined with friends, I could not put the woman out of my mind. What peculiar secret lurked in her past?

About a month later I was surprised to see that same face staring at me from a photograph on a back page of the St. Louis *Post-Dispatch*. To fill space, the paper had run a short feature article on American traitors and what had become of them. Side by side with Alger Hiss, the Rosenbergs, and several World War II traitors was the woman who had waited on me in Chicago. The face in the picture was younger than the one I had seen, but there was no mistaking it. The caption identified her by a name I had not expected: Tokyo Rose.

I was a child in Japan during the years of the American Occupation, and I remembered the name of Tokyo Rose, but I had not known that a person by that name had been tried for treasonous activities. My curiosity was aroused. I went to the library to learn more about her, but all I found were books of a sensational sort that described her briefly along with Mata Hari and other famous women spies. I was disappointed that I could not learn more about the woman or how she had become involved in treason.

In 1973 my husband and I moved to the San Francisco Bay area. In the library one day, intending to begin a study of the history of Japanese Americans in the United States, I suddenly decided to look up entries on Tokyo Rose in the *New York Times Index*. At that moment the research for this book began. The *New York Times* led me to local Bay area newspapers, and they in turn led me deeper in the story of the Tokyo Rose trial. I was hooked. My research continued for the next three years. I was especially lucky to discover that the transcripts of the trial were located in nearby San Bruno, and so I began to commute there every day, working my way through the long and complex stack of trial documents.

Along the way, many people have helped with the research and writing of this book. I am indebted first of all to the staffs of the Stanford University Library, the Hoover Institution, the National Archives Repository at San Bruno, the National Diet Library in Tokyo, the NHK Library in Tokyo, the Australian National Archives, and the National Archives in Washington, D.C. I am grateful to Clarence Kelly, former director of the Federal Bureau of Investigation, for releasing FBI investigatory files on the case.

I would also like to thank a number of individuals. Dr. Clifford I. Uyeda of the Japanese American Citizens League was extremely helpful in discussing the case with me and putting me in touch with many of the principals involved. Without his cooperation and support the research on this book would have been difficult indeed. Among the many people who consented to talk with me personally about the case, I would especially like to thank Wayne Collins, Ruth Hayakawa, Stanton Delaplane, Frederick G. Tillman, Tetsujiro Nakamura, Norman Reyes, Edison Uno, Katherine Pinkham, Ken Murayama, Leslie Nakashima, Nicholas Alaga, Michi Onuma, Paine Knickerbocker, Dwight Ryerson, and Joe Gorman.

Iva Toguri d'Aquino kindly consented to meet with me, and she talked with me many hours by long-distance telephone. Without her help I would not have been able to confirm many of the details that were part of the public record or to learn of some that were not. It must have been trying for her to recapitulate memories of her unhappy experiences, especially since we usually talked at the end of her busy working day. I was glad to learn more about the person behind the eyes that first startled me, and to know that there is often humor in those eyes too.

For other kinds of help I would like to thank my sister-in-law, Louise Duus, for having the manuscript typed, and my son, Erik, for his patience at those times when he wished his mother were not writing a book. My husband, Peter, was a constant source of good suggestions, useful information, and moral support; I am also indebted to him for taking time to render the original Japanese version of the book into English.

Finally I would like to thank Professor Edwin O. Reischauer for kindly consenting in the midst of a busy schedule to write an introduction to the book.

Masayo Duus
Stanford, California

Tokyo Rose

Prologue

On July 5, 1949, the last World War II treason trial opened in San Francisco at the Federal District Court for the Northern District of California. The defendant was a slender, alert-looking Japanese American woman named Iva Ikuko Toguri d'Aquino. She is remembered today by another name—Tokyo Rose.

The trial of Iva d'Aquino proved to be one of the longest and costliest on record. It lasted nearly three months and cost the government more than half a million dollars. On September 29, 1949, the jury rendered its verdict: innocent on seven counts, guilty on one. The prosecutor told inquiring reporters that the United States government thought the verdict a just one, rendered after patient and persevering deliberation. Most of the public agreed. There were others who did not. Iva's family did not, her lawyers did not, reporters who covered the trial did not, and the jury foreman did not. But nothing happened. There were no protests in the liberal press as there were for Alger Hiss, nor worldwide demonstrations as there were for the Rosenbergs. Iva d'Aquino never became a cause célèbre for anyone, not even for the Japanese American community, which regarded her indictment as a shameful blot on its otherwise unblemished record of wartime loyalty.

Yet the trial and conviction of Iva d'Aquino may have been one of the most egregious miscarriages of justice in American legal history. Just a

year before the trial took place, both federal attorneys who served on the
prosecution team—Tom DeWolfe and Frank J. Hennessey—had come
to the conclusion that the government did not have sufficient evidence for
a prima facie case against Iva d'Aquino, and both had opposed trying a
case that the government might not win. The Department of Justice decided to prosecute anyway. The Truman administration was facing a
difficult election, and it was anxious to dispel mounting criticism that it
was soft on treason. So Iva became a victim of politics, and of a government bent on bringing in a guilty verdict by whatever means it could.

The government brought Iva to trial in a city with a long and deep-
rooted history of anti-Japanese feeling; the government took pains to select an all-white jury; the government had no tangible evidence—recordings or broadcast transcripts—to prove Iva had made treasonous broadcasts, so it relied on witnesses who themselves had repudiated American
citizenship; the government may have known that two of these witnesses
gave false testimony; and in the end, a tired but patriotic judge, convinced of Iva's guilt, refused to rule a hung jury when the jurors at first
could not reach a verdict.

Yet if Iva was a victim of injustice, it was because she was also victim
of a legend. In 1945 she had become identified as Tokyo Rose, the sinister Japanese radio propagandist who lured American fighting men in
the Pacific to surrender and death. No such person as Tokyo Rose ever
existed. She was a figment of the imagination, a GI-created legend em-
bodying the American stereotype of the Japanese as sadistic and sub-
human. But legends are often more powerful than truth, and before she
was ever convicted in court, Iva d'Aquino had been found guilty by the
press and by a public that had not forgotten Pearl Harbor.

How did it all happen, and why? The following pages tell the story.

CHAPTER 1

The Search for
Tokyo Rose

Race for a Scoop

General Douglas MacArthur, Supreme Commander of the Allied Powers, alighted from his plane at Atsugi Airfield in Kanagawa, Japan, on the afternoon of August 30, 1945. It was a historic moment, the first time a conquering commander had set foot on Japanese soil.

Early that morning a group of Allied journalists had flown in from Okinawa by B-17 to cover the event. Prominent among them was Clark Lee, thirty-eight-year-old correspondent for the Hearst-controlled International News Service. Lee, a handsome six-footer with smooth black hair, heavy-lidded eyes, and a suntanned complexion, was one of the most glamorous correspondents on hand. After graduating from Rutgers with a journalism degree in 1929, he had worked for Associated Press on a series of overseas assignments. His fame had come in 1941, when the outbreak of war caught him in Manila en route home for a vacation. He stayed on in the Philippines, sending highly regarded dispatches from the besieged island fortress of Corregidor. After barely escaping on the

last submarine out, he had covered the beginning of the American coun-
teroffensive.

Some thought his 1943 book, *They Call It Pacific,* an account of his
experiences, was one of the best on the Pacific war. Rumor had it that
Lee might even win the Pulitzer Prize that year. Lee was hired away
from Associated Press in May 1943 by International News Service,
whose president told him, "I'm going to make another Richard Harding
Davis out of you." Armed with a better salary and the prerogatives of a
roving reporter, he went on to the European front. By the closing days of
the war he still had not won his Pulitzer, but he had become one of the
best-known American correspondents, like Ernie Pyle, a "trained seal"
who sent back vivid and personal accounts of the war's progress.

Sitting beside Lee was a rather different sort of man, a short, chubby,
balding fellow with a whiskey-reddened face. His only distinctive feature
was a thin and well-tended mustache. This was Harry Brundidge, a forty-four-year-old reporter for *Cosmopolitan* magazine, which like INS
was part of the Hearst empire.

In contrast to the dashing Clark Lee, Harry Brundidge was something of a has-been, a flamboyant leftover from the freewheeling journalism of the Prohibition era. He was a character out of *Front Page.* Brundidge had made his name in the 1920s as a crime-busting reporter for
the St. Louis *Star Times.* His specialty was dramatic exposés of crime
and corruption, and he built a reputation as a hard-hitting investigative
reporter with a string of sensational crime scoops: he had exposed the
notorious Egan gang, a St. Louis murder and extortion ring, by extract-
ing a confession from one of its leaders; he had worked as a deckhand on
a rum-running ship to expose its operations between Havana and New
Orleans; he had investigated narcotics smuggling on the Mexican border;
he had exposed a medical diploma mill by posing as a student; and he
had written a series of articles that eventually helped solve the kidnap-
ping of Adolphus Busch Orthwein in 1931. Brash, sly, and self-drama-
tizing, he was always on the side of justice—and always a step ahead of
the police.

By the late 1930s Brundidge had shifted to reporting international
news for the *Star Times.* He first went to cover the China war in 1939,
then to London to cover the blitz in 1941. The next year he left the *Star*

Times to become associate editor of *Cosmopolitan,* spending most of his time at the European front. But his work as a foreign correspondent showed considerably less panache than he had displayed as a crime buster. He was clearly not in Clark Lee's class. He was also known to have a fondness for alcohol, and sometimes reeked of it early in the day.

Lee and Brundidge were both old Japan hands, and they had become acquainted while reporting on the Japanese campaigns in China. They had met again in Okinawa as the Americans were preparing for the final move into Japan. The evening before their departure for Atsugi, the two men had struck a bargain to work together when they got to Japan. Lee had received a telegram from his home office telling him to find Tokyo Rose.

"When we get to Atsugi, let's scram for Tokyo," said Lee.

"Right," answered Brundidge.

"And grab Tokyo Rose."

"It's a deal," agreed Brundidge.[1]

When the reporters landed at Atsugi just before dawn, the air was tight with apprehension. Although advance parties had arrived in Japan without incident two days earlier, the Americans found it hard to believe they would be able to land on Japanese soil so easily. They had seen their fill of kamikaze attacks and Japanese soldiers fighting to the death rather than surrendering. Everyone was tense with doubt and uncertainty. "The atmosphere," Lee recalled, "was that of an invasion, a beachhead, an assault landing."[2]

As it turned out, the anxiety was misplaced. After gingerly walking across the landing field to the mess hall where breakfast was waiting, Lee suddenly found himself face to face with an old acquaintance. "To my amazement," Lee wrote, "the first white-coated waiter in the wooden mess hall called out my name, 'Ree-san! Herro, herro. So grad you returning to Japan.' "[3] Lee recognized him as a former waiter of the Imperial Hotel grill room in Tokyo. The Japanese government, knowing that hotel waiters usually spoke a few words of English, had rounded some up and taken them to Atsugi to make the Americans feel at home.

It was difficult for the reporters to relax during breakfast, for each of them wanted to be the first to write an eyewitness report of war-devas-

* Notes begin on page 234.

tated Tokyo. No sooner had breakfast ended than the correspondents rushed out to the fleet of old-model cars the Japanese had assembled for them. Lee, Brundidge, and Joe McGlincy, a special correspondent for United Press, climbed into a battered old Plymouth and ordered their driver to Yokohama.

The American military headquarters, uncertain about conditions in Tokyo, did not know whether dangerous or hostile elements were still active there. The military authorities had advised that it would be best not to enter Tokyo until the formal surrender ceremony had taken place. Only one road was officially opened to Yokohama, and Japanese sentries stood posted all along the way, their rifles pointing outward to protect the arriving Americans from trouble.

Lee and his party were determined to get to Yokohama quickly, so they told their driver to ignore the prohibition and get there by a back route. As they drove along they surprised a number of Japanese who were up and out of doors, not expecting the American army to go by. "Seeing us," said Lee, "the women covered their faces and turned their backs, the children scattered in terror, and the men stood stonily."[4] The conquered Japanese were as apprehensive as the conquering Americans.

The reporters' spirits began to rise. They did not sense much danger, and they began to see some of the American airborne troops who had landed earlier. By the time they reached Yokohama the reporters decided to stop at the Yokohama Grand Hotel for a beer, just to see what would happen. They got not only beer but the proper change, too. If things were this safe in Yokohama, they could be no different in Tokyo. "Let's get going," said someone, and off they sped—or rather, limped. So did several other parties of reporters.

As the decrepit cars bumped along crater-pocked Route Number 1 from Yokohama to Tokyo, some began to boil over. Whenever one broke down the other reporters would speed by, jeering their hapless colleagues—only to stop themselves a few hundred yards down the road. It was a bizarre scene, a Mack Sennett chase unfolding amid the charred ruins. The Japanese drivers began to get into the spirit of things, urging on their gasping cars like jockeys.

On the edge of Tokyo at Rokugobashi, the first bridge into the city, stood a barricade guarded by a cluster of Japanese soldiers carrying bayoneted rifles. An English-speaking soldier told Lee and his friends that Americans would not be allowed to enter the city until the official occupation had begun. The reporters kept pressing him, until he finally waved them on. Unfortunately they had lost their lead to another car, and their race to become the first American reporters in Tokyo failed.

They drove on through the devastated city to the Imperial Hotel, designed by Frank Lloyd Wright. Part of the hotel had been destroyed by the wartime bombing raids, but some rooms remained in use. Lee asked the clerk for Room 312, which he had often occupied before the war, and Brundidge pulled from his pocket the key for Room 384, a souvenir he had picked up back in 1940. (Brundidge, as we shall see, was an inveterate souvenir collector.)

When Lee told the tale of his race to Tokyo to the court in 1949, the audience was entranced. One reporter commented, "It was a movie script right out of MGM, and could have been played by Clark Gable instead of Clark Lee." (The thought may have occurred to Lee, too. When his book, *They Call It Pacific*, was made into a movie, the leading man was Clark Gable.) In hindsight, however, the reckless rush of the correspondents into Tokyo a scant two or three hours after their arrival in Japan seems foolhardy in the extreme. It can be understood only as a reflection of the relentless drive of the wartime reporters for news.

At the end of World War II print journalism was far more competitive than it is today. Twice as many cities had two or more newspapers then than now, and most daily papers published several editions a day. The fight for readership was intense. Every newspaper, especially those with large newsstand sales, tried to boost circulation with sensational stories and eye-grabbing headlines. Competition was intense among reporters, even those working for the same publication or news company. Everyone fought for scoops, which was what they got paid for. War correspondents were no exception.

In the first days of the occupation of Japan, more than 230 journalists arrived. There were so many they spilled out of their assigned billets in the Dai-ichi Hotel into rooms and houses hastily offered for rent by the Japanese. The occupation, perhaps responding to MacArthur's well-known penchant for managing the news, sent all but seventy-six out of Tokyo at the end of September 1945. In the meantime the same spirit of competition that prompted the car race to Tokyo continued unabated. Reporters seemed to be everywhere. "In the first few days after our entrance to Tokyo," noted one GI journalist, "practically every story was a rat-race of newspaper correspondents, photographers, magazine writers, and assorted trained seals seeking 'exclusives.' "[5] Since the American occupation forces had not yet settled in place, the reporters had the run of the city, often moving more freely, and more rashly, than the military themselves.

The Mysterious Tokyo Rose

Clark Lee later recalled that all the reporters in Tokyo at war's end were after three big stories. One was the first eyewitness report of what the war-ruined enemy capital looked like; another was an exclusive interview with General Hideki Tojo, the man who headed the Japanese government at the time of the Pearl Harbor attack; and a third was to find the mysterious Tokyo Rose, the radio siren whose wartime propaganda broadcasts had angered and amused the Pacific GIs. Of the three, the last presented peculiar difficulties, for no one named Tokyo Rose had ever existed. She was not a person but a legend, with no more substance or reality than Paul Bunyan.

It is not easy to understand how legends begin, even if they are of recent origin. The legend of Tokyo Rose is no exception. By the end of the war there was probably no American soldier in the Pacific who had not heard the name "Tokyo Rose" or met someone who claimed to have heard her broadcasts. But curiously enough, no one knows who invented the name, when it was first used, or even why a Japanese broadcaster should be dubbed "Rose" rather than Sally (as in Axis Sally) or Mary (as in Typhoid Mary) or for that matter something else.

Stanton Delaplane, a San Francisco columnist who covered the trial as a reporter, thinks the name "Tokyo Rose" was probably invented by a journalist. Shortly before the war broke out, "Mexicali Rose," a popular hit song of the 1920s, had enjoyed a revival, and perhaps it suggested to some unknown newsman a name appropriate for a Japanese woman propagandist. The name might also have been a carryover from World War I, when a whole bower of foreign "Roses" blossomed in popular song—"The Roses of Picardy," "My Belgian Rose," "The Rose of No Man's Land," and "The Rose of Montmartre." The last of these "Roses," like the Mademoiselle from Armentières, was a lady of easy virtue, so perhaps there is a clue there. By the 1920s, Tin Pan Alley had found "Rose" a handy name for dusky beauties from far-off lands, among them, "Mexicali Rose." But the fact remains that probably no one will ever know the origin of the name "Tokyo Rose."

Equally mysterious is when the name was first used to describe wartime Japanese women announcers. According to some, it was heard shortly after the Pearl Harbor attack, when "Tokyo Rose" is supposed to have broadcast: "Do you know where all the American ships are? They are at the bottom of Pearl Harbor." At the time of the treason trial, witnesses gave a variety of answers to the question. Clark Lee testified that he probably first heard the name while at Bataan in April 1942, and certainly no later than the time of the Solomon Islands campaign. Another witness, James Whitten, said he heard it around the time of Midway in June 1942. Williston Cox, a former army lieutenant, heard it in New Guinea around January or February 1943; and Mae E. Hagedorn, an amateur radio hobbyist who monitored Radio Tokyo broadcasts from the Pacific Coast, noted the name Tokyo Rose in her log for the first time on July 25, 1943.

Whenever the name was first heard, it was certainly in general use in the Pacific by the summer of 1943 and well established by 1944.

It is not difficult to explain the spread of "Tokyo Rose's" celebrity. For troops in the combat zone, where there were few amusements and no sex, and where the boredom of waiting was punctuated only by the tension of battle, "Tokyo Rose" was perfect as a topic for idle banter. Gradually she became a kind of vocal pinup girl, more interesting and in some ways more real than glossy pictures of Betty Grable or Rita Hayworth. Since no one knew anything about her as a person, she was all the more fascinating, perfectly suited to become the object of imaginative speculation. So the legend grew.

Like Paul Bunyan, the legendary Tokyo Rose was larger than life. She was a seductive and vicious woman who sat far off in the enemy capital ridiculing the GIs as dopes who did not know what their wives and sweethearts were doing back home while the GIs struggled against the

mighty Imperial Japanese army on the lonely islands of the Pacific. She
was scurrilous, she was foul-mouthed, and she was awesomely omni-
scient. She had eyes everywhere. She always seemed to know where each
American military unit was going and when it would get there. She even
called individual soldiers by name and chatted about their hometowns.
Rumor had it that she made some GIs so homesick they were driven to
suicide. Like the Sirens who lured Ulysses, she was a witch who hypno-
tized GIs with her seductive voice and music, enticing them to surrender
or to death.

Legends, like rumors, flourish in time of war. They start with a few
facts, which fantasy then bends out of shape. Japanese propaganda
broadcasts could be heard by anyone within reach of a shortwave radio,
and many of the announcers on the Japanese programs were women. Indeed, the so-called Tokyo Rose broadcasts had become a favorite recreation for many of the GIs by the latter stages of the war. In March 1944
the *New York Times* reported from the Pacific, "If a radio popularity
poll could be taken out here among American fighting forces, a surprisingly large number of votes would go to Tokyo Rose and other of the
programs beamed from the Land of the Rising Sun to the advancing
American bases in the South and Southwest Pacific."[6] Two months later
the *Times* reported that among the enemy broadcast announcers enjoyed
by the Pacific GIs, the two most popular were "Madame Tojo," who
could be heard from the South Pacific to Alaska, and "Tokyo Rose,"
who could be heard mainly in Alaska and the Aleutians.[7]

It should be clear that Americans were not referring to one individual
woman announcer when they talked about "Tokyo Rose." Rather they
seem to have given the name, as well as an occasional variant like "Madame Tojo" or "Radio Rose," to any woman announcer they heard on
Radio Tokyo. Some American GIs later insisted that the voice of Tokyo
Rose was the voice of one particular woman, but there was no agreement
on which one. It seems more likely that the name was attached to a variety of broadcasters—disc jockeys, news broadcasters, and news analysts.
Indeed there is even a strong possibility that some of the so-called Tokyo
Rose broadcasts were made by male announcers.

When the sound of the real women broadcasters mingled with the stories about the sinister Tokyo Rose, it was difficult for the wartime GIs to

distinguish where fact left off and legend began. Spinning stories about Tokyo Rose was a recreation that did no harm. Besides, the stories about Tokyo Rose exactly fit the stereotype the Americans had of their enemy. The Japanese were seen as devious, scheming, cruel people whose arrogant and brutal soldiers sadistically delighted in tormenting their captives.

In 1945, just as the war was ending, Tokyo Rose appeared on the comic pages of American newspapers. In the middle of an episode about a plot to build a Japanese Superman, a sinister, slanty-eyed Tokyo Rose broadcast a challenge to the American superhero: "Attention, Superman. Don't think you're the only superman in the world! A famous Japanese scientist's producing some real competition for you—a real, honest-to-goodness, flesh-and-blood superman—Nipponese version. So look out, Superman in America!"[8] Legend had made Tokyo Rose into a stock Oriental villain, a Dragon Lady or a female Fu Manchu, and the name was fixed in the popular imagination.

At the same time, apart from the sinister and vicious Tokyo Rose of legend, there were also the real women announcers, collectively dubbed "Tokyo Rose" by the GIs, whose broadcasts could be heard from Radio Tokyo. On August 7, 1945, the navy issued a citation honoring this "Tokyo Rose" for her contributions to the morale of the Pacific armed forces:

> While the United States armed forces in the Pacific have been extremely busy capturing enemy-held islands, sinking Jap ships, and killing Japs and more Japs, Tokyo Rose, ever solicitous of their morale, has persistently entertained them during those long nights in fox-holes and on board ship, by bringing them excellent state-side music, laughter, and news about home.
>
> These broadcasts have reminded all our men of the things they are fighting for, which are the things America has given them. And they have inspired them to a greater determination than ever to get the war over quickly, which explains why they are now driving onward to Tokyo itself, so that soon they will be able to thank Tokyo Rose in person.

The citation was tongue-in-cheek, but many Pacific GIs would have agreed with it.

"Tokyo Rose," then, was both the vicious legendary siren and the humorous Radio Tokyo woman announcer. Both had star quality. It is no wonder that finding her was one of the top stories the American news-men were after in 1945.

Speculation about this mysterious lady was a source of diversion for reporters, too, and rumors about her flourished in great variety and pro-fusion. Some said she was the wife of Saburo Kurusu, the last Japanese ambassador to Washington; others said she was General Tojo's mistress; or a hula dancer born in Maui; or a *nisei* woman born in Ottawa; or a white woman from St. Louis married to a Japanese named Oroguchi. And so on, and so on.

The most fascinating rumor of all was that Tokyo Rose might be Amelia Earhart, the famous woman pilot who disappeared in midflight over the Pacific in 1937. During the war rumors circulated that she had crashed near the island of Saipan, then being fortified secretly by the Japanese. After being taken prisoner by the Japanese, she had been forced to make propaganda broadcasts to the United States. Earhart's husband had even gone to the Pacific theater to hear the "Tokyo Rose" broadcasts in order to determine whether or not his wife was the an-nouncer. The Earhart-Tokyo Rose theory continued to tantalize many reporters. Lee later recalled that everyone thought that if Tokyo Rose really did turn out to be Amelia Earhart, it would be the biggest news since Pearl Harbor.

Nevertheless, it is doubtful that the American correspondents believed they would in fact find a real live flesh-and-blood Tokyo Rose when they got to Japan. In early August 1945, for example, the *New York Times* reported the results of a study prepared by the U.S. Office of War Information:

> There is no Tokyo Rose; the name is strictly a G.I. invention. The name has been applied to at least two lilting feminine voices on the Japa-nese radio. . . . Government monitors listening in twenty-four hours a day have never heard the word "Tokyo Rose" over a Japanese-controlled Far Eastern Radio. . . .[9]

Still the news value of the name was a force to be reckoned with. If by some 1,000-to-1 chance a Tokyo Rose really did exist, it would be an enormous scoop for the man who found her. It was a gamble hard to pass up.

The search for Tokyo Rose began on the evening of August 30 when a small group of reporters stormed into the office of the Overseas Bureau of the NHK (Japan Broadcasting Corporation) demanding to meet Tokyo Rose. Only a few employees were left at the station. They were astonished to see the Americans, .45 automatics at their sides, barging into the station in such an excited state, before the war had even formally ended. The reporters were the first of many, and to all of them the Japanese gave the same evasive replies. "We had scores of newspapermen coming into our offices asking for Tokyo Rose," recalled Kenkichi Oki. "This continued for the first week or ten days. We had no particular reason to know, so we evaded the questions about Tokyo Rose as much as possible. We said we don't know what you mean by Tokyo Rose."[10]

Sometimes the Japanese Overseas Bureau staff even turned the question around, asking the reporters who Tokyo Rose was. They were trying to protect the announcers who had participated in propaganda broadcasts to the Americans. Yoshio Muto, chief of the Overseas Bureau, had told his subordinates to be friendly to the reporters but to give only vague answers, and not to mention any names. In fact, since none of the announcers on Radio Tokyo had ever used the name Tokyo Rose, a completely American invention, their claims of ignorance were not wholly false.

Lee and Brundidge at Work

Fact or legend, Tokyo Rose was still one of the hottest stories around, and though some reporters found no such person existed, others still pursued their search.

On September 1 the *New York Times* carried a wire service item:

YOKOHAMA, Japan, Aug. 31 (AP)—The American fighting man has found frustration at the end of the long road to Japan—"Tokyo Rose" is a figment of the fertile brains of the propaganda office. Or is she?

...An American-born Japanese girl who guided reporters through Yokohama said "Tokyo Rose" was any number of different girls who spoke the English language....

...She claimed she knew of at least three who worked at being Tokyo Rose. The story bandied about Tokyo, she said, was that two were *nisei* born in Los Angeles and the third was born in Canada.

Now the guide speaks nice English, was born in Downey, Calif., returned to Japan in 1940, and says she has been working for Domei for two years. Every time she mentioned "Tokyo Rose" to any of the correspondents she smiled slyly.

"Really," she protested. "Tokyo Rose was a mystery even to us Japanese. We never heard her. She was on short wave."

H-m-m-m-m. Come on now, guide, weren't you "Tokyo Rose"?[11]

The obliging guide was Asako Satō, a *nisei* who worked for Domei News Agency. She was not involved in propaganda broadcasts herself, but she knew two of the girls who had been. Their names were Ruth Hayakawa and Iva Toguri. It was an interesting lead, but the reporters in Yokohama never got a chance to pursue it. Clark Lee and Harry Brundidge were already closer to the quarry.

On August 30, after their wild dash into Tokyo, the two Hearst reporters took up temporary residence at the Imperial Hotel in Tokyo, once again enjoying the amenities of civilized life. After lunch they wandered through the burned-out downtown sections, then headed for Domei News Agency to cable out their first impressions of postwar Tokyo. They found to their dismay that they could not. General MacArthur, who had a strong dislike for reporters, had issued orders that all stories filed from areas under his command could be sent out only after clearance by his headquarters. The two newsmen decided to return to Atsugi. According to his later account, Lee suddenly remembered the telegram from his home office to get a story on Tokyo Rose.* The two men did an about-face, returning immediately to the Domei Agency, where they got hold of Leslie Nakashima, an old friend of Lee's, a Hawaii-born *nisei* who had worked at the Tokyo UP office before the war.

Nakashima did not know who Tokyo Rose was, but he offered to help Lee and Brundidge find her. Together the three men went to the NHK Overseas Bureau. They talked with four or five *nisei* who worked there, but received the same evasive replies that other reporters had. "They gave no direct answer—neither yes or no," Lee later testified. "They didn't identify her. . . . [But] we assumed that they would know who it was."[13] Since they seemed to be getting nowhere on the Tokyo Rose story, the two men decided to return to Atsugi to file their other stories. Be-

*Brundidge wrote that the two men had started looking for Tokyo Rose from the time they left the hotel but, as happened so frequently, his memory was at variance with everyone else's.[12]

fore they left, Brundidge asked Nakashima, "Find out who Tokyo Rose `
is for me. If you find her, I'll give you $250."[14] (According to Lee's testi-
mony, the amount was between $250 and $500.)

The sum was tempting. In September 1945 the yen exchange rate was
fifteen to the dollar, so $250 amounted to around 3,750 yen. At the time
many Japanese families lived on less than 100 yen per month. Brundidge's offer was a small fortune. But Leslie Nakashima was not interested in the money alone. He felt an obligation toward Clark Lee, who
had helped his family through some hard times before the war. Mrs. Lee
had been particularly kind to Nakashima's ailing wife when she became
an invalid as the result of tuberculosis. It was natural for Nakashima to
want to return the favor.

According to his deposition, Nakashima had heard the name "Tokyo
Rose" on foreign news broadcasts during the war. On the morning of
August 31 Nakashima went to the NHK offices, where he asked Kenkichi Oki if he knew who Tokyo Rose was. Oki was at first evasive, replying that no female announcer had used that name. But Oki did go on to
say there were five or six female announcers on the popular "Zero
Hour" broadcasts. Nakashima asked for their names. After thinking for
a moment, Oki gave him one—Iva Toguri d'Aquino.

When Clark Lee returned to the Imperial Hotel that morning after
spending the night at Atsugi, he got a telephone call from Nakashima,
who relayed the results of his investigation. Nakashima later testified
that Lee was disappointed. He still did not know who Tokyo Rose really
was. He told Nakashima he would think about the matter, then hung
up. A short time later, Lee called back. Find Iva Toguri, he said. He was
prepared to offer her $2,000 for an exclusive interview.[15]

Lee's recollections, however, were a bit different. He claimed that Nakashima came rushing into the Imperial Hotel on the afternoon of August 31. "We were in the lobby," said Lee, "and he said something to the
effect that he had found a Tokyo Rose. I don't know whether he said *a*
Tokyo Rose or *the* Tokyo Rose."[16] Brundidge turned to Nakashima and
told him to tell Tokyo Rose that if she agreed to an exclusive interview,
Cosmopolitan magazine would pay her a fee of $2,000. The interview
should be arranged if possible, he said, on the following day, September
1, at nine thirty in the morning.

Lee said that the offer of $2,000 for an interview was Brundidge's idea, done on his authority as an associate editor of *Cosmopolitan*. But the two men had agreed that after Lee used the exclusive interview as the basis for a general newspaper article, Brundidge would turn it into a detailed feature story for *Cosmopolitan*. To judge from the fee Brundidge offered, the news value of the Tokyo Rose story was substantial indeed. The sum of $2,000 (or about 30,000 yen) was a staggering amount of money to most Japanese, and it was substantial even by United States standards. An ordinary American white-collar worker could probably live on that amount for six months in 1945.

Clark Lee had not made his name as a correspondent by sitting still. It was his usual practice to get the beat on other reporters by cabling a headline to the home office in anticipation of a detailed story. He would then send the text on by teletype. With a story this big in his hands, he did not change his habits. On the evening of August 31, even before he had interviewed Iva Toguri or checked out the story, he sent a cable to his home office identifying her as Tokyo Rose. So while other correspondents were still speculating about the true identity of Miss Satō, the affable guide in Yokohama, Clark Lee was laying the groundwork for another scoop.

On September 1 (U.S. time) the Los Angeles *Examiner* carried Lee's cabled lead line: "Propagandist Tokyo Rose No. 5, one of the Japanese radio sirens who used to amuse Yanks with clumsy propaganda, was revealed yesterday to be Iva Toguri d'Aquino, L.A. born."[17] The local staff of the *Examiner,* who had done some fast investigation of their own, added a few biographical details about Iva Toguri. According to the article, she was a graduate of UCLA in zoology and had had above-average grades. The paper even ran her graduation photograph, probably found in a university yearbook. The picture hardly matched the image conjured up by the name Tokyo Rose, for it showed a serious-looking young woman wearing steel-rimmed glasses, mortarboard, and academic gown. To be sure, the paper did not identify Iva Toguri as *the* Tokyo Rose, merely as "No. 5."

If there was still an element of uncertainty involved in the identification, however, it was soon to be dispelled with the help of Iva herself. On the morning of September 1 (Tokyo time), Leslie Nakashima visited Iva

Iva Toguri's UCLA graduation picture, 1941

Toguri d'Aquino and her husband, Filipe J. d'Aquino, at their two-room flat in Setagaya-ku on the suburban outskirts of Tokyo. Following Brundidge's instructions, Nakashima explained to the couple that a large number of correspondents had arrived in Tokyo looking for a big story on the identity of Tokyo Rose.

Iva replied that she was not Tokyo Rose. She said there had been a number of female announcers on the "Zero Hour" program, and she was only one of them.

Her name was the only one given out at the Overseas Bureau, replied Nakashima, so there was bound to be a crowd of reporters coming after her soon. If she gave an exclusive interview to *Cosmopolitan,* however, the other reporters were sure to give up the chase. Besides, he said, she would get $2,000 for the interview. She could kill two birds with one stone.

Iva still seemed to be reluctant to go ahead with the interview. But her husband Filipe chimed in, reiterating that giving an interview would help keep other reporters away. So Iva agreed to go with Filipe and Nakashima to meet Lee and Brundidge at the Imperial Hotel.

It was probably merely a matter of time before someone discovered that Iva Toguri best fit the name of "Tokyo Rose." On August 8 the *New York Times* had reported, "When servicemen speak of Tokyo Rose, they refer to the mistress of ceremonies on the Zero Hour dinner-time program. She has a girlish voice and a manner described as gay and clever. Her apparent purpose is to make her listeners homesick. The entertainer calls herself 'Annie of Radio Tokyo,' 'Little Orphan Annie,' or 'Your favorite enemy, Annie.' "[18] Since Iva Toguri d'Aquino was "Orphan Ann," she was the most likely candidate to be the GIs' Tokyo Rose. (The reference to her "girlish voice" presents problems, however, as we shall see later.)

Evidently Iva's name had been uncovered at NHK by reporters on August 31, but the Overseas Bureau staffers pretended they did not know where she lived, so the newsmen began to hunt for her.

One of the first to find her address was Sergeant Dale Kramer, a reporter for *Yank* magazine, who had been given directions by Kenkichi Oki. When he visited the d'Aquino apartment on the evening of August 31, no one was at home, so he left without waiting. "It was a big mistake," he later lamented.[19] But it was even worse luck for Iva herself. Had she been interviewed by the GI reporter from *Yank* rather than Lee and Brundidge, her eventual fate might have been much different.

At the appointed hour of nine thirty on September 1, Clark Lee, looking out the window of his second-floor room at the Imperial, saw Leslie Nakashima enter the hotel with a young man and woman. A moment later the three of them were at his door, and a step behind them was Harry Brundidge. For the first time Iva Toguri d'Aquino met the two men who were to change her life.

The meeting was not particularly momentous, nor did any of its participants have an inkling it would develop into a major public affair. Lee and Brundidge were thinking only of their scoop, and Iva, though bewildered at suddenly finding herself a celebrity, was delighted at long last to meet with some fellow Americans again. The atmosphere, as Iva later testified, was quite pleasant. Little did she know that the meeting was the prologue to the Tokyo Rose witch hunt.

"It Should Have Been Ava Gardner"

Clark Lee and Harry Brundidge were an odd couple, but they did have one thing in common. They had been trained in a school of journalism that prized the big story, the big scoop, the sensational headline. Neither was particularly profound or sensitive, even by the standards of yellow journalism. They knew what kind of news would sell papers for their editors, but they were not especially concerned over the human cost that news might exact.

Although they had missed being the first reporters in Tokyo, Lee and Brundidge scored a number of journalistic coups during their first week or so in Japan. Not only did they manage to find the elusive Tokyo Rose, they also wangled an interview with former Premier Hideki Tojo. Their encounter with him—although ten days after their interview with Iva—reveals a good deal about their methods of operation. They seemed as interested in making news as in reporting it.

During the first confused days after the American correspondents arrived in Japan, the American Counter-Intelligence Corps (CIC) decided to prohibit journalists temporarily from entering Tokyo. To enforce the prohibition, military police were posted at the two main highway bridges leading into Tokyo from the south. The resourceful Lee and Brundidge, as old Japan hands, circumvented the ban by going to Tokyo on the train, which was not under MP scrutiny. By bribing a former member of the Japanese *kempeitai* (military gendarmerie),* they managed to find out Tojo's address and proceeded to pay him a visit. While the three of them sat on chairs in the garden of his modest house, the former premier obligingly gave them an interview.

On September 12, the day after the interview, Lee got word that General MacArthur had ordered the CIC to arrest Tojo as a war criminal. Ever alert, Lee and Brundidge decided on the bold plan of persuading the former prime minister to turn himself in to MacArthur in their company. They arrived at Tojo's house ahead of the CIC, only to find a crowd of other reporters waiting. When the MPs finally arrived to make the arrest, a shot rang out from inside. The waiting reporters, Lee and Brundidge among them, rushed pell-mell into the house, muddy shoes and all. Tojo had shot himself in the chest. In the confusion, while MPs and reporters were milling about, Brundidge noticed that the bullet had gone right through Tojo's body into a chair cushion. He slipped it into his pocket. "Best souvenir of the day," he later whispered to Lee. "There can't be two of these."[20]

Lee was already working on the new scoop. He found a telephone in the office of a nearby lumbermill. While he was calling, his interpreter rushed in sweat-soaked and wild-eyed. "Tojo is dead," he shouted. "Are you sure?" asked Lee. "Yes, I saw him die," replied the interpreter. "It's terrible. Everybody is taking souvenirs. They have no respect for a dead man." Certain that Tojo was dead by his own hand, Lee phoned the story to Bill Dunn, a CBS reporter staying at the Dai-ichi Hotel. He told Dunn to cable a headline back to the States right away: "TOJO SHOT HIMSELF WHEN AMERICANS CAME TO ARREST HIM AND DIED SHORTLY AFTERWARD."[21] The story would follow.

Unfortunately his time-tested technique did not work this time. When he returned to the house once again, he learned that Tojo's heart was

---

*The *kempeitai* was the police agency of the Japanese army. During the war, it was involved in the suppression of defeatist activities, anti-war movements, and even labor unrest in addition to enforcement of military discipline and order.

still beating. What was he to do? The other reporters had already lined up to use the telephone, so he could not call Dunn to cancel the story. The only thing left was to make sure the headline would be accurate. At Brundidge's suggestion he and Lee rolled Tojo's prostrate body over in the hope of hastening his demise. They had the opposite effect. A massive hemorrhage brought on by moving him saved the former premier's life.

Lee was still in a cold sweat, but not about the state of Tojo's health. He was worried about his embarrassing headline cable. He was able to rest easy only after he got back to his hotel and found he still had time to cancel the transmission.

In comparison with this adventure, interviewing Iva Toguri d'Aquino was as easy as twisting a baby's arm.

Lee and Brundidge were a bit put off by Iva's appearance when they first saw her in Lee's hotel room. Tokyo Rose, the GIs' idol, wartime woman of legend, should have been gorgeous and alluring. Instead there stood Iva, slightly tense, looking like a schoolgirl. To Lee and Brundidge she seemed about twenty years old, although in fact she was twenty-nine. "It should have been Ava Gardner," Iva later recalled, "but instead it was me."[22]

Iva stood just a bit over five feet tall, her hair in pigtails. She was wearing a reddish brown vest over a yellow blouse and *monpe*, a kind of pantaloon slacks. She was stocky, her face squarish, her eyes bright and intelligent, her jaw firm. Her only distinguishing feature was a large mole just below her right nostril. She was clearly a person with a good head, and probably a strong will, but even by the farthest stretch of imagination, she was not sexy, nor even very feminine.

After the two reporters recovered from their surprise, Brundidge was the first to speak. "Are you Tokyo Rose?" he said to Iva. According to Lee's trial testimony, Iva replied very clearly that she was in fact "the one and only Tokyo Rose." But his account varies from that of others, including Iva herself. Iva testified that after Brundidge asked the question:

I said, "Mr. Brundidge, there are five or six girls who that name should apply to. I am one of them." He said, "You worked at Radio Tokyo, didn't you?—You announced introductions to records. You were a sort of

disc jockey, weren't you?" I said, "Yes." Mr. Lee said, "Oh. I think she
will do." And he directed his words to Leslie Nakashima. "You went to
Radio Tokyo. Someone at Radio Tokyo gave her name out, didn't he?"
Leslie said, "Yes." "Then she will do. We aim to get a story. We might
as well start getting the story now." . . . Mr. Brundidge went to lock the
door, and Mr. Lee went to get a typewriter.[23]

Filipe d'Aquino's testimony corroborated Iva's, and so did Leslie Nakashima's.

Lee did not swerve from his account under cross-examination, but his
version of Iva's response does not seem very compelling. Given her earlier hesitation to go with Nakashima, it seems unlikely that the first thing
she would say to complete strangers was that she was "the one and only
Tokyo Rose." The phrase sounds more like a journalistic embellishment
than Iva's spontaneous response.

After preliminary greetings were over, and the doors were locked as a
precaution to keep other reporters out, Brundidge proposed that it would
be best to take care of the contract first. Before the interview began Iva
signed the following document:

Tokyo, Japan

September first, 1945

This contract, entered into at the Imperial Hotel, in Tokyo, Japan, on
the above date, between Cosmopolitan Magazine, party of the first part,
and Iva Ikuko Toguri, known as "Tokyo Rose," the party of the second
part, sets forth and agrees to the following:

That Iva Ikuko Toguri is the one and original "Tokyo Rose" who
broadcasted from Radio Tokyo.

That she had no feminine assistants or substitutes.

That the story she had related for publication is to be exclusive for first
publication in Cosmopolitan, with subsequent syndicate rights for King
Features of International News Service, is her own true story, told for the
first time, and not to be repeated to anyone for publication.

Cosmopolitan Magazine, represented by Harry T. Brundidge, agrees
to pay Iva Ikuko, $2000.00 (American dollars) for the above described
rights. It is also agreed and understood that any additional monies which

might accrue from motion picture rights, publication by Reader's Digest, or any other source, shall be turned over to Iva Ikuko Toguri.

Signed (sgd) Iva Ikuko Toguri (Tokyo Rose)
Signed (sgd) Harry T. Brundidge

Witnessed (sgd) Clark Lee
I.N.S.
Witnessed (sgd) Leslie Nakashima
Domei
Witnessed (sgd) Filipe d'Aquino
Radio Tokyo

This contract later became an important material exhibit at the time of the trial.

It seems curious that Iva should have signed a contract as "Tokyo Rose" immediately after denying that she was Tokyo Rose. "I believe it was her vanity that decided her to give the full story," Lee later wrote. "After all, she was thinking—I am an international figure known to millions of American GIs and sailors—I have become world famous during the war—this story will be in nearly every paper in America and in one of the biggest magazines, and my picture will be everywhere."[24]

When Iva was questioned closely on the same point, she gave other reasons. She repeatedly said that she signed the contract because she thought an exclusive interview with *Cosmopolitan* would keep her from being pestered by other reporters. Doubtless this was part of her reason. But in early September 1945, not long after her interview with Lee and Brundidge, she gave another explanation to Sergeant Dale Kramer, the *Yank* magazine correspondent: "I heard that newspapermen had been to Radio Tokyo and that my name had been given out as Tokyo Rose. The station people didn't get in touch with me, though they knew where I was, and I figured they were trying to fix it up for me to take the rap, clearing themselves. Then this fellow from Domei came around offering money. I knew I would have to give an interview sometime, and I thought I'd get it over with. And I figured someone was going to get the money and I might as well be her."[25]

The lure of the money Brundidge offered is undeniable. In the desperately impoverished postwar conditions of Japan, it would have taken an exceptional person to resist the temptation of *Cosmopolitan*'s offer of $2,000. Iva may have thought: If Lee and Brundidge are going to make someone into Tokyo Rose, that's fine—I'll be the lucky girl. But the money offered was not the sole reason she signed the contract. After all, when Brundidge proposed to pay part of her fee on the spot, she refused.

Part of the explanation must lie in her state of mind. Iva was happy that the war had ended in an American victory, and happy that she would soon see her family in the States again. She was in a lighthearted mood, carried away by the carnival search for Tokyo Rose. She signed the contract obviously knowing that parts of it were untrue—that she had no assistants or substitutes, for example. Her husband Filipe also signed as a representative of Radio Tokyo even though he had no connection with it at all. It was almost as if they were playing a game, not realizing the enormity of the stakes.

Ruth Hayakawa, another Tokyo Rose candidate, is still puzzled by Iva's action. "No matter how popular Tokyo Rose was with the GIs," she observed recently, "she was still a Japanese propaganda broadcaster. Iva is an intelligent and sensible woman. I still cannot understand why she put herself forward as Tokyo Rose without fully considering what she was doing."[26] There is no doubt that Iva acted rashly and unwisely, and the responsibility for signing the contract is hers. She may have been after the money, and she may have wanted to return to her family a celebrity. As Clark Lee said, there might have been a streak of vanity in her, too. But whatever the case, her action was certainly naïve.

After the contract was signed, Nakashima, who had been in the room for about half an hour, excused himself and left. Then, while Iva and Filipe sat down on the bed, Lee put his typewriter on the desk and began the interview. He was an old hand at this. He fired questions at Iva, then rapidly typed her answers as she gave them. He seemed to be after a quick sketch of her life history—how she was brought up, why she came to Japan, the circumstances of her employment at NHK, and the like—but he did not go very deeply into detail. Iva did not hesitate to answer his questions. Lee later testified that she even seemed to be enjoying the interview. Brundidge asked no questions himself, leaving everything to Lee and wandering in and out of the room, not even bothering to listen the whole time. Filipe said hardly anything; from time to time he got up to look out the window, but otherwise he sat quietly beside Iva.

By the time the four-hour interview ended, Lee had taken seventeen pages of notes. Then Iva gave her autograph: "To Clark Lee, who interviewed me at the Imperial Hotel on September 1. Iva Toguri 'Tokyo Rose.' "

"I didn't think much about it," she recalled later. "They were in uniform. They always asked me to do it. They . . . said it was a goodwill gesture, so I did it."[27]

Filipe later told Tetsujiro Nakamura, who took his deposition in 1949, that he had begun to feel uneasy from the moment Iva signed the contract so blithely. But Iva herself was in good spirits. Her America had been victorious, and now she had become the celebrated and popular Tokyo Rose, the idol of the American GIs who had fought so hard to win the war.

Celebrity at Yokohama

On September 3, 1945, the front page of the Los Angeles *Examiner* carried the story Clark Lee had sent from Atsugi on the evening following his interview with Iva:

TRAITOR'S PAY—Tokyo Rose Got 100 a Month—$6.60
By Clark Lee

TOKYO, Sept. 1 (delayed)—The one and only Tokyo Rose, a Los Angeles-born American of Japanese ancestry, is willing to take her medicine.

But Iva I. Toguri, 30-year-old graduate of the University of California, Los Angeles, does not feel that she was a traitor to the U.S. for the job of trying to make American troops homesick. She was paid a miserable 100 yen monthly—$6.60 at the present exchange rate.

In an exclusive interview with this correspondent, Iva admitted that she did not think it through when she took the job nor did she consider the possibility of being adjudged a traitor to her country. She said she believed Americans would enjoy her music and laugh at her propaganda. Miss Toguri said that circumstances forced her into broadcasting on Tokyo's Zero Hour.

Iva with her husband, Filipe d'Aquino, in 1949

She was caught in Japan on her first visit in 1941, shortly after her graduation as a zoologist at UCLA, she said, and rather than impose on relatives she went to work first for Domei, then Radio Tokyo.

Two days before, Iva had been identified in the press merely as "Tokyo Rose No. 5." Now she had become "the one and only Tokyo Rose," and for the first time branded publicly as a "traitor." Lee had not intended to write such a story before his interview with Iva, but as he listened to her the word "traitor" flashed into his mind. He later told Stanton Delaplane that he thought the word a good one to embellish his scoop. It seemed natural to use it.

Although Lee was able to make use of his interview with Iva, Brundidge soon found that he could not. On the evening of September 1, as Lee was leaving for Atsugi to file his story, Brundidge had asked him to send off a radiogram to the New York office of *Cosmopolitan*: "Succeeded in getting exclusive interview with the traitor Rose."[28] He asked the home office for authorization to pay Iva the fee of $2,000. After Lee left, Brundidge sat down to write his story, staying up late into the night to work on it.

Lee returned from Atsugi the next day with a long face. In his hand was a telegram to Brundidge from Frances Whiting, chief editor of *Cosmopolitan*. The tone was harsh. The magazine had no interest in an article on a "traitor," and had no intention whatsoever of paying out the enormous sum of $2,000. Whiting ordered Brundidge to inform the home office immediately as to why in the world he made such a contract with Iva.

Brundidge was shocked. He felt he had been slapped in the face. To make matters worse, other reporters in Yokohama, irked at having been beaten out on the Tokyo Rose story by Brundidge and Lee, were passing around copies of the *Cosmopolitan* telegram to Brundidge. He had never been so embarrassed. It is not hard to see why he was so relentless in his pursuit of the Tokyo Rose story in years to come. But more immediately he was faced with the problem of what to do about his commitment to Iva.

As things turned out, Brundidge never had to pay Iva the fee promised in the contract nor did he pay Leslie Nakashima a penny. His excuse was that Iva broke her contract by giving an interview to another reporter.

On September 3, two days after Iva's interview with Lee and Brundidge, Sergeant Kramer of *Yank* magazine paid a second visit to the d'Aquino residence. Kramer had met Kenkichi Oki at the NHK office, and Oki had introduced him to Filipe J. d'Aquino as he was on his way home from work at the Domei News Agency. With Filipe in tow and Sergeant James Keeney, another *Yank* reporter, at the wheel, he drove out to the d'Aquinos' Setagaya apartment. With them was Seizo Hyuga, a co-worker of Iva's at the Overseas Bureau and an old school friend of Filipe's. They arrived at 6:00 P.M., shortly before dinner time. "When we first saw Iva Toguri," reported Kramer, "she was bending over a small open-hearth stove, placing green vegetables in a cooking pot."[29]

The two *Yank* reporters explained to Iva that their magazine was a GI publication. Since Iva had broadcast to American troops, the magazine would like an interview with her even though they could not pay her anything as the Hearst chain could. Iva, who still had her contract with Lee and Brundidge, at first refused, but after thinking quietly for a moment she changed her mind. She realized she was talking to men representing the GIs who had enjoyed her broadcasts, so she consented to an interview.

"If I am Tokyo Rose, which it seems I am," she began, "let me tell about it from the beginning." She began to talk with Kramer, starting with her childhood in California, and covered much the same ground that she had in her interview with Clark Lee on September 1.

After the interview ended, Kramer and Keeney suggested that Iva hold a press conference for all the Allied correspondents. A press conference would be simpler than giving individual interviews to all the reporters bound to come chasing after her. Again Iva hesitated, but finally agreed. Kramer immediately put in a telephone call to Lieutenant Colonel Howell at GHQ in Yokohama. The press conference was arranged for the next day at the Bund Hotel in Yokohama.

On September 4 Iva and Filipe met with Kramer and Keeney at their office in a corner of the *Japan Times*. They set off by car to the Dai-ichi Hotel, accompanied by Kenkichi Oki, Seizo Hyuga, and Hisashi Moriyama, all employees at the Overseas Bureau.

When the two *Yank* reporters stopped in for a moment at the hotel, Oki, whose wife had also been an announcer at Radio Tokyo, turned to Filipe and said, half-smiling to cover his feelings, "I should have told them my wife's name instead of yours."[30] Now that Iva was as popular as a movie celebrity, it did not seem a bad idea to have Tokyo Rose for a wife.

An army jeep sent by GHQ met Iva, Filipe, Hyuga, and the two *Yank* reporters at the Yokohama station. The press conference was held in the main dining room of the Bund Hotel. Iva entered and found herself facing more than a hundred male and female Allied journalists. She later recalled, "The room was so crowded with reporters in Army khaki that they could hardly move. When I came in they all suddenly became quiet for a moment. But everyone seemed quite interested, and I didn't feel any hostility at all."[31]

The reporters began by asking Iva about her background. Then one Australian reporter attached to an American news company raised a more pointed question. Had she ever made a broadcast, he asked, telling Australian soldiers that Yank troops stationed in Australia were sleeping with their wives and sweethearts back home? Others began to ask if she had made broadcasts to American GIs that their wives were carrying on with 4-Fs and defense plant workers. Iva was shocked to hear such questions. She replied that it was the first time she had ever heard any of this, and she vehemently denied ever having made any such broadcasts.

Some of the reporters wondered whether Iva was in fact "the one and only Tokyo Rose." The same Australian reporter who had first asked about the content of the Tokyo Rose broadcasts got up once again. Iva recollected, "He asked me to read a phrase which he heard frequently down in the South Pacific to verify the voice, because he said my voice did not sound anything like the voice he heard in the South Pacific. I read this one phrase. . . . He told me the voice was nothing like what he heard in the South Pacific."[32]

Like Lee and Brundidge, the reporters at the conference were a little disappointed by Iva's appearance. She did not seem to fit the image of the seductive Tokyo Rose at all. But Iva, for the first time surrounded by a crowd of reporters and facing flashing cameras, played her role as Tokyo Rose with aplomb. When the questioning had ended, Keeney set up a table with a microphone on it and Iva posed for a picture behind it, as if in the midst of a broadcast. The photograph was used by many publications as one taken during the war.

When the press conference ended, Sergeant Jack Ruben of the *Pacific Stars and Stripes* took Iva and Filipe to the Yokohama Customs House, which was temporarily being used for offices by the Eighth Army. Sergeant Merrit Page, a noncom from the Counter-Intelligence Corps, politely asked them to meet with Brigadier General Elliot R. Thorpe, chief of Eighth Army CIC, who wanted to ask them a few things. After a few simple questions, Thorpe said he wanted to question them further, but since it was already after eight o'clock in the evening, he would like to continue in the morning.

That night, at Thorpe's request, the d'Aquinos stayed in the New Grand Hotel in Yokohama. An MP was posted outside the door of their room, and the door was kept locked. Wayne M. Collins, Iva's defense counsel, angrily protested at the trial that this amounted to arrest without a warrant. But Iva herself did not regard it as all that serious. On the contrary, she said, the atmosphere was fun, and it all seemed to be a big joke.

On the morning of September 5 Lieutenant Colonel Turner of the CIC took Iva to the ballroom of the hotel, which then served as Eighth Army CIC headquarters. There she was questioned by Sergeant Page from eight in the morning until about two thirty in the afternoon. His questions were not very different from those Lee and Kramer had asked, and the interrogation was carried on in a relaxed, lighthearted manner. But when word got around that the infamous Tokyo Rose was being questioned by CIC, an endless stream of soldiers and officers of all ranks began to parade in and out of the room asking for Iva's autograph. Every time another came in, Page paused in his interrogation. He made no effort to stop either them or the cameramen who slipped in and out to take pictures.

At one point in the midst of the interrogation Lieutenant General Robert Eichelberger, Eighth Army commander, called Iva to meet him in his office. During the war Eichelberger had ordered a B-29 to drop on Tokyo a package of the latest hit records addressed to Tokyo Rose. He asked Iva if she had received it. Iva said she knew nothing about it. Eichelberger thanked her for playing such nice music for the GIs, and had a souvenir photograph taken with Iva (alias Tokyo Rose) standing beside him.

There are some who take the cynical view that Harry Brundidge turned Iva in to the CIC in order to nullify his contract with her. There may be truth to this view. According to an article bylined by Mark Gayn in the San Francisco *Chronicle* on May 6, 1946, the Eighth Army began its investigation of Iva after Brundidge made a secret request that they do so. When *Cosmopolitan* refused to pay Iva the promised $2,000, Brundidge had been extremely worried that he might have to come up with the money himself. He thought he had been taken off the hook when Iva gave her interview to the *Yank* reporters, but to make doubly sure he called on Brigadier General Thorpe, the chief of Counter-Intelligence, and suggested that Iva be jailed.

But it is also possible that the CIC authorities were taken by surprise at the earlier journalistic hullabaloo over the identity of Tokyo Rose. In fact, the correspondents were banned from Tokyo shortly afterward. The CIC authorities now could hardly remain inactive when one of the women wartime propaganda broadcasters announced in a public press conference that she was Tokyo Rose. At this point, however, the CIC was mainly interested in verifying Iva's identity for the record. Consequently, their interrogation appears to have been quite casual, mainly for public show.

After the questioning ended CIC Sergeant James Fenimore took Iva for fingerprinting to the Japan Postal Building, also commandeered by the Eighth Army. After waiting there for about an hour with Filipe, who had sat in a corner of the Grand Hotel ballroom during the interrogation, Lieutenant Colonel Turner and Sergeant Page appeared once again. They told Iva that since her husband was a Portuguese citizen, her nationality status was not clearly established, and it would be all right for her to go home in her husband's custody. They also told her that they might have to call her down for questioning again. The d'Aquinos were taken home in an army jeep.

On September 6, news of Iva's press conference finally appeared in the American press. The *New York Times* carried the following story:

TOKYO ROSE TALKS, M.P.'S ARREST HER

YOKOHAMA, Japan, Sept. 5 (UP)—Military police of the United
States Eighth Army plucked Tokyo Rose from Yokohama's Bund Hotel
today and took her into custody.

The M.P.'s tapped 29-year-old pig-tailed Iva Togori [sic], California-
born Nisei who during the war had regaled United States troops with
honey-voiced chit-chat over the Tokyo radio, immediately after she finished a press conference in the hotel dining room.

It was uncertain whether charges would be filed against her for broadcasting sweet music and sour propaganda on the enemy radio. First it
must be determined if she is still a United States citizen.

Miss Togori, who said she was one of four Tokyo Roses, had just explained to correspondents she had been broadcasting "for the experience"
and did not consider herself disloyal to the United States.

(The National Broadcasting Company in San Francisco reported that
Miss Togori had broadcast again Wednesday, using her customary opening line "Hello, everyone, this is Orphan Annie speaking from Tokyo."
She was quoted as saying that she was not sure she was glad she had retained her United States citizenship, since she had just undergone questioning by the military police.)*

"Just Sitting on the Fence"

"I was just sitting on the fence as far as the war was concerned," Miss
Togori told correspondents. "I didn't think I was doing anything disloyal
to America." . . .

. . . Her voice merely announced record programs from Bach to jive.
She never, never broadcast any propaganda, she insisted.

. . . She said she had never mentioned wayward wives or sweethearts,
and she had never used the phrase "forgotten men." She remembered
hearing it only in the 1932 Presidential campaign, she said.

. . . Other Tokyo Roses included Ruth Hayakawa, another Nisei, and
June Suyama, who was born in Canada, she said.

Once again accompanying the article was a graduation photograph of
Iva in her mortarboard. A small following item reported that Iva's

---

* The report from NBC in San Francisco is particularly curious. On September 3 General Mac-
Arthur had ordered complete suspension of all overseas broadcasts from Japan, and there were no
broadcasts at all on September 5. Even if there had been, Iva could not have made one, since she was
in CIC custody on September 4 and 5.

brother and sister, then living in Chicago, were surprised at the news, and that they had not been able to correspond with Iva during the war.

Less than a week before Iva had been an unknown. But once this article appeared in newspapers across the country, and was picked up by radio news broadcasts as well, she would never be unknown again.

About a week and a half later Iva received a visit from Sergeant Jack Kadeson of the Intelligence and Education Section, Eighth Army. He asked her to cooperate in making a news film for GI audiences about her activities as Tokyo Rose. She agreed. The shooting for the film began in early October. The format was to be an interview with Iva, with flashback scenes played by professional actors showing episodes in Iva's life or scenes of GIs at the front. Iva played a flashback scene, too, showing her making a broadcast.

When the filming took place, the hallway outside the studio was crammed with GIs who had come for a look at the famous Tokyo Rose. A few lucky ones who managed to get inside asked Iva for her autograph. Since they were wearing the same khaki uniforms as the GI film crew, Iva could not tell one from the other in confusion, and so she gave away more autographs as "Tokyo Rose." At Kadeson's request she also autographed some pages of broadcast script she had given him to help in preparing the movie script.

Doubts about her identity as Tokyo Rose still bothered some. Filipe later recalled during the shooting that the movie director asked Iva, "This is your normal voice? It certainly does not sound like anything we heard in the South Pacific." [33]

Filipe had been amazed by all that had happened over the past month. His uneasiness was increasing. Iva was getting herself deeper and deeper into trouble, and Filipe was upset that she was giving away her autograph as Tokyo Rose so freely. He even seems to have thought about bringing the whole affair to a halt by going off into hiding with Iva. But Iva, who thought he was worrying too much, had not paid much attention to him. She was unshakably confident that she had not done anything wrong. Besides, she knew that even if she went into hiding, the American authorities could track her down anytime they wished.

Then even Iva began to have her doubts. As she left the studio when the shooting was over, she found herself suddenly surrounded by a crowd that even the MPs could not handle. Clutching Filipe's hand, she became frightened for a moment. As she said herself, she was not Ava Gardner, but the GIs who came to take a look at her were as excited as if she had been. Iva was learning what it meant to be a star. She was soon to learn what it meant to be a traitor.

Arrest

The furor over Tokyo Rose reached its denouement in mid-October, nearly a month and a half after it had begun. On the afternoon of October 17, Iva, who had just finished washing her hair, went to answer a knock at the door of her flat. "It was about 3:30 in the afternoon," she recalled. "Two officers,* and I think it was a master sergeant, from the Counter Intelligence Corps in Yokohama, came to my house, asked me to go down to Yokohama to be questioned on a few matters, and at the last minute they told me I may have to stay overnight, to take a toothbrush, which I did."[34] The CIC men had arrived without any announcement, while Filipe was still at work. But Iva did just as she was told. She changed her clothes, and without much thought climbed into the CIC jeep.

When Iva arrived at Yokohama, however, she found she was to be detained in the Eighth Army brig. This was Iva's second arrest. There was no warrant. The prosecution argued at her trial, however, that peacetime conditions did not prevail and that under military occupation it was perfectly normal to detain suspicious persons without a warrant. But Iva's arrest was not made simply at the discretion of the occupation army. A public hubbub over Tokyo Rose had begun in the States.

On September 13, Charles H. Carr, United States attorney for the Southern California region, held a press conference in Los Angeles, Iva's hometown. He announced that he intended to ask Washington to bring Iva back to Los Angeles for trial in federal court there. "This infamous woman—born here and educated here—used myriad artifices and devices to spread discontent and dissension among American troops," he said. "This should be a matter for local court action rather than army

---

*Actually there were three.

court-martial proceedings."[35] He said he intended to take the matter up with Attorney General Tom Clark.

The forty-two-year-old Carr, who eventually became judge of the U.S. District Court in Los Angeles, was a man on the way up. His press conference announcement may have been prompted by the newspaper articles about Iva appearing since early September, but it certainly could not have hurt his political future, particularly in an area of California where anti-Japanese feeling was particularly strong.

Carr's announcement was reported nationally the next day. It marked yet another significant step in the identification of Iva as the "traitor Tokyo Rose." It was the first time a public official—and a law enforcement officer, to boot—had so identified her. The announcement may also have precipitated the decision to put her in custody.

Iva was unable to sleep at all during her first night in the Yokohama prison. When word got around that Tokyo Rose was being held there, a constant stream of curious GIs made their way in to look at Iva in her cell. A few brought along newly acquired Japanese girlfriends. Some stood silently watching Iva's every move as though they were seeing something strange and wonderful. Others asked for her autograph. A few came to call her names and to jeer at her. The curiosity-seekers continued to come for two or three days. Iva was able to doze only in the wee hours of the morning after the sightseeing GIs had left, and she was too tired to make her morning exercise walk. She complained to the prison superintendent. From then on, only high-ranking officers were permitted a look at the famous Tokyo Rose.

After her imprisonment the CIC interrogations began again. The questioning was often startling to Iva—"Is it true that you had dinner with Tojo?" "What was your reaction to the leaflets dropped by American planes?" "Didn't you advise the Japanese government on their propaganda warfare?" Surprised to find herself regarded as a central figure in wartime Japan, Iva continued to insist that she was merely a typist who had taken a job as radio announcer. Her interrogators were skeptical. The infamous Tokyo Rose was, after all, a liar and a cheat. The CIC interrogators apparently thought that Tokyo Rose had been connected with Japanese espionage agencies. No matter how hard Iva denied it, the CIC men seemed to regard her denials as pure fabrication.

At the Sugamo prison in Yokohama, Japan

They were also very persistent in questioning Iva about why she had come to Japan in the first place. There must have been a special reason for her to have left the States suddenly in the summer of 1941, just on the eve of war.

The CIC was confused about Iva's nationality. At the press conference announcing her arrest, CIC officials stated that she had been arrested because she was an American. But in fact they had not established that with any certainty. The prison authorities were confused also. She spoke English like a native American, but looked Japanese. No matter how hard Iva protested that she was an American citizen who had not set foot outside the country until she was twenty-five years old, they had trouble deciding how to treat her. Should she be given a bed or should she sleep on a Japanese *futon* (quilt)? Should she be given American food or should she be given Japanese? It began to get on Iva's nerves.

Even worse, she was allowed no contacts with the outside. Her requests to get a lawyer or to meet with her husband were denied.

For the first ten days or two weeks after she was jailed, Iva had to wear the same clothes she had arrived in. She had brought only a toothbrush from home. By a stroke of luck she got in touch with a Swiss Red Cross worker who had been a fellow student at a Japanese language school with her during the war. He brought her some pajamas and a few other personal effects from Filipe.

Filipe, of course, had rushed down to the Eighth Army CIC office in Yokohama when he found that Iva had been taken away by CIC men. Not until several days later was he informed that his wife was being held in Yokohama prison. "I tried to see her," said Filipe, "but I was denied a visitor's pass."[36]

There was one other woman prisoner besides Iva, Dr. Lily Abegg, a husky, florid-faced German-Swiss woman who had spent several years in Tokyo before the war as a correspondent for the *Frankfurter Zeitung*. Extremely pro-Japanese, she had returned during wartime to take part in propaganda broadcasts the Germans had made from NHK studios, allegedly under the alias of Sybille Abe.

Dr. Abegg had been imprisoned about a month earlier, the only woman among the thirty-eight war criminals (including Tojo) whose arrest had been ordered by MacArthur on September 11. She was charged with cooperating with the Japanese army during the war and was suspected of being the author of Tokyo Rose broadcast scripts. For a time it was even reported that she probably was "the real Tokyo Rose."[37]

In fact, however, Dr. Abegg had no connection with the "Zero Hour" program, nor did she have any connection at all with propaganda broadcasts made by the Japanese themselves. She did not know Iva and only met her for the first time in the Yokohama prison. Nevertheless, the CIC interrogators kept insisting to her that she had written scripts for Iva, and they kept insisting to Iva that she had read scripts prepared by Dr. Abegg. The persistence with which the CIC attempted to establish a connection that did not exist tells a good deal about their investigative techniques.

The arrest of Dr. Abegg also shows the importance the American authorities attached to finding "the real Tokyo Rose." In the first days after their arrival in Japan the American authorities had discovered that several women announcers might correspond to the description of Tokyo Rose. Only Iva had stepped forward to identify herself, but it was not certain that she was "the real Tokyo Rose." Indeed the CIC had not even bothered to detain her after questioning her on September 4. Instead the army authorities apparently decided it was more important to arrest the person who wrote propaganda radio scripts than the persons who read them over the air. Unfortunately, possibly acting on rumor, they ended up arresting Lily Abegg. When they discovered their mistake, they wanted to pick up someone, anyone, connected with the name of Tokyo Rose. So they arrested Iva again. Otherwise it would have been difficult to calm public opinion.

From the time of Iva's arrest and imprisonment in mid-October, the press stopped reporting that there were several Tokyo Roses. Instead they began to deal with Iva as "the one and only." From then on, the label was to stick to her alone.

On November 16, after she had been in prison about a month, a Major Bressler appeared with two MPs to escort her to a new place of detention. Both Iva and Lily Abegg were taken to Sugamo Prison, where Japanese war criminals were held. After the transfer Iva repeated requests she had made to the prison authorities in Yokohama. She asked the superintendent, Colonel Hardy, and later other prison officials, for an explanation of the reason for her arrest, for legal counsel, for a speedy trial, and for the right to see her husband. All these requests, based on rights guaranteed to any American citizen, were, if not rejected, at least ignored. The occupation authorities were vigorously urging Japanese citizens to respect civil rights, but they showed little concern for Iva's. The CIC, for example, publicly announced that Iva had been arrested on charges of treason, but they did not tell Iva herself.

In late December, after about three months, she was allowed to see Filipe. Still she was not permitted to write to her family back in the United States. Like the Japanese nationals imprisoned as war criminals in Sugamo, she was permitted to send letters only within Japan.

Iva was questioned again by CIC after moving to Sugamo—twice in November and twice again in December. The interrogation covered the same ground as before. Otherwise her situation remained unchanged. Iva was getting anxious.

In the outside world the full force of American occupation policies had begun to strike Japan at a dizzying pace. The Americans were hard at work teaching the Japanese how to be democratic. Only two weeks before the CIC had arrested Iva without a warrant or an explanation, MacArthur's headquarters had ordered the abolition of restraints on the political freedoms. All political prisoners were freed; all laws restricting freedom of thought, religion, assembly, or expression were nullified; the right to criticize the Imperial family and the government was permitted; the thought-control police were abolished; and all top police officials in the Home Ministry were dismissed. By December 21, 1945, the Americans were able to announce that they had finally eliminated the old authoritarian order that had led Japan into war.

The occupation army had been busy, and so were the ordinary Japanese, who were struggling to survive food and fuel shortages as the hard winter months approached. Most people had their hands full keeping body and soul together. Few had time to worry about anyone else's problems. Isolated and alone in prison, Iva began to fear that she would be forgotten.

CHAPTER 2

From L.A. to Radio Tokyo

A Girl from L.A.

Iva d'Aquino was the eldest daughter of Jun and Fumi Toguri. She was born in Los Angeles, by an ironic twist of history, on the Fourth of July, 1916. The date was singularly appropriate, since Iva was the first American citizen in her family. Like most *issei* (which in Japanese simply means "first generation"), the Toguris did not have American citizenship, nor did their eldest son, Fred, who was born in Japan. All were citizens of Japan.

So for a time was Iva. Two months after her birth, Jun entered her name on his family register in Japan, an act that made Iva legally a Japanese citizen. This was not an uncommon practice. Many American-born *nisei,* registered as Iva was, had dual nationality. But in January 1932, shortly after the Japanese invasion of Manchuria, her name was stricken from the family register. In an effort to Americanize the *nisei* community and allay suspicions aroused by dual nationality, many Japanese American leaders urged the *issei* to make sure their offspring were

100 percent American. So from the time she was sixteen, Iva held only American citizenship.

The Toguri family was not very different from millions of other first-generation immigrant families. Jun Toguri, a native of Yamanashi prefecture, had come to the United States at the age of seventeen after graduating from high school. When he arrived in Seattle in 1899 he was given permanent residence in the United States. But even after he had lived here for several years he still could not get American citizenship. Thus in 1906, although he retained his Japanese citizenship, he took out Canadian citizenship as well.

The following year he returned to Japan. On June 8, 1907, at a ceremony in Yokohama, he married nineteen-year-old Fumi Iimuro. She did not return to the United States with her new husband right away. Jun made several visits back to Japan, and in 1910 a son, Fred, was born to the couple. In 1913, six years after the marriage, Fumi and her three-year-old son arrived in San Francisco. Fred, like his parents, remained a resident alien, unable to become naturalized until after passage of the McCarran-Walter Immigration and Nationality Act in 1952.

Like most *issei* immigrants, Jun worked hard, holding a series of jobs. When Iva was three years old the family moved to Calexico, a little town on the California-Mexican border, where Jun went into the business of raising cotton. The business did not prosper, so Jun packed the family off to a new home in San Diego. A second daughter, June, had been born in Calexico, and a third, Inez, was born in San Diego.

The family did not really settle down until 1928, when Jun moved back to Los Angeles. There he started a small import business, which developed into a retail grocery and variety store selling mainly imported goods from Japan. It was the kind of "mom-and-pop" enterprise that so many immigrants, from Japan or elsewhere, have used to launch their families into a better life. All the Toguri children helped out. Fred was his father's main assistant, but the three daughters often tended the store after school.

It was a good family, centered on the father, Jun. Iva described him as a generous and helpful man—*sewazuki* is the Japanese word—always willing to help out when he saw someone else in trouble. The family's main worry was Fumi, whose health was quite poor. She suffered from diabetes and high blood pressure, and even when Iva was very small she had to help take care of her mother.

Otherwise the family was in all respects normal, making its way in Jun's new homeland without much interest in or nostalgia for his old one. Iva described her childhood and youth in 1948:

> Our family home was located in a typical American community. I went to the neighborhood grammar school and attended church in the neighborhood. [Both Iva's parents were Christians.] I took part in normal activities at school and at church. . . . There was some Japanese spoken in our family until we started to attend public school, thereafter English dominated.
>
> We followed both American and Japanese customs at home. We had both Japanese and American cooking in the home. My parents tried to raise us according to American customs. We celebrated all the national holidays, all Christian holidays . . . anniversaries, birthdays, etc.[1]

Although Jun's store sold Japanese groceries and variety goods, the Toguris did not mix much with other Japanese Americans. Jun did not like the idea of bringing up his children in the Japanese community. The family rarely went to Japanese American gatherings, and if anything Jun tried to limit their contacts with other Japanese. He wanted to raise his children to belong to a wider world. Some in the Japanese American community criticized him for his stand-offishness, but Jun did not mind. When he chose a house, he always tried to find a neighborhood where there were many Caucasians, not neighborhoods where the Japanese immigrant families clustered together. As a result, in contrast to many *nisei* of her generation, Iva's playmates were nearly all Caucasian.

Since Jun was determined that his family be brought up as Americans, he did not send his son, Fred, back to Japan for schooling as *issei* fathers often did once they managed to accumulate some savings and property. Many *issei* hoped to return to Japan someday, and they wanted their children to grow up as Japanese. Others sent their children back to show other Japanese Americans that they were financially successful, even if in fact it meant making financial sacrifices to do so. It was a source of pride for many *issei* to tell their friends, "Yes, my son is off to study in Japan."

Iva was a competitive child. She was *maken-ki*—she hated to lose. But she was also firm and reliable, as oldest daughters and sisters often are. Iva grew up like most American teenagers in the early 1930s. She went to local junior and senior high schools, she joined the Girl Scouts, she took piano lessons, and she had a crush on Jimmy Stewart. She was very involved in high school sports, taking part in as many as she could, from badminton to field hockey, and she even made the tennis team.

In high school, Iva recalled, her grades were only "fair,"[2] but the Toguris had high hopes for their eldest daughter. Fumi had wanted to be a doctor when she was a girl, and apparently she passed on some of her ambitions to Iva. Barely 10 percent of Iva's generation of *nisei* went on to college, and for *nisei* women the rate was even lower—around 5 or 6 percent. But the Toguris were determined that Iva pursue her education.

In 1934 Iva enrolled at Compton Junior College. After attending for about half a year she transferred to UCLA, where she could get better preparation for medical study. She had to drop out for two years because of a ruptured appendix and complications that developed from it, but once her health had improved she plunged back into student life.

Iva majored in zoology, a field that was to provide her with some of the happiest memories of her college days. She often spent her weekends, and frequently part of her Thanksgiving, Christmas, and Easter vacations, on desert field trips in Southern California and Arizona, camping out overnight and spending the days looking for specimens.

Dwight Ryerson, a retired biology professor who was then a graduate student at UCLA, recalls that he made field trips to the Mojave Desert with Iva and a number of other students in Professor Roy H. Miller's paleontology class. Ryerson occasionally brought along his wife. The other students got the impression from Iva that her parents permitted her to go only because there was a married couple to chaperone. Ryerson remembers Iva as a lively and lighthearted person, no different from the other American girl students. "Iva was an extroverted, outgoing personality, and she was full of energy. She had a good sense of humor, always kidding and making jokes. It was fun to be with her. She was *nisei*, but in every way she seemed like 100 percent Yankee. I never got the feeling that there was anything Japanese about her, and I also got the feeling that she did not have any interest in Japan at all."[3] Ryerson's wife had the same impression, and neither could quite believe the news when they read that Iva was accused of treason.

Equally surprised was Joe Gorman, another fellow student of Iva's, now an environmental consultant in California. Gorman remembered Iva as more mature and more relaxed than the other students on the field trips, perhaps because she was older. Like Ryerson, he recalled her as a completely average American girl, and he never got the slightest impression that there was anything particularly Japanese about her. But he especially remembered arguing with Iva about his commitment to pacifism. "I was a conscientious objector," he said recently. "In my case it had nothing to do with religion. It was simply a matter of conscience. . . . I talked with Iva many times about it. She never used strong words, but she never budged from the idea that if it were she, she would go and fight for her country, America."[4]

Apart from her field trips, Iva's life was like that of most other UCLA coeds. She was fond of sports, often went to UCLA football games, and even on field trips sat with the other students crowded around a portable radio listening to game broadcasts. She dated, usually Japanese American boys, and she continued to play tennis. At home Iva was not particularly interested in housework, but she did find time to help out with the family business. During summer vacation she often helped her father drive on long business trips.

Politics did not play much of a role in her life. She was too young to vote in the 1936 election, and when she did register as a voter in July 1940 she gave her party preference as Republican.

In 1948, shortly before her case went before the grand jury, Iva stated, "I never felt racial prejudice while in schools. I never felt there was prejudice among teachers or schoolmates. Racial prejudice was never discussed at home and therefore [I] never was aware of the existence of it."[5] At her trial she repeatedly insisted on this point.

Many reporters covering the trial were skeptical about Iva's statements on lack of prejudice, since California, where Iva had been born and raised, had a long history of anti-Japanese discrimination. Most Japanese immigrants to the continental United States had settled there, and California contained about 80 percent of the Japanese American population before World War II. Precisely for this reason, anti-Japanese feeling had strong and deep roots. Anti-Japanese sentiment sprang not simply from racist xenophobia but from the fear and resistance of white working-class people toward the diligent Japanese laborers as competitors for jobs. The economic fears of white workers eventually found expression in politics. Legislators, responding to the resentment of their white constituents, passed laws preventing *issei* from owning or leasing land (Alien Land Law of 1913), repressing Japanese language schools, prohibiting the in-migration of "picture brides," and ultimately prohibiting further Japanese immigration into the United States (1924). During the years of Iva's childhood, anti-Japanese feeling grew even stronger, for the industrious *issei,* who earlier had worked as laborers, began to set themselves up as small businessmen or farmers.

The *issei* put up with anti-Japanese sentiment, doing their best to improve the position of the Japanese American community and their families. They were especially concerned to provide their children with good educations. By the 1930s many *nisei* began to move upward in American society. But they still encountered prejudice and hostility. *Nisei* who had graduated from college with the help of their parents' hard work were often unable to find suitable jobs. A few gave up hope of a future in the United States and moved to their parents' homeland in hopes of finding something better.

There can be little doubt that Iva knew about the existence of anti-Japanese discrimation. Still, there is a difference between knowledge of racial prejudice and direct hurt by it. Partly by circumstance and partly by character, Iva escaped its impact. Her family had lived outside the Japanese American community, usually in Caucasian neighborhoods, and Iva herself had many Caucasian friends and playmates. If she met with prejudice, she may have made little of it, avoided it, or even resisted it.

Aunt Shizu Was Ill

Iva went to Japan more by chance than by choice. Her own plans were to continue preparing for a medical career. Her grades at UCLA had been better than average, so after graduating with a B.A. in zoology in 1940, she decided to go on to graduate work. By the following June she managed to complete a couple of courses in zoology and premedical studies.

In the middle of June 1941 Iva's mother received a letter from Hajime Hattori, the husband of her only living sister, Shizu. Like Fumi, Shizu had long suffered from diabetes and high blood pressure, and Hattori had written that his wife very much wanted to see her older sister, whom she had not met for nearly thirty years. He asked whether Fumi could return to Japan for a visit while Shizu was still alive.

It was clearly impossible for Fumi to return. She had been bedridden for a year and a half. Jun could not leave his business on such short notice, and neither could Fred, who had given up hope of becoming a lawyer and was working as his father's right-hand man at the store. So the family decided that Iva, who had the fewest commitments, should go to Japan in her mother's place.

There was another reason to send Iva to Japan. Her parents were anxious to see their homeland again, but it had been nearly a generation since either of them had been there. They hoped that while visiting her aunt Iva could report back on living conditions there. If everything worked out, Jun could go to Japan the following spring and then accompany Iva back to the States. If Fumi were well enough, she might go also.

Iva was not enthusiastic about the prospect of a sudden and unexpected trip to Japan, but she agreed to her parents' request. Her father hurried to make arrangements for the trip. One of the first things he did was to write to the State Department in Washington to request that Iva be issued a passport.

The early summer of 1941 was hardly an auspicious time for a trip to Japan. Relations between Japan and the United States had deteriorated sharply over the past six months. In Washington Ambassador Kichisaburo Nomura and Secretary of State Cordell Hull were engaged in talks to stave off a possible collision between the two nations, but many Americans thought that the outbreak of war was merely a matter of time. Iva later testified that at the time she had no sense of a crisis between the two countries, and that her family had not made a problem of it at all. Perhaps they were victims of wishful thinking, or perhaps of misplaced hopes that relations between the two countries would improve. Perhaps Jun, who had left Japan when it was still a weak and backward nation, thought his former homeland would never start a war with a powerful country like the United States.

Jun rushed about finishing the arrangements, booking passage for Iva on the *Arabia Maru*, an Osaka Shipping Company vessel scheduled to sail from Los Angeles on July 5. But still no reply came from Washington about Iva's passport. As the date of departure grew closer, Jun finally decided to ask the immigration office in Los Angeles what to do about Iva's travel documents. He was told that it would be all right for Iva to take a certificate of identification along with her when she left, and that once she arrived in Japan she could apply at the consulate in Tokyo for an American passport, which she would need to return to the States.

Four days before her departure, on July 1, 1941, Iva made out a certificate of identification to take along when she left the United States. The document was not issued by the Immigration Office. It was simply a notarized statement that Iva was leaving the United States temporarily to visit her aunt. Neither Iva nor her father had any idea that leaving the country with this certificate of identification instead of a regular passport would make much difference, as long as she could apply for a passport once she arrived in Japan. Iva also left the States without an entry visa for Japan. Remembering his own experience thirty years before, Jun seems to have thought that she did not need one. But the world had become more complex, as Iva was to find out.

The day before departure was Iva's twenty-fifth birthday. Usually the Toguris had a big double celebration on the Fourth, for Iva's birthday and for the nation's. This year things were a little different. The big celebration had come a few days before, when friends of Iva and the family had gathered at a Chinese restaurant for a farewell party. When the Fourth came around, the Toguris, pausing after the hustle and bustle of getting ready for Iva's departure, celebrated with a quiet meal at home by themselves. Jun and Fumi were worried about their daughter. It was the first time she was leaving home, and she knew little of the country to which she was going. They wondered what would happen to her. But Iva was relaxed. She chatted gaily with her sisters about the Fourth of July next year when she would be able to see the Los Angeles fireworks once again. In fact, she would never again spend an evening with all her family together.

The Toguris went to San Pedro the next day to send Iva off on the

Iva and her father, Jun Toguri

Arabia Maru, en route to Kobe via Yokohama. Jun, who had taken care of everything so far, bustled about looking after Iva's luggage. She was taking a lot with her: fruits, chocolate, and other food as presents for Japanese relatives and friends; insulin, aspirin, and medicine for Aunt Shizu; and a sewing machine for Iva's cousin. Jun, concerned about Iva's complete dislike of Japanese cuisine, had also packed American food for her to eat during her stay—sugar, coffee, cocoa, jam, canned meat, tomato paste, chocolate, and even flour and baking powder so that Iva could make her own bread instead of eating rice. Then too there was yarn, and soap, and a typewriter for her to use. All together Iva had some thirty pieces of luggage.*

As the boat pulled away from its berth, paper streamers cascaded from the departing passengers to well-wishers on the docks below. Iva stood at the rail, wearing the white sharkskin suit her sister June had made for the trip. She waved to her family and friends until they dwindled to tiny specks in the distance.

Iva had a traveling companion, eighteen-year-old Chieko Ito, a girl Iva had known since childhood. When Chieko's parents heard that Iva was going to Japan, they decided to send Chieko to visit her uncle, and they asked Iva to look after her. Like Iva, she left the country without a passport.

The first week of the voyage was miserable for both young women. They were homesick and seasick. Iva had begun to worry about what lay in store for her in Japan. Aside from what she had studied in geography class at school, she knew little or nothing about her parents' homeland. Indeed, her interest in Japan was scant. She found it hard to relax as each day the *Arabia Maru* drew closer to the country that had become the object of both anticipation and anxiety.

"All the Customs Were Strange"

Iva and Chieko spent their first night in Japan on board ship. The *Arabia Maru* docked at Yokohama at three o'clock on the after-

---

*At the trial prosecutor Thomas DeWolfe suggested that so much baggage was excessive for someone planning to spend only six months in Japan, and he hypothesized that Iva was really planning to stay in Japan for several years so she could attend medical school. But, as Iva pointed out, more than one-third of the luggage consisted of presents for her aunt.

noon of July 24, 1941, nineteen days after leaving San Pedro. Iva and
Chieko had trouble disembarking. Both were American citizens, yet neither had a proper passport or visa. By the time they managed to get visas
issued, it was too late to get them stamped.

When Iva disembarked the next day she found her uncle and cousins
waiting for her. She had never met any of them before. To help break
the ice they took her to the New Grand Hotel in Yokohama for lunch,
and Uncle Hajime was pleased at Iva's delight to learn she could eat real
Western food even in Japan.

Iva's first impressions of Japan were not all pleasant, however. It was
especially hard to get used to the midsummer heat and humidity. Loaded
with Iva's luggage, the Hattoris took the train to their house in Setagaya,
a suburb of Tokyo. For Iva, who was used to getting everywhere by car
in the States, the short trip was something of a trial. The train was sti-
fling, and smells from the lavatory drifted into the car. But her strongest
impression was that everywhere she looked there were Japanese faces.
She still recalls being surprised at seeing so many Japanese.

Aunt Shizu, her mother's sister, had not been able to come to Yokohama, but she was in better health than Iva expected. More surprising,
she looked exactly like Iva's mother, Fumi. Even their voices sounded the
same. Iva was so happy that she felt like weeping. Aunt Shizu seemed as
if she were welcoming home a daughter. Iva's cousin, Rinko, a year
younger than she, was an almost uncanny look-alike for Iva. Only Uncle
Hajime, who ran a clothing store, seemed different. Unlike the gregar-
ious Jun, he was a quiet person, passive and not inclined to push his
own ideas forward, but he did his best to take care of her, Iva said later.

Iva had trouble shaking the feeling that she was an outsider. "Japan
impressed me as very, very strange," she recalled in 1948. "All the customs were strange to me, the food was entirely different, wearing appar-
el different, houses different, people were stiff and formal to me. . . . I
had no idea of what the country was going to be like until I hit Yokohama. . . . I felt like a perfect stranger, and the Japanese considered me
very queer."[6]

Aunt Shizu and Rinko did their best to teach Iva the ordinary daily
customs of the country. Iva later reflected that she must have seemed an
unusual twenty-five-year-old. Her face was Japanese, but the inside of

her head was not. It was as though she were a child again. She had to learn everything—how to take off her shoes before entering a house, how to sit properly on a mat floor, how to eat without knife and fork. Her spoken Japanese was nearly unusable, so someone, usually Rinko, had to accompany her every time she left the house. Iva thought this was ridiculous. Determined to learn enough Japanese to get around by herself, in September she started going every morning to the Matsumiya Nihongo Bunka Gakkō (Japanese Language Culture School) in the Shiba section of Tokyo.

Iva's bewilderment was like that of any stranger new to a foreign land, but the culture shock she experienced was greater than if she had visited Japan thirty years later. In 1941 the gap between Japanese and American living standards was enormous. Iva had arrived in a Japan that had been at war in China for four years, and the ordinary people of Japan, like the Hattoris, had to bear the economic burdens. Consumer goods were often cheap and shoddy, made with ersatz materials. But it was the food, which Iva did not like much anyway, that got to her the most. "I have finally gotten around to eating rice three times a day," she wrote her family. "It's killing me but what can I do? I can't buy an oven to bake any bread and since I didn't bring one, the flour which I brought just sits in the kitchen."[7]

The Hattoris continued to do what they could for Iva. She received a rice ration card in September, but since she did not eat much her uncle began to worry about her. In October, much to Iva's delight, he went to the government office and had her ration changed from rice to bread.

Iva's cousins were about her age and did their best to be friendly to her. She found them nice enough, but somehow could not get used to their sense of humor or their idea of a good time. Iva tried to keep her spirit up, but she missed her family and life in the United States. "I have gotten used to many of the things over here and I think that in a few more months that I will be able to say that I don't mind living in Japan. It has been very hard and discouraging at times but from now on it will be all right I'm sure. I sure miss being away from home. There isn't a day that goes by without thinking about home and everybody. I hope things are going along all right with all of you."[8]

Iva was especially worried about her family because communications with the United States had become more and more difficult. On October 9 Iva received a letter that her family had mailed to her a month before. She was astounded to learn from it that none of the letters, postcards, and packages of photographs she had sent from Japan had reached the United States. She entrusted a long letter to her family to a *nisei* acquaintance about to sail for America. She wanted especially to discourage her mother from coming to Japan the following spring.

"Normal healthy people are striving to live with what little they can get," she wrote,

> so Mother would have twice as difficult a time. The heating problem is big enough to discourage anyone coming to Japan. June, Hisa, Fred, Mom you couldn't stand the kind of living you have to put up with here. I'm telling you, you have to grit your teeth and like it. . . . Now with Dad, it is probably a little different with you. You probably can stand to live here for a while. . . . You have half an idea of what Japan and living in Japan is like, but for the rest of you, no matter how bad things get and how much you have to take in the form of racial criticisms and no matter how hard you have to work, by all means remain in the country you learn to appreciate more after you leave it. Fred, settle down and get married and do the best you can with the business and be content and never think of coming to Japan. June and Inez, you both do the same. Eventually settle down and get married and plan to live and die in the country which can give you so much.[9]

Iva was anxious to return to the States herself. Since she could not read the Japanese newspapers and since the Hattoris were rather vague about the news, Iva did not clearly understand the diplomatic situation between Japan and the United States. Some of her *nisei* friends in Japan urged her to return to the States right away. Certainly there was good reason for their uneasiness. On July 25, the day after Iva arrived in Japan, the Roosevelt administration had escalated its economic warfare against Japan by freezing Japanese assets in the United States. Although the public did not know it, the Japanese government had decided in early September to go to war with the United States if negotiations with the Americans remained deadlocked.

Ever since arriving in Yokohama, Iva and Chieko Ito had worried about their lack of passports. At the time the young women were given temporary visas in Yokohama, the Japanese immigration officials said they would be permitted to stay in Japan no longer than six months. If they wanted to extend their stay even a bit longer, they would need passports. In early August Iva and Chieko had gone to the American consulate in Tokyo to apply for passports. Both said that they planned to return to the States within a year. The consular officials said it would not be possible to issue passports until their identity and references had been checked with Washington, which would probably take some time.

September came and went, then October. By November there was still no word from Washington about their passports. The newspaper reports kept getting worse and worse. Japan seemed to be moving toward a major crisis with the United States. Iva began to wonder whether she would be able to get a boat back to the States if she waited until spring, when her father was planning to come to Japan.

On November 25, the day that the Hull-Nomura talks came to a standstill in Washington, Iva and Chieko put in international telephone calls from the Hattori house to their families in the United States. Iva told her father that there was no telling when something was going to happen between Japan and the United States and that she wanted to come home right away. Jun, surprised at receiving a call from Iva, who was usually so stouthearted, told his daughter that he did not get much sense of danger from the American papers, but if she wanted to come home right away it was all right with him. Iva was relieved to hear his promise he would get to work on the formalities right away.

At 3:00 P.M. on December 1, Iva received a telegram her father had sent two days before from Los Angeles. It told her to book passage home on the *Tatsuta Maru,* scheduled to leave Yokohama for the States the very next day. The news was welcome, but with less than twenty hours to spare before the ship left, Iva and her uncle had to move quickly to make preparations for her departure. The next few hours were hectic, and desperately frustrating.

When Uncle Hajime phoned the NYK steamship office he was told that Iva could not buy a ticket on the *Tatsuta Maru* unless she had either a valid passport or a letter of identification from the American consulate. Iva rushed right off to the consulate, where she succeeded in getting the needed letter, but when she called her uncle she found that the trail of paper had only just begun: she had to go to the language school to get documentary proof that she had not been employed in Japan and that she had been going to school. Iva rushed over to the Nihongo Bunka Gakkō, where she got the required documents. Much relieved, she went to meet her uncle at the NYK office to buy her ticket.

There she found another hurdle. The company, she was told, would not sell her a ticket unless she had a permit from the Ministry of Finance allowing her to leave the country. Iva and her uncle managed to arrive at the Ministry just before closing time, only to find that all their frantic activity was to no avail. The Finance Ministry officials told her they had to check on how much American currency she had brought to Japan, how much she had spent, and how much she had left. ". . . They wouldn't give me clearance because they said it would take three or four days to ascertain whether all my expenditures were true. They refused my application."[10] Iva was trapped by the chains of red tape.

Iva testified calmly about these events in court, but at the time she was bitterly disappointed at failing to get on the *Tatsuta Maru*. The Hattoris could hardly bear seeing how discouraged she was.

The *Tatsuta Maru* left Yokohama the next day with a full passenger list. It would have done Iva little good to be on board. In midvoyage, on December 7, the Japanese attacked Pearl Harbor, and the *Tatsuta Maru* turned back to Japan. Iva had no way of knowing that, however, and it would have been little consolation to her if she had.

War

"I just did not have enough knowledge of Japanese to understand what was happening that day the Japanese radio announced war between Japan and the U.S.," Iva recalled in 1948. "I could understand the word 'war' but could not believe that war had really broken out. I could not understand enough Japanese to listen to the radio and get the full story from this source. I could not read the Japanese newspapers. I could read only the English newspaper printed in Tokyo. But I was warned by my uncle and aunt not to be seen reading a paper written in English. . . . I went around in a daze for several days. I could not believe war had broken out."[11] She tried to act as though nothing had happened, going to her Japanese school as usual, denying the awful reality.

On December 9 Mr. Fujiwara, a plainclothes officer from the Foreigners Section of the Special Security Police (*tokkō keisatsu*)* in Setagaya-ku, came to the Hattoris' house to question her. He asked Iva at great length about what she did every day, when she went to school, how much money she had, and so on and so on. Finally he looked up and said, "If you keep your American citizenship there will be all kinds of trouble for you from now on, so it would be smart for you to enter your name on your family register and become a Japanese citizen."[12] Iva immediately refused the suggestion. But Mr. Fujiwara was very persistent. For the next two weeks he came to the Hattori house nearly every other day for more interrogations. At the end of his visits he always urged Iva to take Japanese citizenship. One day she finally blurted out angrily, "I want to be interned as a foreigner." Mr. Fujiwara appeared surprised. He forced a smile. "Well," he said, "since you are of Japanese extraction and a woman, I do not think you will be very dangerous. So we will not intern you. For the moment we will just see how things go."[13]

Mr. Fujiwara's visits continued twice a week in January, and so did his persistent suggestion that Iva change her nationality. "It won't take twenty minutes," he said to her one day. Iva gave him another heated reply: "A person born and raised in America doesn't give up his citizenship for a piece of paper."[14] Her aunt and uncle, who had to interpret for her, were quite upset.

At the time of Pearl Harbor there were about 10,000 Japanese Americans who, like Iva, were forced by the outbreak of war to remain in Japan. Those who had not already had their names entered in the family register were urged to do so by the Special Security Police. It was part of the effort by the Japanese government to conscript Japanese Americans into the army and to make them pledge their loyalty to Japan. Those who refused were subjected to considerable economic and psychological pressure. As belligerent aliens they had trouble getting jobs or even rations. Many stranded *nisei* eventually registered themselves as Japanese, with the result that after the war ended they had considerable trouble returning to the States. Iva was one of the few who held on to

---

*The *tokkō keisatsu* was the internal security branch of the national police force, charged with the investigation of domestic political radicalism and other subversive activities. It was well supplied with secret service funds, and it was known to conduct rigorous and cruel interrogations, which gave the agency a fearful reputation.

their American citizenship throughout the war, despite continual pressure by the Special Security Police and the military gendarmerie (*kempeitai*) to register as Japanese.

Iva felt alone, with no one to rely on. Without success she tried to contact her family through the International Red Cross. The Hattoris had
become nervous about having Iva, an enemy American, living in their
midst. Her only real consolation came from talking and complaining to
her young friend, Chieko Ito, also stranded in Japan. At the end of January 1942 Chieko entered a special Japanese language training school at
Waseda University. Every now and then Iva would meet Chieko after
her classes, and the two would stroll to Takadanobaba station, where
Chieko boarded the train for home. Iva enjoyed these meetings, for she
could chat away in English without worry. Sometimes the two young
women were joined by a classmate of Chieko's, Yoneko Matsunaga, a
New Jersey–born *nisei*. None of the three had given up her American
citizenship, which made them all feel a bit closer.

Iva was the most outspoken of the trio in her dislike of Japan. "She
didn't like Japan at all," recalled Chieko. "She couldn't stand the people, the customs, the food, everything about Japan. She didn't like it, and
so the first chance she had she would try to get back to America. . . . She
was going to keep her U.S. citizenship and she was going to keep it no
matter what happens. . . . She could not become a Japanese citizen overnight."[15] Iva strongly advised Chieko and Mieko never to give in to pressure by the police, and she told them that America was certain to win the
war soon.

In the middle of February Iva read in the *Daily Mainichi,* an English
newspaper, that the Swiss consulate was accepting applications from
stranded Americans who wished to be repatriated. Iva and Chieko went
there immediately. They were told that without passports there was only
a slight possibility that they would be able to return on the first repatriation ship, scheduled to carry Ambassador Joseph Grew back to the
States.

Iva had hardly touched the money she had brought for return passage,
and she still had enough for a return fare, but since it was not at all clear
when or whether a second repatriation ship would be leaving, she wanted to return on the first one. She asked the Swiss consulate to telegraph

the State Department at her expense to establish her American citizenship. The reply from Washington a few days later indicated there were some doubts about her citizenship. The State Department's doubts were curious indeed, since Iva had been born and reared in the United States: she had never set foot outside the country before the age of twenty-five. Yet the State Department appears not to have discriminated against Iva alone, for it also refused to certify Chieko's citizenship. So Iva and Chieko were frustrated once again. Most of those who did sail on the first repatriation ship were American embassy officials, journalists, and businessmen.

Iva had to face long, tedious days waiting for another chance to leave Japan. She plugged away at her Japanese language study, but she had nothing to do in the afternoons. Her aunt and uncle warned her to remain as inconspicuous as possible, so she spent most of her time at home, huddled over the *hibachi*. On top of all her other problems, the California-bred Iva was experiencing her first Tokyo winter, enduring a cold that seemed to cut through her body despite the several layers of heavy wool clothing she wore.

By the spring of 1942 Iva had also begun to worry about money. Even though she knew she probably would not be able to return to the States for a while, it was getting harder and harder for her to pay for her Japanese lessons. Her own expenses were substantial too. Iva had been giving the Hattoris 50 yen a month for food, and she had to pay for all her transportation expenses. She had brought about $300 plus her return fare, and she had managed to make a little money by selling some of the wool yarn and cotton socks she had brought with her. After failing to get passage on the first evacuation ship, she began to dip into her little nest egg of dollars.

No matter how she scrimped, the money she had brought from the States seemed to be trickling away bit by bit. But she was anxious above all not to touch the money she had set aside for her return fare, so she did what she could to conserve it.

Tuition at the school was 30 yen a month. When Iva asked Kazuya Matsumiya, the head of the school, to reduce her fee a bit, he agreed to do so if she typed up the manuscript of a Japanese grammar textbook he had written in English. Since she knew how to play the piano, he also asked her to give lessons to his son and daughter, and to some of their friends as well. She got 5 yen a lesson for each pupil, but she had to pay Mr. Matsumiya rent for the piano so she netted only 2.50. Still, Iva was thankful to have the 20 yen or so she earned every month.

At the end of March she decided to look for a real job. Translation work seemed one possibility, but Iva's inadequacy at reading and writing Japanese ruled that out. Then, too, she was an American citizen, and people were reluctant to hire her. Her spirits began to sink as day after day she was refused work.

It was getting increasingly difficult to remain at her aunt and uncle's house. The police continued to drop by to check on Iva's comings and goings. Some of the neighbors were disturbed at having an American around and complained to the Hattoris through the local neighborhood association (*tonari gumi*). When the local children saw Iva go by they often jeered at her, calling her a "spy" or, worse, a "prisoner of war"—a particularly strong epithet. The wartime Japanese regarded nothing as being more dishonorable than capture by the enemy. Some of the children even threw stones at her. The whole situation began to take its toll on Aunt Shizu. It was nearly impossible for Iva to remain, but her aunt and uncle were reluctant to ask her to leave.

Tactfully, Iva finally brought matters to a head herself by asking if it would be all right for her to move out. Her aunt and uncle were embarrassed at the awkwardness of it, and abashed at the thought of making her go, but there seemed to be no other solution. "I did not think badly of my uncle and aunt," Iva later recalled. "I decided to leave myself. It was awful for them." But it must have been awful for Iva, too. She was on her own for the first time in her life, in an enemy country whose language she could not yet really speak and whose life she really did not understand.

Her reaction to the famous Doolittle raid, the first American bombing of Tokyo on April 18, 1942, perhaps summarized her situation. She was overjoyed to see the American planes, but she did not like the idea of being attacked by them, and she simply wanted them to fly off and disappear. It was a strange and unsettling feeling.

"Go Get Yourself Registered"

In early June Iva moved into a boardinghouse near her language school run by a Mrs. Furuya, who provided her with room and board for 65 yen a month. She had been introduced by Mr. Matsumiya. About a week and a half later, with the help of a fellow student, Iva found a job in the Monitoring Division of the Domei News Agency located at Atago Hill, not far from her lodgings and her school.

In wartime, news travels from one enemy country to another by way of neutral countries, but during World War II all the belligerents, including Japan, tried to pick up news by shortwave radio broadcasts from the enemy as well. In Japan the Foreign Ministry, the army, and the navy, as well as Domei, all had monitoring facilities. At Domei the monitors worked in shifts around the clock listening to Allied broadcasts, principally from Australia and the United States. Their reports were sent on to the main offices of the Domei Agency. Iva's job was to listen for news about the movements of Allied armies.

The hours were not convenient—she had to work late at night—and the pay was not good. Her salary was 110 yen a month, but after taxes and other incidentals were deducted, only 82 yen remained in her pay envelope. Still, after looking for work for nearly three months, Iva was glad to have a job even though it was only temporary. At least now she could support herself without having to draw on the money she had saved.

By this time Iva had found out what had happened to her family. She had learned by way of the International Red Cross that Japanese Americans on the West Coast had been sent to relocation camps. A short time later she saw the names of her family on a list of those interned at the Gila River Relocation Center in Arizona. Iva had no clear idea of what all this meant, nor did she understand what was going on in the United States. She certainly did not believe anything that the Japanese told her about conditions there, and for a time she even thought that the news about the relocation centers was propaganda put out by the Japanese government or a rumor spread by the Special Security Police. She still hoped to get home.

On August 27, 1942, Iva got word from the Swiss consulate that another repatriation ship was scheduled to leave Japan in September. She hurried down with Chieko to make arrangements to leave, but once again there was a problem. The consulate officials told her she would not have to pay any fare for the first part of the trip, but from India to New York the fare would be $425. The money was a problem. "I had been reading in the papers where all my family had been put in relocation centers and I couldn't contact them to know whether they had $425 for me," she later testified. "I had not one dollar to my name because I had been living on the money I had brought. . . . I could have gotten on [the first evacuation ship], but six months later I didn't have the money to pay for the passage. . . ."[16] So Iva canceled her application for evacuation in September.

Shortly afterward Iva returned home from work one day to find her landlady's daughter waiting for her. Her face was ashen. Silently she pointed in the direction of Iva's room. Iva hurried up to see what the matter was. The room looked as though it had been struck by a typhoon: her suitcases were thrown open, her books scattered all over the floor. Three men Iva had never seen before were ransacking her room, hardly aware that she was standing there, rigid with fear, watching them.

They were plainclothesmen from the *kempeitai,* the military gendarmerie. When they finally noticed Iva they simply told her they were looking for English-language books. But they also seemed to know that Iva had canceled her application for evacuation on the second repatriation ship. "No more reason not to become a Japanese citizen," they said. "Go get yourself registered." Iva told them she would not, and she asked to be interned with the other Allied-country nationals. The *kempeitai* officer replied, "If we had to intern all the *nisei* and feed them, it would cost just too much. So we'll just see what happens. In the meantime, think it over, and don't keep any English-language things around."[17] They would come again, they said.

The police, especially the Special Security Police *(tokkō keisatsu),* continued to harass Iva because of her failure to register as a Japanese citizen. After she had left her aunt's house in June, she had had difficulty getting a ration card. The police issued her one only in September. In the meantime she had great trouble buying food.

There was one bright spot in this dreary and lonely period of her life. In the middle of July, about a month after she had started at Domei, Filipe J. d'Aquino began to work there, too. He was a slender young man of medium height and pale complexion, and rather handsome. He was a gentle sort of person who always seemed calm and rarely raised his voice. At the time he was twenty-one years old, about five years younger than Iva.

Filipe was only part Japanese. His grandfather was a Portuguese national who had married a Japanese woman. Their son, José F. d'Aquino, Filipe's father, had married a Japanese, and Filipe had been born and had grown up in Yokohama. From primary school through junior college he had attended a Catholic mission school, St. Joseph's, where classes were taught in English, so he was quite fluent. He could also speak Japanese, but was not proficient at reading and writing it. He knew no Portuguese at all, but because of his ancestry, from birth he had been formally registered as a citizen of Portugal.

Iva, in 1948, recalled her growing friendship with Filipe: "The fact that he was educated at a Catholic college in Yokohama—priests and brothers from the U.S. were instructors there—started conversations between us. He was interested in the U.S. and I was able to give him some kind of picture of the sections of the U.S. I had been in. . . . He understood my predicament and tried to help me as much as possible. We had to be very careful not to cross the police as we were both alien nationals and were registered as such."[18]

In contrast to most of the other Domei monitors, many of whom were pro-Japanese Japanese Americans, Filipe was pro-American in his sentiments, and he was the only person at the Monitoring Division who sided with Iva when she made her own strong pro-American views known, often too clearly, to the other employees. Filipe later testified that his sympathy for the United States came partly from his dislike of the militaristic atmosphere of wartime Japan, which was very much out of tune with his own temperament, and that after listening to Allied news broadcasts as a monitor he came to think that Japan was going to lose.

Filipe's mixed-blood heritage may also have made him pro-American. He had grown up among the Japanese, a provincial and insular people who tended to look down on those of mixed ancestry, and although he had gone to school where many of the students were foreign, he had his share of unpleasant memories. Then too, he was much taken by Iva's reminiscences about the United States, and about the freedom she had enjoyed there, and he soon became her ally. Aside from Chieko, whom she saw less frequently, Filipe was the only person Iva could speak freely and openly to without having to worry she would be reported to the police.

Both Iva and Filipe knew that the fortunes of war were beginning to turn against the Japanese. After a series of brilliant early successes, the Japanese had suffered a major naval setback at Midway in June 1942, and an equally serious military loss in the Solomon Islands in August. The Imperial General Headquarters official announcements made no mention of these unfavorable developments and continued to claim a string of heroic victories for the Japanese. But Iva, who was getting quite different reports over the Allied shortwave broadcasts, doubted the truth of the Japanese army announcements. The news she heard led her to continue hoping that the Americans would eventually win. Often the Japanese would grudgingly confirm news broadcast over the Allied airwaves. In mid-April 1943, for example, the Americans announced that Admiral Isoroku Yamamoto, commander of the Japanese fleet and the architect of the Pearl Harbor attack, had been shot down. Although the Imperial Headquarters made no mention of it at the time, they did confirm his death two months later by official announcement.

In June 1943 Iva became seriously ill. Ever since arriving in Japan she had been troubled from lack of vitamins and an improper diet. She had had bouts of scurvy and beriberi. Finally in June she had to be hospitalized for malnutrition and beriberi at the Amano Hospital, run by a Dr. Amano who had studied medicine in the United States and had served as Ambassador Grew's physician. Dr. Amano knew Iva very well. "She was definitely pro-American," he later recalled. "She said Japan will lose the war at the time nobody . . . said that. She brought me the Allied news."

The illness, which kept Iva in the hospital for six weeks, added to her financial difficulties. To pay for her medical expenses she had to borrow money from Filipe and Mrs. Furuya, her landlady. When she got out of the hospital she went back to her job at Domei. But since she was working only part-time, her pay was just barely enough for her own subsistence, so she decided to get another part-time job to pay off her debts as quickly as she could. She did not really like borrowing money, and she was anxious to square her accounts.

In late summer she saw an ad in the *Nippon Times* announcing that there were a few jobs for English-language typists at Radio Tokyo. Iva responded immediately by postcard, took an employment examination, and two or three weeks later received word that she had the job. It was her first step into the legend of Tokyo Rose.

CHAPTER 3

"Zero Hour"

Radio Tokyo

On August 23, 1943, Iva reported for work as a part-time typist in the administrative section of the American Division of the Overseas Bureau at NHK.* The NHK offices were located in downtown Tokyo at Uchi-saiwai-cho, not far from where Iva lived. The American Division was on the third floor of the building in a large room divided into clusters of desks.

Iva worked only a few hours in the afternoon, usually from three o'clock to around five or six o'clock, after she had finished at the Domei monitoring service. Her main work was to type English-language broadcast scripts written by Japanese scriptwriters, correcting any grammatical or other mistakes as she went along. Her salary was 100 yen a month

* The Overseas Bureau was divided into five major divisions: the American Division, which broadcast to North and South America; the European Division, which broadcast to the European area; the Asia Division, which broadcast to the rest of Asia; the Editorial Division, which was in charge of general news and information; and the Administrative Division, which took care of routine business matters.

The American Division, where Iva worked, was in turn organized into a number of sections: the News Translation Section (editing of news scripts); the South American Section (broadcasts in Spanish and Portuguese); the Broadcast Section (announcing staff); the Commentary and Drama Section; and the Administrative Section. Eventually another section, the Front Line Section reportedly under direct control of the army, was added to these others.

(about 78-80 yen after deductions), but with her salary from Domei it was quite enough for her to live on.

At first, propaganda broadcasts from the NHK Overseas Bureau had been supervised by the Foreign Ministry and the Government Information Office. The military services had carried on their own propaganda activities independently without much liaison with one another or with NHK. Indeed, a fair amount of rivalry developed among the various competing propaganda agencies, with the result that Japanese propaganda warfare often became quite ill-coordinated.

To remedy these problems, an Information Liaison Conference Committee was set up to develop overall plans for Japan's propaganda activities. Representatives came from the army, the navy, the Foreign Ministry, the Government Information Office, the Cabinet Information Bureau, the Home Ministry, the Great East Asia Ministry, the Transportation Ministry, Domei News Agency, NHK, and several other smaller agencies. The committee, which met at nine every morning to select the news to be used in propaganda activities, was supposed to function like a general editorial board, giving some focus and direction to Japan's propaganda efforts. But like all such bureaucratic compromises, it worked better on paper than in fact.

The army, the navy, and the Foreign Ministry carried on a struggle for leadership within the committee. Gradually interagency cooperation disintegrated. In the end it was the army that came to have the strongest voice in determining foreign propaganda broadcasting policy.

At first the army had not shown much interest in propaganda work—it was thought to be beneath the dignity of soldiers and not in accordance with the spirit of *bushidō*—but gradually its importance in modern warfare became clear. The General Staff lodged responsibility for propaganda warfare, or "psychological warfare" as they preferred to call it, in the Eighth Section, G-2. Major (later Lieutenant Colonel) Shigetsugu Tsuneishi, a Military Academy graduate who joined the Eighth Section in November 1941, was put in charge despite the fact he was a complete amateur who had never done propaganda work before.

Tsuneishi's first efforts at "psychological warfare" concentrated on print propaganda. His staff produced an illustrated photo magazine called *Front*, which somewhat resembled *Life* magazine, and they designed leaflets to demoralize the Allied enemy forces. Tsuneishi apparently believed that American men were always thinking about women and sex, so the leaflets usually showed bosomy hometown girls languishing in diaphanous nightgowns, pining away for their absent boyfriends—and often succumbing to fleshy temptations with other men. The Allied troops found these leaflets amusing but ridiculous, and were far more demoralized by pamphlets that showed homey scenes of families round the dinner table.

As the war progressed, army propaganda efforts increasingly centered on radio broadcasts. Tsuneishi, as the army representative on the Information Liaison Conference Committee, even had an office set up for himself in the NHK office building and began issuing orders to the various sections of the Overseas Bureau through the Bureau Chief, Yoshio Muto.

The English-language broadcasts remained rather moderate in tone before the attack on Pearl Harbor. The Foreign Ministry and the Government Information Office instructed NHK not to make broadcasts that might hinder negotiations going on in Washington in mid-1941. But when war finally broke out between the United States and Japan, the character of the broadcasts changed suddenly, taking on the violently anti-American and anti-Western tone of domestic Japanese broadcasts.

The Japanese radio propaganda efforts were plagued with problems. The more fanatic patriots insisted that the broadcasts include the mystical nationalism characteristic of domestic propaganda. This was not likely to have much effect on overseas audiences. The station constantly spouted pieties about the "sacred soldiers of Japan" who were fighting a "holy war" and did not fear death in the service of the Imperial Son of Heaven, descended from Emperor Jimmu, grandson of the Sun Goddess Amaterasu. At one point Tsuneishi and his staff even came up with the idea of getting together a group of actors to recite Shinto prayers over the radio. If this was "psychological warfare" it showed precious little understanding of the psychology of listeners in enemy countries, who were not likely to be persuaded of Japanese superiority by this sort of broadcast.

Furthermore, news broadcasts had to be based on the official announcements of the Imperial General Headquarters. As the war dragged on, these official announcements retreated more and more into a world of wishful thinking. Propaganda succeeds only if based on the truth, and as a result the news broadcasts began to lose credibility. No one was going to believe or listen to propaganda that reported defeats as victories or disasters as triumphs. Most Allied soldiers regarded the wartime Japanese news broadcasts as a big joke.

But more than anything else, the radio propaganda efforts suffered from lack of talented personnel. One student of the Japanese radio warfare has observed, "Probably the most important of all prerequisites for successful propaganda is to have capable propagandists, and it was in that very requirement that Tokyo was sadly lacking."[1] Whereas the United States drew on its ablest announcers and journalists for its radio propaganda efforts, the Japanese had difficulty finding anyone either to announce or to write scripts. There were few professionally trained English-speaking announcers in Japan. Yuichi Hirakawa, who headed the American Division announcers section, lamented that his subordinates were rank amateurs who could speak English but had no training in radio work. Hirakawa, a native Japanese with a degree in dramatics from the University of Washington, was one of the few exceptions.

Many of the announcers were former American *nisei* who had come to Japan after giving up hope of finding work in the States. Some of them had journalistic experience, but most got jobs at Radio Tokyo simply by saying they had done news work or had been in the theater. A handful had natural talent, but the rest did not.

Among the announcers were a number of women. Perhaps the ablest was June Yoshie Suyama, born in Japan but reared in Canada. She had been with NHK since before the war. A good broadcaster with a deep and attractive voice, she was nicknamed "the Nightingale of Nanking." Ruth Sumi Hayakawa, also born in Japan, had lived in the United States from the age of two until graduation from junior college in Los Angeles. Her voice, in contrast to June Suyama's, was light and pretty, like a young girl's. Margaret Yaeko Kato, Japan-born but brought up in London, had a rather marked British accent. Occasionally when the bureau found itself shorthanded, women announcers were drafted from the typists' section. Among those who became announcers in this way were Katherine Kei Fujiwara (*nisei*), Katherine Kaoru Morooka (*nisei*), Mieko Furuya (*nisei*), and Mary Ishii (half-English, half-Japanese).

Even if the announcers were not professionals, it might have been possible to produce effective propaganda broadcasts with good scripts. Unfortunately the scripts were often worse than the announcers.

News scripts were assembled in a particularly cumbersome way. News materials provided by the Domei News Agency, the information bureaus of the army and navy, the Foreign Ministry, the German DNB News Agency, and the Italian Stefani News Service were translated from English and other foreign languages into Japanese. The Editorial Division used the translations to draft news and news analysis scripts. These were then handed over to the news translation sections for each geographical area for retranslation into the language in which they were broadcast. By the time the news got through this double translation process, the final version was often rather far removed from the original. This obviously produced problems, but the system remained uncorrected until the end of the war.

Part of the problem also lay in the fact that while there were some *nisei* scriptwriters, most were native Japanese whose grasp of English was not always firm. Their results were often startling. Allied monitors compiled catalogs of their howlers. A few samples: one broadcast referred to the "chimney" of a naval vessel; another, reporting the aftermath of an air attack, said, "The remaining planes took to their heels"; one alleged that "Japanese men look furious but they are sweet on the inside"; another, reporting on the repatriation of belligerent nationals, asserted, "With the exception of one dead, all on the exchange ship were in the best of spirits." Had the Japanese been willing to trust the foreign-born *nisei* a bit more, some of these errors might never have been broadcast. But the *nisei* were second-class citizens at the bureau, and the bloopers continued.

To make matters worse, a number of the announcers, basically amateurs and untrained, were none too certain of English pronunciation. According to Australian monitors they made what seem to have been incredible errors: "imitation" instead of "intimidation," "defied" instead of "deified," and hardest of all to believe, "slumbering" for "submarine."

Despite their clumsiness, the Japanese propaganda broadcasts proved quite effective during the early phases of the war. Simply by broadcasting the truth—the incredible string of Japanese victories—it was not difficult to attract an audience. But after the Japanese military fortunes took a turn for the worse in mid-1942, things were not so easy. From about the time of the Midway defeat, Japan's propaganda machine began to intensify its efforts. At NHK the Overseas Bureau was expanded. Broadcasts in new languages were added and broadcasting hours were extended.

But there were those in the army who realized that mere expansion was not enough. If the propaganda was to be effective, it would have to improve in quality, too. The staff that had been assembled at the Overseas Bureau was simply not up to the job. Colonel Yoshiaki Nishi, Tsuneishi's superior at the Eighth Section, came up with the idea of recruiting radio professionals from among the Allied POWs captured in the early days of the war. Orders were sent out to the front-line regions, and gradually the army began to assemble a group of POWs to use in enemy propaganda broadcasts. By late 1942 three were already working at Radio Tokyo.

"I Just Feel Sorry for Them"

The day after Iva went to work at the American Division, she noticed three rather emaciated foreigners being escorted through the office. Two were Caucasian and the third looked Asian. They wore dirty-looking short-sleeve shirts, khaki canvas shorts, and old tennis shoes. Iva asked who they were. In a low voice Ruth Hayakawa replied that they were Allied POWs who had been captured in Southeast Asia. They had been forced to come to Japan and take part in broadcasts from Radio Tokyo, she said.

Iva's interest was aroused. She told Ruth that she would like to meet the prisoners. When Ruth asked why, Iva replied, "It is just a natural instinct with me. I would like to meet with them and talk with them if I can. . . . I just feel sorry for them."

"Don't ever say that at Radio Tokyo," Ruth warned her, "because there are too many plainclothes *kempeis* in here."[2] Someone else who had expressed sympathy for the POWs had been called down for questioning. But Ruth promised to arrange for Iva to meet the POWs if she really wanted to. The next day, August 25, 1943, she did.

The three POWs were Major Charles Hughes Cousens, an Australian; Captain Wallace E. Ince, an American; and Lieutenant Norman Reyes, a Filipino. Iva greeted them and shook Cousens's hand. "I told him to keep his chin up and I would come and see them as often as I could," she later testified.[3] The three prisoners exchanged glances, somewhat surprised at seeing Iva's beaming face. Orders had been given that no one was to talk to them without a good reason, and that was why they were kept isolated in a small room on the second floor of the building. So the prisoners were a bit wary of Iva's unnatural friendliness. "We didn't talk much," recalled Cousens. "She talked mostly. She was very friendly, so much so that we were very suspicious." Indeed, they even thought that Iva might be a *kempeitai* spy.[4]

Iva guessed how the three men felt about her, but she continued to drop by to chat on one pretext or another. Partly it was just a matter of personal sympathy. The three men always looked underfed and overworked. Iva wanted to do what she could to cheer them up. She was also glad to see Allied soldiers who had been fighting on "her" side in the war.

Iva did her best to allay the POWs' suspicions of her. She told them that she was an American still, that she had not given up her citizenship as many other *nisei* working at the station had done. But the POWs did not really begin to trust Iva until she began to bring them news of how the war was going.

Ordinary Japanese were forbidden to listen to shortwave broadcasts during the war, and even the employees at NHK were not allowed to listen without good reason. There were shortwave receivers at the station, but staff members were permitted to use them only to familiarize themselves with the equipment. In her job at Domei, Iva was able to listen to Allied news broadcasts every day, and she knew that the war was starting to go well for the Allies. When visiting with the POWs, Iva would pass along news reports of the Allied advances, sometimes whispering in a low voice and sometimes writing on scraps of paper. She also began to bring the three POWs little bits of food, and gradually they began to trust her. Cousens later remarked that she was the only loyal person he worked with at NHK, and Norman Reyes said at her trial, "I would have trusted her with my life."[5] Ince, a man with a contrary disposition and strongly anti-Japanese sentiments, later testified that he did not really trust anyone with a Japanese face, but even he seemed to mistrust Iva less than he mistrusted other members of the staff.

Three POWs

Iva was most impressed by Major Charles H. Cousens, who seemed to be the leader of the group. At their first meeting, when Iva asked him how long he was going to stay at the Overseas Bureau, he had replied quietly but firmly, "Until the Allies win." That made a deep impression on Iva, and her feelings of respect and trust for him grew as she came to know him better.

Major Charles Hughes Cousens, then forty years old, was the perfect picture of an English gentleman. He was six feet tall, with a splendid mustache, a piercing gaze, and a military bearing. A graduate of Sandhurst, he had been posted to India after receiving his commission, but at the age of twenty-two he had decided to leave the army and seek his fortune in Australia. He had bounced about for a while, working first as a stevedore, then as a professional boxer, a sportswriter, and manager of an advertising agency. Finally he went to work for 2GB, a Sydney radio station, and soon became the chief announcer. He also got married, fathered two children, and acquired Australian citizenship.

In June 1940, at the age of thirty-seven, Cousens enlisted in the Australian army. As the Japanese continued to advance in Asia, Australia began sending forces to augment the British Far Eastern army forces at strategic points in Asia. Cousens had responded to the call of his adopted country. When the Pacific war began, Cousens was stationed in Singapore. During the next three months he commanded an infantry battalion in the battle for Malaya. On February 15, 1942, two days after he was promoted to major, he was taken prisoner when Singapore fell to the Japanese.

Cousens had feared that if the Japanese discovered he was a radio announcer they might try to use him for their propaganda purposes, so he tried to conceal his professional past. He simply told Japanese interrogators that he had been a journalist before the war. However, when the Japanese gave permission to let the Australians broadcast home that the captured troops were safe and healthy, one of Cousens's commanders

asked him to do it. At first Cousens refused, but since he had to obey orders from a superior officer, he finally agreed.

The local Japanese army authorities, now that they knew who Cousens was, sent word back to the General Staff in Tokyo that one of the
Australian POWs was a famous radio announcer. Orders were issued to
bring him to Tokyo. Cousens refused to go. He soon found himself in
solitary confinement, then shipped off for heavy labor in South Burma.

The Japanese did not give up so easily. Cousens was brought back to
Singapore, where one of his superior officers, under pressure from the
Japanese, persuaded him to go to Tokyo to report by broadcast that the
Australian prisoners were well. After receiving a written order that he
was to transmit POW messages and to appeal for help to the International Red Cross, he finally agreed. In June 1942 he left for Japan—by
a strange coincidence on the *Arabia Maru,* the ship that had brought Iva
to Japan a year before.

On the morning of August 1, Cousens was brought to meet Major
Tsuneishi at General Staff headquarters in Tokyo. A small, trim man,
ruddy-faced and sinewy, looking every inch the Japanese military man,
Tsuneishi was a sharp contrast to the thin and ailing Cousens, weakened
by dysentery, who stood before him in a soiled khaki uniform stripped of
insignia.

Tsuneishi came right to the point. Cousens was to make propaganda
broadcasts for Japan under the orders of the Japanese Imperial army.
Cousens, weak and tired though he was, protested. He had received orders from his superiors only to send POW messages and to make appeals
to the International Red Cross. Tsuneishi barked back that he could not
guarantee the personal safety of a prisoner who did not obey the orders
of the Japanese Imperial army. Cousens replied, "Give me a pistol and a
cartridge. That would save time for both of us."[6] Instead, Cousens was
taken to the Dai-ichi Hotel, where for the first time since he had left
Singapore he was allowed to shave.

Later that day Cousens was led to the NHK offices, where he was
handed a script and ordered to broadcast it that evening at six o'clock. At
once Cousens saw that it was a virulent attack on President Roosevelt,
and he refused. He said that as a POW he would be glad to sweep the
floors or do any other kind of work, but he simply would not broadcast

such a script. When Tsuneishi got word that Cousens was being stubborn, he replied simply, "Do whatever you have to do, but he must make the broadcast." To make sure that Cousens did, Tsuneishi set out for the NHK building himself.

As soon as he arrived, Tsuneishi sat down and scrawled out a written order, attaching Cousens to the NHK Overseas Bureau in the name of General Gen Sugiyama, army chief of staff. The chief staff members of the American Division assembled in his office and Tsuneishi ordered Cousens brought in. Akira Namikawa later testified that Tsuneishi turned to the group and said, "If he does not listen, we will simply dispose of him."[7] As Cousens walked in, Tsuneishi stood up silently and with deliberate care placed his officer's saber on the desk in front of him. In a drill-ground voice that stunned even the Japanese staff members, he barked out, "ATTENTION!" Namikawa, who was supposed to interpret, stood speechless, and it took a few minutes to find another staff member who could capture Tsuneishi's tone of voice in translating the order to Cousens.

Tsuneishi was acting out a little drama to impress Cousens that he had no choice but to accept the order. Cousens, desperately alone, a prisoner in the midst of the enemy, was profoundly shaken. The Japanese in the room saw the blood drain from his face, and as he left he seemed to be faint with dizziness. The confrontation impressed even the Japanese civilian staff members, who had never seen Tsuneishi bellow out orders like a line commander before. Indeed, everyone was now rather in awe of Major Tsuneishi.

The confrontation had served its more immediate purpose. That evening Cousens sat before the microphone to read the propaganda script. Even so, he had not quite given up the fight. His broadcast delivery was so slipshod that Namikawa, who had been listening in the control room, sat fuming with anger after the program ended. But Cousens was undaunted. Since sabotage had worked once, Cousens decided to try it again. For the next two weeks he read the news analysis scripts given him in such a clearly dispirited way that the bureau staff began to wonder if he would be any use at all.

The Japanese were not the only ones who noticed the sloppiness of Cousens's first performances. Peter de Mendelssohn, an Allied analyst of the Japanese propaganda effort, noted in a study published in 1944: "Cousens, formerly a Sydney announcer, gives the impression that he is merely reading a script already written for him, probably by a Japanese, as his phrasing rather resembles the peculiar style affected by Japanese when speaking English."[8]

But Tsuneishi, who had decided that Cousens was too valuable a resource to waste, began to pursue another line of attack. If threats did not work, then a gentler approach might. He thought that it might not be a bad idea to provide Cousens with some female companionship. Namikawa was ordered to get to work on it, but whenever he invited Cousens to visit a nightclub with him, he got a firm but polite refusal. Tsuneishi kept badgering Namikawa, however, until Namikawa finally one day importuned Cousens to go with him so he could save face with Tsuneishi. Ever the gentleman, Cousens agreed to go on an excursion to a geisha house in Honmokugai, a red-light district in Yokohama. Cousens was simply there to help Namikawa out, and he left rather quickly after dancing with one geisha.

So Tsuneishi had to give in. Like the other bureau staff members, he had come to understand that Cousens was a man of particularly strong character who acted in accord with his own sense of propriety. Cousens was put to work writing "radio essays" about the need to have high ideals as a human being. He broadcast them himself. He had taken stubborn refuge in platitudes.

In the middle of October 1942, about two and a half months after Cousens arrived at the Overseas Bureau, he was joined by Wallace E. Ince, an American army captain, and Norman Reyes, a Filipino lieutenant. Both had been captured in the Philippines. The thirty-year-old Ince had been in charge of "The Voice of Freedom," a propaganda program that the Americans had transmitted from Corregidor. He had broadcast under the name of Ted Wallace. Norman Reyes, then not yet twenty, had served on his staff. When the Japanese learned that the two men had propaganda broadcasting experience, they were taken to Santiago Prison in Manila for lengthy interrogations. They were then brought to Tokyo on orders from Major Tsuneishi, who told them when they arrived that they were to be attached to the Overseas Bureau. "You will regard orders from the Overseas Bureau as orders from the army," he told them. "If you do not follow these orders, I do not think I need to explain to you what will happen."[9]

Tsuneishi, having had difficulty with Cousens, was somewhat apprehensive about how the two new POW recruits would perform, but neither showed much inclination to protest. Reyes, whose mother was American, seemed to take to his new work with some enthusiasm. He had always been interested in radio, and after graduating from high school he had gone to work in broadcasting. As far as many bureau staff members could determine, it seemed he was happy to be doing radio work in Japan as well.

At first Reyes and Ince were put to work rewriting and correcting news analyses scripts, but before long they were writing their own scripts. Ince took charge of a program called "From One American to Another," and Reyes oversaw a program called "Life in the East."

Like Cousens, both Reyes and Ince stayed in private rooms at the Dai-ichi Hotel. In accordance with the Geneva Convention, all were paid salaries appropriate for Japanese officers of their rank. Major Tsuneishi also continued his "soft" policy of humoring the POWs with small favors. He had special ration cards issued for them, and twice had suits made for Cousens—one for fall and one for spring—at a Tokyo department store.

The treatment the POWs received caused some resentment among the *nisei* employed at the Overseas Bureau, many of whom were not paid or treated as well. Billeting the POWs in the same hotel as visitors from friendly countries caused objections elsewhere, too, so in March 1943 Major Tsuneishi moved his valuable charges to the Sanno Hotel, used to house army and *kempeitai* officers.

The presence of the POWs caused some friction at the bureau, particularly among the female staff members, who did their best to fraternize with the three men. The outgoing Norman Reyes was particularly popular among the typists. Higher-ups at the bureau looked on with much disapproval, and issued warnings to those who got unnecessarily friendly with the prisoners. To make sure that contact was kept at a minimum, the three were assigned an office on the second floor of the NHK, always under surveillance. Even so, some women staffers would make their way downstairs on various pretexts. The POWs, who had heard that some of the bureau personnel were *kempeitai* spies, were often less than cordial.

"Zero Hour" Begins

The Overseas Bureau staff did not take long to realize that, compared to themselves, Cousens was a true professional who knew what he was doing. At first the POWs read over the scripts written for them by Japanese staff members, but since these scripts had to be vetted for mistakes in grammar, syntax, and the like, the POWs began to insist that it would be easier for them to do their own scripts from the start rather than wasting time correcting the enormous number of errors the Japanese staff writers made. So the POWs were allowed to prepare their own scripts directly from news materials.

Cousens, Ince, and Reyes all later testified that as a result of their new freedom they began attempting to sabotage their broadcasts. Sometimes they would try to get messages to the outside world by using strange expressions or putting words with double meanings into the broadcast scripts. Sometimes they slipped news items out of the file of items to be broadcast. Probably these acts of sabotage were undetectable to anyone listening to the broadcasts, but the POWs regarded every minor change of wording as a part of their secret war against the Japanese. It helped keep up their morale.

In 1943 the Eighth Section embarked on a new project for the POWs. The Japanese army had developed facilities to monitor medium-wave domestic radio broadcasts from the United States. As a result Japanese listening posts were able to pick up news of local disasters in the States— floods on the Mississippi, forest fires in California, major automobile accidents, train wrecks, and the like. Major Tsuneishi and his colleagues decided it would be a good idea to have the POWs broadcast a news program of these items to demoralize American front-line troops. The news would be true, and the GIs probably would not hear it otherwise.

On March 1, 1943, Radio Tokyo began broadcasting a brand-new program to the Pacific. It was called "Zero Hour." The title was loaded with intimidating significance: "Zero Hour" was the moment before an attack; the Zero was the best-known and most feared Japanese fighter plane; and the red round sun in the middle of the Japanese national flag looked very much like a zero.

The basic purpose of the program was to make the GIs homesick, demoralized, and discouraged by broadcasting disaster news from home. The Japanese had become sophisticated enough by now to realize there ought to be a teaser or lead-in to get the GIs interested in listening, so it was decided that Norman Reyes, who knew quite a bit about jazz, would start off by playing popular song records. The "original Zero Hour"—as one of Iva's lawyers later called it—was a disc jockey show. Reyes played records, and between selections he read a script written from news items given to him that day. The program began at 7:15 P.M. (Tokyo time), so it could be heard by the GIs just as they were relaxing after dinner.

Since the music was good listening, and Reyes's delivery relaxed, "Zero Hour" became quite popular with the Pacific GIs. In June 1943, just four months after it had begun, the first American news report of the program came from Guadalcanal:

> Between the Tokyo radio and Japanese bombers, the nights are not always dull here. Tokyo has been beaming a program called "the Zero Hour" direct to the Russell Islands and Guadalcanal. The fellows like it very much because it cries over them and feels so sorry for them. It talks about the food that they miss by not being home and tells how the war workers are stealing their jobs and their girls.[10]

Major Tsuneishi was quite pleased with success of the new project. He decided to use "Zero Hour" as bait to expand the audience for other Radio Tokyo programs. In the first week of August 1943 the program was lengthened from fifteen or twenty minutes to forty or forty-five minutes, and Cousens and Ince were put to work helping Reyes. "Zero Hour" became the POWs' program. George Mitsushio, a former *nisei* born in San Francisco, and Oki furnished materials for news scripts, and sometimes wrote scripts themselves, but the three POWs controlled the tone of the program. Reyes continued playing records interspersed with commentary, Cousens read POW messages, and Ince read domestic news items for the United States.

The three POWs were in a far better position to subvert "Zero Hour" than they had been to sabotage any other programs, and that is precisely what they tried to do. Their idea was to make "Zero Hour" into an entertainment program that would boost GI morale rather than destroy it. The POWs did their best to downplay propaganda, reading objectionable news items hurriedly or in a joking tone of voice. Judging from the fact that a good many GIs found "Zero Hour" propaganda more amusing than demoralizing, the POWs succeeded to some extent.

The bureau staff had been told by Major Tsuneishi that the program was bait to lure listeners to Radio Tokyo, so they did not interfere much with the POWs' work. Although the POWs were supposed to be under strict supervision, often it was quite perfunctory. Some bureau staff members criticized the program because it was pure entertainment and because the POWs were given so much latitude with it, but everyone recognized its quality. It was the only Radio Tokyo program that approached the standards of Allied overseas broadcasts.

In November 1943 Major Tsuneishi decided that it was time to expand "Zero Hour" once again. George Mitsushio was ordered to work up a plan. Around Armistice Day 1943 he got together with the three POWs. They were not pleased at the news. As Cousens later testified, "We protested because we had the thing, as we thought, fairly well under our control. [The program] was comparatively useless to the Japanese, and further change in the thing might make us reassess our plans for it."[11]

If the program were expanded, new staff would have to be added, and more demoralizing propaganda would be put into the scripts. The whole tone of "Zero Hour" as an entertainment program would be lost. But when the three men protested, according to Cousens, Mitsushio said that expansion was an order from the Imperial Japanese army. "It is my neck as well as yours," he said, and made a little chopping gesture with his hand, as the staff members often did.[12]

Cousens asked Mitsushio to let him think the matter over for a while. "But please leave the plans for expansion to me," he said. He was beginning to think that "Zero Hour" could be expanded without changing its basic tone and format. If new staff members had to be added, he thought, it would be best to get someone the POWs could trust, a woman announcer whose voice was a bit different from the others. It was then he decided to recruit Iva Toguri, the friendly new typist.

When Cousens told Ince and Reyes his idea, they were rather surprised and opposed to it. Cousens paid no heed. He went to Mitsushio. At first Mitsushio thought it a joke, but when it became apparent that Cousens was serious, he objected. "You can't use a voice like that," he said. It was Cousens's turn to insist. "If all our necks are at stake, trust me, just leave everything to me," he said. "I won't do anything bad."[13] Not entirely convinced, Mitsushio grudgingly gave in.

"A Voice Like That"

One afternoon in mid-November 1943—probably between the eleventh and the thirteenth—Iva was at her desk typing when George Mitsushio walked over to talk to her. "He came up to me and told me that army orders had come through, that I was to be taken down to be put on a new entertainment program put on by the prisoners of war," Iva recalled in court. "I told him I had been hired [at NHK] as a typist. I didn't know the first thing about radio or radio announcing or anything about scripts or records. I said, 'I do not want to be an announcer.' . . . He said, 'It is not what you want. Army orders came through and army orders are army orders. If you want details go see your boss.' "[14]

Iva, flustered and upset, quickly went over to talk to her supervisor, Shigechika Takano. He looked up and said, "I meant to tell you when you first came in this morning that we had received army orders that you had been selected by the prisoners of war to put on this new entertainment program." Iva, who hardly knew what a microphone or a studio looked like, told Takano she did not want to do it. "You better not forget that you got a job at NHK even though you're a foreigner," he said. "You have no choice. You're living in a country under the control of the army. You can't do anything but follow the army's orders. I don't think there is any need to tell you what will happen if you don't do it."[15]

Around four-thirty or five that afternoon Iva was taken to a studio on the second floor, where Cousens (and perhaps Reyes, according to some testimony) was waiting for her. "I asked what was the reason for me being called down for a voice test when I didn't know the first thing about radio," Iva later testified. Cousens replied quietly, "Don't worry about that. We chose you for a specific reason. Just go out there and take a voice test. It is a formality." And a formality it was, for the voice test lasted only a minute or two.

When she was done, Cousens explained the format of "Zero Hour" to her, and then went on in a low voice. "This is a straight entertainment program," he said. "I have written it and I know what I am doing. All you have got to do is look on yourself as a soldier under my orders. Do exactly what you are told. Don't try to do anything for yourself and you will do nothing that you do not want to do. You will do nothing against your own people. I will guarantee that personally because I have read the script."[16] Iva was still dubious, but she trusted Cousens, so she decided to go ahead.

At six o'clock that evening Iva sat down in front of the microphone to introduce the records Cousens had selected and to read the script he had written. It had been nearly two and a half years since she had left San Pedro harbor. Now she finally was talking to other Americans again, but in a way she could not have imagined possible then—as an announcer on a Japanese propaganda broadcast.

Major Cousens' Plan

The choice of Iva as the new woman announcer for "Zero Hour" surprised nearly everyone in the American Division. "What is the idea?" someone asked Mitsushio. "Why pick a farmer like Iva? No experience. Terrible voice. Even her English is not laudable."[17] Mitsushio shrugged his shoulders. The POWs had recommended her, he said.

The rest of the staff could not understand the choice either. There were other women announcers with excellent voices—June Suyama, "the Nightingale of Nanking," or Ruth Hayakawa. They would have been happy to appear on "Zero Hour." But instead the choice was Iva, a typist with no broadcast experience, whose voice was deep and cracked. Ince and Reyes, when they first heard Iva speaking into the microphone, thought she sounded awful. She had a voice like a crow, thought Ince.

Only one person in the American Division was pleased at the choice, and that was Charles Cousens. He had a very clear purpose in choosing Iva. As he later testified, "With the idea that I had in mind of making a complete burlesque of the program, [her voice] was just what I wanted—

rough. I hope I can say this without offense—a voice that I have described as a gin fog voice. It was rough, almost masculine, anything but a femininely seductive voice. It was a comedy voice that I needed for this particular job."[18]

He explained this to Iva. "Major Cousens said my voice is not what you call a gentle and sweet voice," she later testified, "but he wanted a Yankee voice with a certain personality to it, with a little touch of a WAC officer's voice in it that would have a lot of cheer."[19] He promised to bring out that cheer by daily coaching.

Indeed, from the first day on Cousens began to coach Iva very carefully on her delivery. The sight of the two of them huddled together was familiar to the bureau staff. Cousens would first read Iva the script he had written for her portion of the broadcast. Then he would have her go over it again and again, imitating his accent and intonation exactly for every word and phrase until he was satisfied that she had it down pat. He did his best to correct her own peculiar habit of speech. Iva had a tendency to talk in a rapid chattering voice, so every day Cousens tried to get her to speak slowly and cheerfully. He urged her to talk as though she were in the midst of a group of GIs kidding with them.

Cousens put a great deal of effort into his coaching, and Iva, who knew that the other staff members complained about her voice and made fun of her, worked hard to improve her delivery. The coaching paid off. Gradually Iva's rather harsh, throaty voice was transformed into one that was comical but cheerful, lively, and gay, perhaps somewhere between Gracie Allen and Shirley Booth. Filipe later described it as being like the voice of Molly on "Fibber McGee and Molly." The other Radio Tokyo woman announcers had voices that were sweet and mellifluous but without any special character. Iva's delivery and patter were distinctive, and were liked by the GIs. Indeed, with the appearance of Iva on "Zero Hour," the program's popularity began to rise even more.

At first Iva did not want to use her real name, so she broadcast anonymously. But in December Cousens suggested that she take the name "Ann," the abbreviation used for "announcer" on the NHK scripts. It was a completely casual suggestion, a name with no significance. When Cousens learned that even American broadcasts were calling the GIs "orphans of the Pacific," he proposed that Iva change her name to "Orphan Ann" or "Orphan Annie." He was even more pleased when he found out from Ince that "Little Orphan Annie" was a well-known comic strip character in the United States.

The format of the new "Zero Hour," with Iva as its female announcer, was different from the original "Zero Hour." It now began at 6:00 P.M. Tokyo time and lasted until 7:15 (sometime at the end of 1944 it was shortened to an hour, 6:00 to 7:00 P.M.). According to pieced-together accounts of various later trial witnesses, it seems to have had more or less the following format at the time Cousens worked on it.

1. Opening theme song: a record of "Strike Up the Band" played by Arthur Fiedler and the Boston Pops orchestra.

2. POW messages (5–10 minutes). The messages, read by Cousens, were about twenty-five words long. A typical message might go something like this: "Hello Mom. This is Corporal So and So. We need socks, food. We are doing all right. Blooey is here with me. Tell his folks. Haven't seen Charlie since Singapore. Keep your chins up. We are all right."[20]

3. "Orphan Ann" disc jockey segment (15–20 minutes). With the words, "Here comes your music," Cousens would introduce "Ann." After reading a greeting Cousens had written, Iva played three 12-inch or four 9-inch 78 rpm records, prefacing each with a few pert comments. The music was mainly classical or semiclassical, with some dance records. Iva never ad-libbed or made comments of her own, but simply read the script written for her by Cousens. Her voice was on the air only two or three minutes.

4. "American Home Front News" (5–10 minutes). Mitsushio wrote the script from items picked up on army-monitored American domestic newscasts. The announcer was usually Ince. Often there was not enough news to fill the segment, so records were played to kill time.

5. "Juke Box" (15–20 minutes). Norman Reyes played popular or jazz records. This portion was basically the original "Zero Hour."

6. "Ted's News Highlight Tonight" (5–10 minutes). News items from overseas shortwave broadcasts supplied by a Japanese staff member and edited by Ince.

7. An occasional news commentary read by Charles Yoshii, a *nisei* dubbed as a Japanese "Lord Haw-Haw."

8. A military march or song.

9. Sign-off by Ince.

All the witnesses connected with "Zero Hour" unanimously testified that Iva's portion of the program was under the control of Cousens, who wrote her scripts and selected records for her to play. The scripts Cousens wrote were filled with shorthand expressions, slang words, jokes, and puns that would be difficult for a non-native speaker of English to understand. None of the Overseas Bureau staffers, except the *nisei,* knew English well enough to understand most of what was in the script. It was all the more difficult to understand when Iva read it, for although she spoke more slowly than she normally did, her delivery was still fast-paced.

To keep on the safe side of the censors, however, Cousens's scripts for Iva had her address the GIs as "honorable boneheads." But Cousens coached her to use the phrase in a bantering way. The Japanese were not supposed to be able to pronounce a clear and rolling *r*—the Japanese *r* often sounds close to a *d*—so Iva pronounced "honorable" as "honable." Following Cousens's scripts, she occasionally called herself "Your favorite enemy, Ann." The tone was self-mockery, not seriousness.

"Zero Hour" was on the air seven days a week, but Cousens, Ince, and Iva never came to the studio on Sundays. Ruth Hayakawa usually took over then, along with Norman Reyes, whose "Juke Box" segments were rebroadcast, and Kenkichi Oki, who replaced Mitsushio as supervisor. Just who wrote the Sunday scripts remains unclear, but it is certain that Iva never participated in the Sunday "Zero Hour."

Bunka Camp

Having enjoyed such success with the "Zero Hour" program, Major Tsuneishi and the Eighth Section decided to expand use of Allied POWs for propaganda broadcasts. In November 1943 fifty-three such POWs were brought to Omori prison camp in Tokyo. To keep them isolated from other POWs, the army prepared a special facility at Surugadai in the Kanda section of Tokyo, famous today for its used-book stores and publishing houses.

The facility was the former Bunka Gakuin (Cultural Institute), an educational institution closed down for "liberalism." In the spring of 1943 the army decided to turn the building into a dormitory and workshop for POWs engaged in propaganda work. Officially it was known as the Annex Office of the Eighth Section. To camouflage its real character, the plaque in front of the gate identified it simply as the "Surugadai Technical Research Center." It was so secret that many within the General Staff did not know of its existence.

To the POWs, however, the place was known simply as Bunka Camp. It was an unpretentious square structure built around an inner courtyard. Military guards stood in front of the gate, but ordinary passersby would have no idea what went on behind it. The staff, numbering about thirty, were told never to talk about their work on the outside.

The first contingent of fourteen POWs arrived at Bunka Camp on December 1, 1943, and twelve more arrived the following month. On their first day they were assembled in the courtyard, where Imperial Army Captain Koimai told them he could not guarantee their lives if they did not follow his orders. This ritual injunction was repeated every morning for the next three months.

About a week and a half after their arrival, Major Tsuneishi gave a speech of his own. "Unfortunately for both of us," he told them, "a war has developed between Japan and America.... The war is a matter of extreme loss to both sides.... It is my desire and wish, therefore, that this war be terminated as soon as possible."[21] He asked the prisoners to help end the war quickly by broadcasting these wishes and ideas to the American people. "If there is anyone who does not wish to do this, please step forward," he concluded.

George Williams, an English civilian who had been captured on the Gilbert Islands, did so. He was immediately led off by the guards, and Major Tsuneishi returned to his office in a rage. Williams was sent immediately to another POW camp, where he survived until the end of the war, but the POWs remaining at Bunka Camp assumed that he had been killed by the Japanese.

The psychological pressure put on the prisoners had its effect. When Cousens and Ince—who had been separated from Norman Reyes after he became a "friendly alien" instead of a POW*—were transferred to Bunka Camp on December 18, Cousens was surprised to see what a timorous group they were, frightened at everything, skulking like whipped dogs. As the highest-ranking officer among them, he automatically became their leader. He began to do what he could to put some spirit back into them. As with Iva (and perhaps with himself as well), he urged them to use the broadcasts as a way of fighting back at the Japanese. He told them to put double meanings into the broadcast scripts. Since Kazumaro ("Buddy") Uno, a former *nisei* on the Bunka Camp staff, censored the scripts quite carefully, it is unlikely that this sort of sabotage was very effective, but Cousens's constant sermons about "fighting" the Japanese probably helped boost the POWs' own morale.

Three of the POWs—Lieutenant Edwin Kalbfleisch, Ensign George Henshaw, and Sergeant John David Provoo—were put to work right away as announcers on a new program Japanese staff writers had put together on the model of "Zero Hour." Broadcast from one to one thirty in the early afternoon (later from one thirty to two), it consisted of POW messages, music, news analyses, and occasional radio dramas. Provoo was the master of ceremonies, and Kalbfleisch did the news analysis. With a desperate want of imagination the new program was called the "Hi no maru Hour"—*hi no maru* being the zero-shaped round red sun on the Japanese flag. The name was so ridiculous that a staff member urged Tsuneishi to change it, and eventually it became "Humanity Calls." The Japanese staff wrote all the scripts at first, but since they were not very good, the POWs eventually began to write their own material. Later the POWs took complete charge of the program, as Cousens and the others had with "Zero Hour."

Gradually a number of other POW programs were put on the air— "War on War," "The Postwar Call," "The Australian Program" (or "Australian Hour"), "Civilian Air Program," and the like—but the content and format were generally the same.

---

* Reyes had become a "friendly alien" when the Japanese established a puppet government in the Philippines in November 1943. Reyes had requested that he be sent to Manila to do broadcast work there, but Tsuneishi put pressure on him to remain. Cousens and Ince told Reyes that since he could not get back home, he should stay on to do what sabotage he could at Radio Tokyo. "Get anything you can out of the Japs," they said. He did—his salary jumped from 60 yen to 500.

Life at Bunka Camp was by no means pleasant. On the slightest excuse Japanese guards beat the prisoners, who had forfeited their honor by allowing themselves to be captured. Cousens seemed to be the only one who escaped this treatment. Uno often complained to Tsuneishi that beating the prisoners was not a good way to gain their cooperation or to produce effective propaganda programs. Tsuneishi agreed to transfer one of the more brutal guards, but he kept on Lieutenant Hamamoto, who once knocked Ince unconscious, even though Ince was desperately ill. Eventually, after more complaints by Uno, he too was transferred to other duties.

Two Bunka Camp staffers, Tamotsu Murayama and Suisei Matsui, often urged Nobuo Fujimura, the camp's civilian chief, to treat the POWs in accordance with the Geneva Convention. Fujimura talked to Tsuneishi about it, but Tsuneishi saw no need to bother with such matters. (Japan had signed the convention in 1929 but had not ratified it formally.) Cousens asked Tsuneishi to get in touch with the neutral Swiss, but since the General Staff wanted the existence of Bunka Camp kept secret, the Swiss were not allowed to visit.

The POWs found the food as hard to stomach as the beatings. Nicholas Schenck, a Dutch POW, later testified, "We got a ration of three teacups of kaoliang per day and three bowls of soup to get that down with. The bowls of soup were a little bit larger than the teacups. The soup merely consisted of daikon [radish] . . . a little salt, a little soya, to which water was added."[22] It was hardly enough to keep them alive. On a diet of kaoliang, a grain often used as chicken feed, human beings suffer from beri-beri or pellagra. According to some witnesses, the POWs often ate the buds from trees on the camp grounds or a luckless stray animal. Schenck recalled making meals of at least two dogs and two cats. The POWs used their pay to buy what food they could on the black market with the help of an old couple who served as caretakers at the camp. One or two of the Japanese staff members helped, too.

And Iva helped. At Cousens's request she began bringing food, medicine, and other supplies for the prisoners almost daily. On her holidays she often went to the countryside, sometimes trading old clothes for food. Drugs she bought at pharmacies wherever she could find them in supply—quinine, aspirin, vitamins, yeast pills. She got her friends to help also. Filipe's grandmother in Atsugi bought things for her, and an agricultural student living at her boardinghouse gave her fresh vegetables and fruits his parents sent from the countryside.

Smuggling drugs and medicine to the POWs was not so difficult, but bulky food was another matter. Often she took food to the NHK office in an aluminum mess can. Cousens and Ince would eat what Iva had brought and then would share their nightly rations with the other POWs at Bunka Camp.

In February or March 1944 one of the POWs, Larry Quille, came down with a high fever and severe chills. The POWs were issued only one thin *futon*, a quilt which was barely enough to keep them warm even on early spring nights. The Bunka Camp authorities refused to give Quille another quilt. When Iva heard the story from Cousens, she brought in a blanket that she had been using to cover a trunk. Ince wrapped it around his own body and smuggled it into camp under his coat. Filipe was surprised when she told him she had given the blanket away. In wartime Japan a good wool blanket was worth more than gold.

"America Was Winning"

Iva finally quit her job at Domei monitoring service at Atago Hill in late December 1943. Her blunt and unconcealed attachment to the Allied cause in the war led to a falling out with the other *nisei* employed there. All of them had registered as Japanese citizens, and their sympathies were as clearly pro-Japanese as Iva's were pro-American.

"[F]or about three or four months previous to my quitting the Domei job, I had reasons for becoming involved in a lot of discussions with the other employees at Domei . . . about the truthfulness of the news that came through the shortwave and also the other United States government reports," Iva later recalled. "I never read Japanese papers, because I couldn't read them. Occasionally I would buy an English paper, but their reports on the progress of the war were entirely the reverse of what I heard on the San Francisco and the London stations."[23]

The other Domei monitors accepted the announcement of the Imperial General Headquarters as the gospel truth. While these announcements were quite accurate during the first six months of the war, report-

ing both victories and setbacks, they had become detached from reality
by mid-1942. Iva did her best to convince the others at Domei that the
Japanese announcements were false. "I said the Japanese from [the time
of Coral Sea and Midway] had never announced the names of any ship
that they claimed to have sunk, never could name any aircraft carrier
that they claimed to have sunk, whereas the Americans could bring out
the exact name of the Japanese aircraft carriers that they had sunk, and
I told them just that fact alone should be proof enough of the fact that
America was winning."[24]

But instead of convincing the others, Iva merely irritated them. Filipe
was the only one who took her side. One day he even got into a fistfight
about it. Although the other *nisei* threatened to turn Iva into the Special
Security Police, they never did for fear of getting into trouble themselves.
After the fistfight it was difficult for Iva to stay on at Domei. In a way
her quitting proved fortuitous. In response to an English-language newspaper ad she was able to find more congenial work as a secretary at the
Danish legation.

Lars Pedersen Tillitse, the Danish minister, was interested in the
United States, and Iva later surmised that he decided to hire her because
she was American. The pay was good—initially 150 yen a month, later
160—and there was really not a great deal of work to do. Aside from the
maids she was the only employee at the legation.

Iva's acquaintance with the Tillitses was one of the pleasantest experiences she had in wartime Japan. After the war Tillitse recalled, "She
told me she had great difficulty adjusting to Japanese life at the beginning. She also repeatedly said she wanted to go back to America. She
wanted to go back in the fall of 1941. She was very sorry that she was
stranded in Japan during the wartime. I remember she often talked
about the war. She said America will win the war and that it was mad-
ness on the part of Japan to try and attack the U.S., and I always took it
for granted that she wanted America to win the war."[25] Iva did not tell
the Tillitses about her job at NHK, and after the war, when Tillitse
heard that Iva was "Tokyo Rose," he was astounded.

Her day at the legation ended at 4:00 P.M. Iva would rush off to
NHK, usually arriving about five. Occasionally when she had to work
late at the legation she would barely get to the studio in time for her

broadcast. Oki and Mitsushio, who were directly in charge of the program, were not pleased, but Iva did not tell them about the legation job.

Although she enjoyed her work with the Tillitses, Iva did not want to quit her work at the Overseas Bureau. For one thing, as the result of Cousens's coaching she was enjoying her broadcast more and more. She felt fortunate to be learning the business from a pro like Cousens. She even thought that after the war was over she might like to go into radio work.

Considering the small amount of time she put in at Radio Tokyo, her salary was quite good too. The other regular women announcers worked all day, but Iva was at the studio for only two or three hours a day. Her basic salary was 80 yen with a special allowance of 20 yen for her English-language skills. Even June Suyama, the best-paid woman announcer, got only 150 yen plus bonuses.

By staying at NHK, Iva could continue to secretly smuggle medicine and food to the POWs. Buying food had become a little easier since the Tillitses shared with her their special diplomatic rations of soap, sugar, matches, and other scarce items. Iva exchanged them for food and medicine to give to the prisoners.

She could also continue to give the POWs reports Filipe heard on the Allied broadcasts. She worked out a kind of code to pass the news on under the watchful eyes of the Japanese guards. If the Allies had captured another island, Iva made a V-sign with her fingers. Sometimes she could be more direct. When Iva and Cousens were in the studio broadcasting records, they could talk rather freely in low voices. The NHK staff people in the control booth could hear only the sound of the music. When she whispered, "Praise the Lord and pass the ammunition," it was a signal to Cousens that she had some news to tell him.

Who Is Tokyo Rose?

The Overseas Bureau staff heard the name "Tokyo Rose" for the first time in March or April 1944. Both Iva and Cousens testified that the report had come through a neutral news source, either Lisbon or Sweden, and that Mitsushio brought a copy of the item to the room newly set aside for the "Zero Hour" staff on the third floor. They testified the report indicated that the "Tokyo Rose" broadcast resembled "Orphan Ann" broadcasts. Since it had been on a Sunday, however, Cousens and Mitsushio concluded it could not be Iva but perhaps was a broadcast originating in the South.

Kenkichi Oki's testimony on the matter was a bit different. He recalled that the news item clearly identified "Tokyo Rose" as "Orphan Ann," and that afterward everyone at the bureau secretly called Iva "Tokyo Rose." He even insisted that Iva seemed to be inwardly happy at her new celebrity. But according to Ruth Hayakawa, that is not what he thought at the time. She remembered very clearly talking to Oki about the report: ". . . He showed me a copy of the news that came in from the Foreign Office, which said the GIs in the South were enjoying the radio programs from Tokyo, especially the music and voice of a young lady. . . . This article said that the woman's voice was very soft and appealing, and they liked her program, and they wondered who Tokyo Rose was. So I recall asking Ken who was Tokyo Rose and Ken told me that it was I, because the article said Sunday evening and I was on the Sunday evening program. . . . Ken also pointed out that my voice was soft and appealing, whereas Iva's voice was not."[26]

Most Overseas Bureau staff thought that Iva, Ruth Hayakawa, and also June Suyama were the most likely candidates as the popular Tokyo Rose, but when all was said and done, her identity remained a mystery to them. Many, like Cousens and Mitsushio, surmised the voice might be a woman announcer broadcasting from a station in the South Pacific regions. There was a string of Japanese-controlled stations from Burma to the Dutch East Indies, and while most broadcasts were in local languages, the Japanese army tried to reach English-speaking peoples in India and Australia as well as the American troops in the Pacific with English-language broadcasts. Some of these originated in Manila. So there were good grounds for surmising that the report about "Tokyo Rose" referred to a woman announcer on one of these southern stations.

War's End

The staff of "Zero Hour" began to change bit by bit in the spring of 1944. In April, Ince, who always seemed to be in trouble, got into a disagreement about a "Zero Hour" script with a Bunka Camp staffer named Hishikari, who was quite proud of the fact that he had once slapped General A. E. Percival, the defeated British commander in Malaya. Hishikari gave Ince a beating, and he was taken off the "Zero Hour" program. Rumors circulated that he might be executed. He reappeared at NHK in September to work on a POW message program, "The Postman Calls."

New members began to join the staff. Ince was replaced by Kenichi Ishii, a Japanese national whose mother had been an Englishwoman. He spoke with an English accent, and his voice so much resembled Cousens that it surprised Cousens himself. Another addition to the staff was Mieko Furuya, a *nisei* typist and translator who did administrative work connected with the program. She replaced Iva as an announcer when Iva was absent. Mitsushio and Oki also began to do broadcasts from time to time. Oki was rather inept as an announcer, but he had wanted to broadcast for quite a while and Ince's departure gave him the opportunity.

In late June, Cousens left "Zero Hour" and Bunka Camp as well. He collapsed with a heart attack. The physical and mental strain of his POW experience had finally caught up with him. He was sent to a POW hospital in Shinagawa, where he had to share a cell-like room with an American POW suffering from a nervous breakdown. This was too much for the even-keeled Cousens to bear, so eventually he managed to have himself transferred to the Juntendo Hospital near Bunka Camp.

Cousens's departure from the station was a great shock to Iva. She had gone to work on "Zero Hour" in large part because she trusted and respected him. It was he who had written her scripts, had coached her on delivery, and had been her "commander" in their small struggle against the Japanese. Her role as Orphan Ann had been Cousens's creation, and now that he was gone she was an orphan indeed. Without Cousens, "Zero Hour" was meaningless for Iva.

"Zero Hour" was ceasing to be the same program it had been when only Iva and the POWs had been involved. Mitsushio, Oki, and then Norman Reyes, now a "friendly alien," began to make more and more suggestions about Iva's portion of the program. The content began to change: Mitsushio began to play a new character, "Frank Watanabe," a role modeled on "Artie and Watanabe," a comic strip that enjoyed mild popularity on the West Coast before the war. New staff were added: Satoshi Nakamura, a Canadian *nisei,* as master of ceremonies; Shinichi Oshidari and George Teruo Ozasa as writers; and Hisashi Moriyama as announcer.

Iva began to think she would like to quit the program. When she told Mitsushio, he replied that she had better reconsider whether she could quit a program directly under the control of the army simply for her own personal reasons. Major Tsuneishi was not likely to let go of the popular Orphan Ann so easily.

Since she could not leave, Iva asked for a raise. Two months later she got one. Tsuneishi felt it wise to keep such an important star by offering a hook baited with money. In July 1944 her salary went to 140 yen in basic pay and 40 yen in language allowance. She was earning 180 yen altogether.

Even so Iva began to absent herself more and more as her interest in "Zero Hour" dwindled. She had taken a good deal of time off already— a week at New Year's, three weeks in late January and early February when she had an ear infection. Her absences increased noticeably after May 1944, when she moved from her Tokyo lodgings to live with Filipe's family at Atsugi. The commute from Atsugi to Tokyo was rather long—nearly two and a half hours. Iva had to get up at 5:00 A.M. and often did not get back until 10:00 P.M. Since she was anxious to get back to Atsugi as quickly as possible in the evening, she started leaving the NHK studio around 6:30 p.m. when her portion of "Zero Hour" was over. She also began to miss her Saturday broadcasts more and more frequently.

After Cousens left the station, her absences and vacations became much more frequent. In July she took off from work at the station for two weeks after her birthday, and absented herself again in late August when she went to spend two weeks at the Danish minister's villa in Karuizawa. She stopped coming on Saturday altogether. Iva's absences were well known at the station, and Mitsushio and Oki often complained about them. (By contrast, she was extremely regular in her work at the Danish legation.)

After her return from Karuizawa Iva went to visit Cousens at the hospital several times. She complained that Mitsushio and Oki were meddling with her scripts, and she told Cousens she would like to quit if she could. Cousens tried to encourage her. He told her to use the record introductions he had written and to hold on until he was well enough to get back to work. But Cousens never did return to "Zero Hour." After being released from the hospital he was sent back to Bunka Camp, and Iva never saw him again until after the war.

Since Iva did not like the scripts that Reyes and Mitsushio prepared, she began to write her own. "I used a more or less standard pattern," she later testified, "using Major Cousens' old script as the basis or foundation for the script. By changing the records, I changed the name of the vocalist and also the name of the orchestra. I used most of his phrases as best I could, because I had no experience in radio work at all, especially scriptwriting. I hadn't any idea what to do with the script, and I used his almost word for word."[27] Reyes and other witnesses corroborated this testimony.

Things continued to go downhill at the station. In October or November 1944 Mitsushio became chief of the news analysis section, and Kenkichi Oki took over Mitsushio's responsibilities for "Zero Hour." The program was now run as an independent section, the "Front Line Section," more or less under the direct control of Major Tsuneishi. Mitsushio dropped by from time to time to see how things were going, but from mid-autumn 1944 until the end of the war the central figures of "Zero Hour" were Oki and Reyes. The quality of the broadcast gradually deteriorated. It ceased to be simply an entertainment program and was now used more and more for propaganda purposes. Only the "Orphan Ann" segment, based on Cousens's old scripts, preserved the earlier flavor of the program. Even within the American Division the program's reputation suffered after Oki took over.

The atmosphere at the American Division was rather peculiar, especially since many former *nisei* were employed there. The *nisei*, insecure because of their American origins, often tried to curry favor with their Japanese superiors, and there was a good deal of factionalism. Generally less well paid than the Japanese employees, many *nisei* used applepolishing to get extra work translating in order to earn extra pay.

Apart from this office backbiting and petty rivalry, there was much suspicion in the air. Some bureau employees were rumored to be *kempeitai* spies. This made it hard for staff members to trust one another, since there was no telling what kind of reports might be going to the police.

Despite the alleged *kempeitai* supervision, some Japanese employees thought the moral atmosphere of the American Division was a bit too relaxed. The women typists continued to make a fuss over the young POWs who came to broadcast at the station, and some, like Iva, smuggled things into Bunka Camp. At least two romances blossomed on the "Zero Hour" program: in November 1944 Norman Reyes married Katherine Morooka, a typist who had been promoted to announcer, and in March 1945 Kenkichi Oki married Mieko Furuya. The affair between Norman Reyes and Katherine Morooka raised many eyebrows. Their relationship seemed rather free to most Japanese, although it was probably not much different from the kind of dating the two might have done back home.

Iva's reputation at the station was not particularly good. Most of the staff held their tongues because Major Tsuneishi regarded her presence on the "Zero Hour" program as essential, but they resented her frequent absences, her short working hours, her high salary, and her aloofness toward the former *nisei* at the station. All this was understandable: Iva acted rather superior toward the *nisei* who had given up their American citizenship. She herself says that she did not have even one friend at the station.

There was also gossip about Iva and Filipe, who always seemed to be with her. For a while during the spring and summer of 1944 she had lived with his family near Atsugi, but tiring of the long commute she had moved in the fall to lodgings in the Tokyo suburbs with Mrs. Unami Kido, a friend of Chieko Ito's uncle. (Mrs. Kido at first had worried about having an American in the house, but a cousin in the *kempeitai* assured her there would be no problem since Iva was a *nisei* and a woman.) The friendship between Iva and Filipe that had begun at Domei two years earlier had become more serious. Around New Year's 1945 they decided to get married.

In late January the couple visited Heinrich Dumoulin, a Catholic priest at the Sophia University Church where Filipe usually attended services. Iva, brought up as a Methodist, said she wanted to convert before she married Filipe. Dumoulin, who did not speak English very well, introduced her to a Father Kraus for instruction. From the end of February to the end of April 1945, after her day was over at the Danish legation, Iva went to the Sophia Church to meet with Father Kraus instead of going to NHK. Her absences were not authorized, but since Allied bombing raids on Tokyo had increased in intensity from the end of 1944, Iva used them as an excuse for not going to the station.

On April 18, 1945, Father Kraus baptized Iva at the Sophia Church, and the next day he presided over her marriage to Filipe. It was a small ceremony but a warm one, attended by the Portuguese minister, Filipe's sister, and a few close friends such as Chieko Ito. The only mishap was an Allied bomber raid that forced the wedding party to take refuge in a shelter.

After the wedding Iva continued to absent herself from the station. Perhaps she hoped that since she had been absent so long the station would simply let her go. Before they were married Filipe told Iva several times that she should quit her job. He wanted her to be waiting for him at home when he got back from work. Iva herself did not want to go back to work, particularly now that "Zero Hour" was under Oki's management.

In late April she received a postcard from the station telling her to report for work. She ignored it, but three or four days later a man from the American Division came to the house to see whether something had happened to her. When he found her safe and sound he told her that he had "orders from above" to tell her to report to work the next day.

During Iva's absences Mieko Furuya, now married to Kenkichi Oki, substituted for Iva on "Zero Hour." At the time of the trial Oki, perhaps anxious to cover up her involvement, testified that Mieko had quit working at the station in November 1944. The attendance records in the NHK archives clearly show that she worked at NHK until May 23, 1945, however. It is not clear what was in her scripts, but some former Radio Tokyo staffers state they were heavily laden with propaganda. Mary Ishii, Kenichi Ishii's sister, also substituted for Iva after Mary joined the "Zero Hour" staff in late March 1945.

Oki probably preferred working with Mary or Mieko, who were easier to use than Iva. But Tsuneishi evidently had his heart set on having the original "Orphan Ann" continue as the female announcer, and so "orders from above" had been issued to get Iva back to work. "Orders from above" meant "orders from the army," so Iva glumly went back to work at the station. Even so, she still took time off whenever she could, using the Allied air raids as an excuse.

The last months of the war were a depressing period. In May Denmark broke off relations with Japan and the Tillitses left for home. It was a sad farewell for Iva.

The Allied raids became increasingly severe. Food, clothing, and the simplest necessities of life were becoming scarcer and scarcer in the bomb-ravaged city.

By now many American Division staffers knew that the end of the war was near. Women and children were being trained to use bamboo spears in the coming "battle for the homeland." The time allotted for record music on "Zero Hour" lengthened, and the propaganda softened. The feeling of waiting for the end intensified. The American Division staff members were worried not only about what would happen after the defeat, but about what the right wing might do before the war ended. Kenkichi Oki even warned Iva and Norman Reyes, neither of whom was a Japanese citizen, not to come near the station as the Japanese defeat approached.

And suddenly it was over: Hiroshima, Nagasaki, and then the emperor's final decision to "endure the unendurable." On August 15 crowds listening to the emperor's high-pitched voice wept with shame, with shock, and with grief. But Iva and Filipe, clasping each other's hands, wept with relief and gladness that the stupid war was over. It was the day that Iva had awaited four long, hard years. She was happy. She had kept her American citizenship, she had never lost hope that America would win, she had fought her "secret war" under Cousens, and she had helped the POWs. For her, August 15 was not a day of surrender but a day of victory.

CHAPTER 4

The Tokyo Rose Witch Hunt

Sugamo Prison

Sugamo Prison was just a few minutes' walk from the Yamate Line that circles central Tokyo, but for those behind its gates the rest of the city might as well have been miles away. The walls bristled with barbed wire and "keep away" signs. Inside, the only people visible were American MPs or Japanese guards in khaki uniforms. Sugamo Prison, like Spandau Prison in Berlin, housed war criminals.

Iva was held in the cell area designated Blue Block, where Japanese diplomats or women accused of war crimes were kept. Her cell was small, about six feet by nine feet, with a toilet and a wash basin that could be covered by a board for use as a table. Here Iva lived nearly a year, spending her days studying Japanese or reading prayer books sent from home. About the only thing she could be grateful for in prison was steam heat. She hated the bone-chilling Tokyo winter more than anything else about Japan. The only break in the dreary year was an incident that Iva could never forget. One day, while taking the bath she was permitted every three days, Iva suddenly noticed several faces pressed against the frosted windows of the bathing area. When she let out a scream, the guard who came rushing in to see what had happened found a group of visiting Congressmen who were in Japan to observe the American Occupation at work. They had dropped by Sugamo to look at General Tojo and other well-known war criminals, and when they found that the famous Tokyo Rose was taking a bath at just that moment, they decided to take a peek. The guard, Sergeant Martin Pray, was so irate at the incident that he sent off a letter of protest to the prison commander. Iva herself even today is still astounded that "representatives of the people" could behave in such a fashion.

Imprisonment was a shame Iva found hard to accept. She simply could not understand why GHQ had arrested and jailed her on suspicion of treason. She had held on to her American citizenship to the very end of the war, despite continued pressure from the Special Police and the *kempeitai*. It seemed like a bad joke. She must have regretted her mistake in thinking that Tokyo Rose was a popular star among the GIs. But the fault was not hers alone. The correspondents had their share of responsibility for raising all the ruckus about Tokyo Rose.

Still it was pride and excessive self-confidence that had involved her with them in the first place. She had been too confident that she had done nothing to be ashamed of in her broadcast work, and that there was no reason she should not face her fellow countrymen again. She even believed, as Cousens had told her, that she had helped boost GI morale through the programs. So imprisonment was hard for her to bear. All the while her hurt pride kept asking her: What are they saying I have done?

Shortly after being moved to Sugamo, Iva finally learned what had happened to her family in the States. Filipe brought her the sad news that her mother, Fumi, had died in May 1942 at the age of fifty-four in the Tulare Assembly Center. Iva had been prepared for this. In May 1943, exactly a year after her mother had died, Iva had a dream of her mother's death so clear and so vivid that she cannot forget it to this day.

The personal tragedy of her mother's death was part of a larger national tragedy. In February 1942, under Executive Order 9066, all persons of Japanese ancestry living on the West Coast, even those born in the U.S. with full citizenship, were forcibly interned by the government, scapegoats of the public shock and hysteria that followed the Pearl Harbor attack. Within a few weeks they had been herded into jerry-built wooden barracks thrown up on racetracks, fairgrounds, or livestock pavilions. The barracks were crowded, flimsy, and without any privacy. Even the toilets were communal. The strain of being suddenly forced to live in such circumstances was too much for Fumi Toguri, and she died a few months later.

Shortly after Fumi's death the rest of the Toguri family had been sent to the Gila River Relocation Center—the American government, for obvious reasons, avoided the more appropriate term "concentration camp." It was located in the midst of the Arizona desert, where the summer temperature often reached 110 degrees. They stayed until 1943, when internees were given the choice of remaining in the camps or moving to some part of the country other than the West Coast. The Toguris, like many others, decided to move to Chicago. Jun had been employed by the relocation camp administration to buy supplies, and in the course of his business trips across the country he had found that city most to his liking.

The Toguris, led by sixty-two-year-old Jun, had to start a new life from scratch. After about a year they managed to open a small Japanese grocery and variety store. They worked hard, waiting for the war to end, and then learned that Iva, about whom they worried so much during the war, was accused of treason against the United States.

Filipe came to the prison once a month, bringing Iva as many little gifts and food as he could manage. Iva had asked him to find her a lawyer, but despite all his efforts, it was not easy to find one familiar with American law. He tried to get an ordinary lawyer, but the prison authorities would not permit an interview with Iva.

The CIC questioned Iva twice in Sugamo, once on January 3, 1946, and again on February 3, 1947. They covered the same ground as before. Iva continued to think that some terrible mistake had been made. But she was growing impatient, anxious to know what the army authorities planned to do with her.

At the end of April FBI agent Frederick G. Tillman came to question her. Iva welcomed the opportunity to talk. "If I tell things honestly," she thought to herself, "they will understand." It was a naïve and misplaced hope. Frederick Tillman was a dyed-in-the-wool G-man who had been in the FBI during its gang-busting days in the 1930s. In September 1945 he arrived in Tokyo as the FBI representative in Japan, one of his first jobs being to carry on an investigation related to the Pearl Harbor inquiry.

Iva's first meeting with Tillman on April 29 was relatively simple. He asked for a general rundown and told her to order her thoughts for a more detailed questioning the next day. Iva asked him why she had been detained for six months already without being told the reason. She said if she was accused of something she wanted a speedy trial. Tillman replied that in fact the authorities were carrying on an investigation to determine whether or not she should be indicted for treason.

The main interrogation took most of the next day. Tillman found Iva quite cooperative. "She was willing to talk," he later testified. "She was very self-possessed, she did not look nervous to me."[1] During the first half-hour or so Tillman wrote down Iva's answers to his questions in longhand, but since the interrogation seemed to be going smoothly he switched to his typewriter, taking down her answers in a narrative form. Every time he finished a page he had Iva read it to make sure there were no mistakes, and at the end of the interview she looked over the whole document and signed it.

In taking the statement, which ran to twelve pages, Tillman made sure Iva went on record as stating that "she did not broadcast under duress."[2] The statement became rather important at the trial, so it is interesting to hear Iva's version of how it came to be included in the document. "Mr. Tillman," she said, "asked me if there was any gun held against me or whether I was beaten to broadcast. I told him no. And he said, 'Well there were no threats.'"[3]

Tillman brought along some broadcast scripts that Filipe had handed over to the CIC right after the war. When he showed them to Iva she mentioned that the three POWs had hidden double meanings in the script. At the trial Tillman insisted he tried to pursue the matter further. "I asked her repeatedly if she could recall such double meanings. She could not. . . . I had her review the scripts which the Army received from her husband and point out if any of them had double meanings. She could not point out or state whether or not there were double meanings in them."[4] Iva, in her own testimony, had a somewhat different recollection of this part of the questioning. "Mr. Tillman did not ask me to point out anything in those scripts," she said. "All he asked me to do was initial them, and that was all. May I add something here, please? Because when I mentioned that I knew the phrases had double meanings, he laughed at me and he ridiculed me. He never asked me to point out anything from the scripts which could be considered to have a double meaning."[5]

By the time the interview was ended, Iva's head ached. Tillman asked the same things over and over again, often in a mocking and sarcastic tone of voice. Iva felt he was teasing her.

Tillman probably had no particular hostility toward Iva. Questioning her was simply another job for him. But for Iva the interview was a chance to tell her whole story. The questioning might determine whether or not she was to be tried, so she was eager to explain everything. To Tillman she simply appeared to be a garrulous know-it-all who kept talking without listening. He did not notice that she grew more tense and nervous as the day wore on. He became irritated himself. When Iva found that Tillman seemed to doubt everything she said, she became quite weary and discouraged. She thought she would sign anything to be rid of him.

After the questioning ended, Iva asked Tillman what he thought about the legal status of her citizenship. He replied that he thought she probably had dual Portuguese and American citizenship. As he was leaving he also told her that she would know the results of the investigation—whether or not she was to be indicted for treason—in about six weeks. Iva had to believe him, but the weeks passed and still no word came. There were no more interrogations either.

War Criminal or Traitor?

There was good reason why Iva was not interrogated again. Even before Tillman had come to question her, GHQ had already come to its own conclusions about the Tokyo Rose affair.

On March 14, 1946, the Eighth Army CIC had put together an investigative report on Iva for GHQ G-2. Rather interestingly, the bureauc-

racy was a little confused about what to call her. The report referred to
her as Ikuko Toguri, with "Iva" in brackets. As the report progressed
through official channels, a bracketed subtitle "Tokyo Rose" was added
as well. The GHQ authorities ignored the fact that she was married, indeed occasionally referred to her as "Miss Toguri," and gave her the
alias that Lee and Brundidge had pinned on her.

On April 3 the Office of the Chief Civil Intelligence Officer, a G-2
subsection, sent the report on to GHQ Legal Section requesting a decision on the case. G-2 wanted to know whether Iva should be kept in
prison and whether there was enough information to warrant a trial.
Two weeks later, on April 17, the Legal Section replied that "Miss [sic]
Toguri" might be subject to trial by military commission for violation of
Articles of War 81 and 82, but that the available evidence indicated no
violation of those articles. It added, however, that perhaps Iva had violated American treason laws. If that were the case, then civilian courts
would have to decide whether an indictment should be sought. The Legal Section recommended that the whole matter be sent on to the Justice
Department in Washington for an opinion.

On April 27 the file on Iva went to the GHQ Chief of Staff, with a
G-2 recommendation that the case be submitted to the Justice Department in Washington and that in the meantime Iva be released from
Sugamo. The Legal Section agreed to this, and the International Prosecution Section, responsible for the prosecution of war criminals, said it
had no interest in the case. The lower echelons of the GHQ bureaucracy
were willing to wash their hands of Iva's case for the time being.

The upper echelons were more cautious, however. On April 29 the
Deputy Chief of Staff approved all of G-2's recommendation *except*
Iva's release from prison. The reason he gave for keeping her there was
that "her immediate *release would cause wide publicity, sure to be unfavorable* [italics added]. . . ."[6] He recommended that she continue to be
held until orders were received from the War Department. GHQ was
worried that newsmen would stir up another public fuss if "the traitor
Tokyo Rose" were released from prison without trial. That, of course,
would tarnish GHQ's image, which was to say General MacArthur's
image. So Iva was to be kept in jail until the buck stopped one way or
another in Washington.

By this time it was clear to the Legal Section that Iva was not "Tokyo Rose," if indeed such a person existed at all. After screening the evidence gathered by CIC, the section had concluded:

> There is no evidence and subject denies, that she ever referred to herself, or was referred to, on the Zero Hour program, as "Tokyo Rose." There is no evidence that she ever broadcast greetings to units by name and location, or predicted military movements or attacks indicating access to secret military information and plans, etc., as the Tokyo Rose of rumor and legend is reported to have done.[7]

But all that was beside the point. As long as the press and the public thought Iva was Tokyo Rose, it would be potentially embarrassing to set her free without permission from Washington.

Mark Gayn, correspondent for the Chicago Sun Service, summed up the GHQ predicament rather well in a dispatch he sent home early in May. Iva, he wrote, was a "victim of circumstances":

> ... No charges have been preferred against her and none ever will be if responsible officials can persuade themselves they will not be universally condemned for freeing her.
>
> The Allied prosecutors here feel they would have a tough time making charges against her stick, because broadcasting prepared propaganda is not regarded as a war crime. If it were, hundreds of broadcasters in Tokyo would have to stand trial. . . .[8]

In other words, GHQ itself was in a bind—it could not release Iva without adverse publicity, but it could not prosecute her without prosecuting everyone who had worked at the Overseas Bureau, including at least one former *nisei* woman announcer who was working in a GHQ staff section.

Gayn spoke with authority. A few days before, on April 24, he had paid a visit to Colonel H. I. T. Creswell, Chief of the CIC, who complained about the harm that the journalists had done in the Tokyo Rose case. "We've had her in Sugamo Prison for months, and now we find we have no solid evidence against her," he said. "She was just taking orders. Yet we don't dare release her, because we know that you boys will promptly jump on our necks." Gayn and a companion protested, "You're wrong, Colonel. If you have no evidence, you let her go, and the two of us anyway will say nothing against you." Colonel Creswell was skeptical. "You're just saying this now, but if we let her go . . .," he replied.[9]

The CIC file took nearly five months to inch its way through bureaucratic thickets in the States. The buck finally stopped at the office of James M. Carter, the U.S. attorney in Los Angeles, the logical place to prosecute Iva in the United States. On September 13 Carter wired the Justice Department: "RE YOUR WIRE IVA TOGURI FURTHUR INVESTIGATION MENTIONED IN CORRESPONDENCE HAS NOT STRENGTHENED THIS CASE PD WE FEEL EVIDENCE INADEQUATE PD RECOMMEND TREASON PROSECUTION BE DECLINED PD." Someone had finally made a decision regarding what to do about Iva.

On September 24 Assistant Attorney General Theron L. Caudle sent Tom C. Clark, the Attorney General, a memo that read in part:

> Considerable investigation has been conducted in this case and it appears that the identification of Toguri as "Tokyo Rose" is erroneous, or, at least, that her activity consisted of nothing more than the announcing of music selections. . . . A few recording cylinders of her broadcasts and a large number of her scripts were located, and they, as well as the transcripts of the only two broadcasts of her program which were monitored by the Federal Communications Commission, do not disclose that she did anything more than introduce musical records. In addition it appears that "Tokyo Rose" was broadcasting prior to the date of Toguri's employment.
>
> It is my opinion that Toguri's activities, particularly in view of the innocuous nature of her broadcasts, are not sufficient to warrant her prosecution for treason. The United States attorney at Los Angeles concurs in this opinion. I believe that the case should be closed, subject, of course, to be reopened in the event more information is received at a later date, and that the War Department should be advised we no longer desire her retention in custody.[9]

On October 4 Caudle informed FBI Director J. Edgar Hoover that Iva did not warrant prosecution for treason on the basis of evidence available. All bases had been touched.

Finally, on October 6, nearly a year after Iva had been imprisoned, the War Department cabled Tokyo: DEPT OF JUSTICE NO LONGER DESIRES

IVA TOGURI BE DETAINED IN CUSTODY. NO PROSECUTION CONTEMPLATED AT PRESENT. Nearly three weeks later, at eleven o'clock on the morning of October 25, Iva was informed that she was to be released that day.

Interestingly enough, GHQ was still timorous about its decision. Iva was not allowed to leave the prison until seven that evening. The choice of the unusually late hour reflected the continuing desire of GHQ authorities to avoid the attention of newsmen. They wanted Iva to fade away without a fanfare of publicity.

Their caution was to no avail. Three days before, American newspapers had already reported Iva was to be released. When a smiling Iva walked out the gates of Sugamo flanked by two MPs and clutching a bouquet of cosmos flowers, she found a crowd of journalists waiting in the semidarkness for one last look at "Tokyo Rose." Shielded by Filipe, who had come to take her home, Iva stepped into a waiting jeep amidst the popping of flashbulbs and sped off into the night.

Iva's troubles were over—at least, so it seemed. After a thorough investigation by the CIC and the FBI, the authorities had finally agreed to her release from prison "without condition." She had been found innocent, it had been established that she was not Tokyo Rose, and she could go back to a normal life again. Just as she had thought, it had been a mistake, and now it was all over, a bad dream to be forgotten.

Wanting to Go Home

Iva was surprised to see how much had changed in Japan during her year in prison. The food situation was much worse than it had been in wartime. Foodstuffs were still scarce, prices had skyrocketed, and the black market flourished. Iva and Filipe were barely able to get by on the wages he earned at his new job as a linotypist for an English-language newspaper.

Tokyo had changed, too. American GIs seemed to be everywhere, and street signs had been put up in English all over the city. Yet Tokyo was not an American city. It was the city of a defeated people under foreign occupation. Prostitutes, called pan-pan girls, roamed the areas frequented by the GIs, and gaudy bars with names like "Manhattan" or "Florida" were thrown up to entertain the footloose young American soldiers.

For the Japanese, life was grim. Hastily built wooden slums were constructed in the devastated downtown sections, but the streets at night still were filled with the homeless and the destitute who had lost property and family during the war. Crime, theft, gang violence—all flourished in the humbled city.

Iva had never liked living in Japan, and now more than ever she wanted to go home as quickly as she could. Her father frequently wrote letters urging her to come back. But Filipe was opposed to her return so soon after her release from prison. He thought that Iva had better act cautiously after all the excitement that had been stirred up over Tokyo Rose. She should wait until the fuss had quieted down and people had forgotten about her. Then she could return to America quietly without telling anyone. Time and again, he told her that would be the easiest way for her to get back.

Iva was stubborn and did not listen. She wondered why Filipe was so cautious. After all, she had been released unconditionally by the authorities, and it had been proved clearly that she was not the Tokyo Rose of wartime legend. She had done nothing wrong at all. There was no need for her to be apologetic about returning to her own country. Now that her self-confidence had returned, Iva had become a bit self-righteous. She set herself the goal of "seeing the Golden Gate in '48."

In early December 1946, a little over a month after getting out of Sugamo, Iva set off for the American consulate in Yokohama to have her citizenship verified and to apply for repatriation to the United States. She found herself confronted with the same problem that had stranded her in Japan in 1941—lack of documents to prove that she was in fact an American citizen. Vice-Consul Harry F. Pfeiffer told her he thought she was a stateless person. If she wished to return to the States she would have to reestablish her citizenship.

It was all very vexing to Iva. She had been born in America, she had never repudiated her citizenship, and she believed that she was an American. But the American military and civilian officials had trouble accepting that fact. This was all the more curious since she had been thrown in prison on suspicion of treason, a crime she could have committed only if she were an American citizen. Sergeant Page, the CIC man who had questioned her, had told her she might have Portuguese citizenship as a result of her marriage to Filipe. The American prison commander, Colonel Hardy, had treated her as a Japanese national, keeping her in a cell block set aside for Japanese and forbidding her to send letters to the United States as other American prisoners were allowed to do. Tillman, the FBI man, told her she might have dual citizenship. Then the Portuguese consulate told her that it recognized her as a Portuguese national as the result of her marriage to Filipe in 1945, and GHQ had issued her a ration card as a Portuguese citizen. And now finally the American vice-consul was telling her that she was a stateless person.

Iva was confused. She did not fully understand what her legal status really was. But she did know one thing—she wanted to go home, and if she had to reestablish her citizenship to do so, then she would.

Not until the end of May 1947 did Iva manage to get her file together. When she went to Yokohama again, she found there would be more delays. Vice-Consul Pfeiffer told her that since applications to reestablish citizenship had to be referred back to Washington, it usually took three or four months for a reply to come back, and in her case it might take as long as six months.

Part of the reason for the delay was that the consulate was deluged with a flood of applications like Iva's. Although the precise figure is not clear, there were from 7,000 to 10,000 *nisei* stranded in Japan during the war, most of them young people who had left their families in the United States to come to Japan for two or three years of study or to find employment that they could not find in the United States. When war broke out they had been caught between two homelands, and rejected by both. They were forgotten by the American government, which was busily rounding up their parents and siblings to ship off to internment camps. The Japanese distrusted them as foreigners, and even those who registered as Japanese citizens were kept under surveillance by the Special Security Police and the *kempeitai*.

When the war ended, the majority of the stranded *nisei* wanted to return to the United States. American consular officials were astounded to see how strongly they wanted to go home despite the wartime relocation and the anti-Japanese prejudice that prompted it. Roger Baldwin, head of the American Civil Liberties Union, on a trip to Japan in 1948 tried to console a young *nisei* man who feared he might not be able to get back. "Why do you want to go back to the United States and face the life of a Japanese American?" he said. "You know what you'll be up against." The young man's eyes filled with tears. "Can't you understand," he replied. "I was born there. It is the only real home that I have."[11]

About half the stranded *nisei* were able to return to America ultimately, but the rest had to remain in Japan whether they wanted to or not. Some *nisei* had been forced to serve in the Imperial army and a few had inadvertently taken jobs that lost them their citizenship. But the majority of *nisei* who remained in Japan were forced to do so because they had been registered as Japanese citizens. Indeed, some had been children when their parents entered their names in the family register, and had lost their citizenship by no conscious act of their own.

The Japanese American Citizens League set up an office in Tokyo after the war to help some *nisei* with family register problems by having them bring suits in Japanese courts to cancel acts of their parents which they had not approved. The rest found themselves cut off from home and family because they had become Japanese citizens out of rashness, ignorance, confusion, or *kempeitai* pressure. They were yet another group of victims in the tragic history of the Japanese Americans.

Iva's attempt to return home brought her once more to public attention. When word got to the press that she was trying to get back to the United States, Iva again emerged in the public eye, not as Iva Toguri d'Aquino but as "Tokyo Rose." On August 1, 1947, a story appeared about her in the *Stars and Stripes:*

> Mrs. Iva Toguri d'Aquino, better known as "Tokyo Rose," yesterday told Pacific Stars and Stripes that she is "seriously contemplating" the writing of a book in which she will defend her wartime activities and "correct" a lot of false statements that have been printed against her. . . .
>
> The book . . . will reveal the reason why she did her alleged "treasonable" broadcasts as an American citizen when "I could have conveniently renounced my American citizenship in twenty minutes and not be liable for charges of treason."

The *Stars and Stripes* also reported that she had applied for repatriation to the United States. The story, as usual, was picked up by newspapers in the United States.

As Filipe said, Iva should have kept quiet. But she lacked the prudence and the patience to wait until the time was right for her to return. On the contrary, supported by her confidence that accusations against her had been proved without foundation, she once more stepped out into the open gaze of the mass media. She should have learned her lesson in 1945, but she had not. She carried her sense of wounded innocence like a shield.

Retired FBI agent Frederick G. Tillman recently put it more bluntly. Iva got herself arrested in the first place by presenting herself as Tokyo Rose in hopes of making money, he said, and she should have kept herself hidden quietly afterward. "She was stupid," he went on, "and all her trouble came from her own stupidity."[12]

Walter Winchell's Crusade

As Filipe had feared, the American public had not forgotten "the traitor Tokyo Rose." Or perhaps it would be more accurate to say that it was now that the real witch hunt for Tokyo Rose began. Had there not been a witch hunt, Iva might have returned to the United States to live happily ever after.

On October 20, 1947, the Chief of the Passport Divison at the State Department wrote to the Justice Department asking for an opinion on Iva's application to reestablish citizenship and return to the United States. The Justice Department, which had reviewed all the evidence just a year before, responded rather quickly. On October 24, T. Vincent Quinn, the Assistant Attorney General wrote: "After a careful analysis of the available evidence, this Department concluded that the prosecution of this individual for treason was not warranted, and we so informed the War Department. Therefore this Department will have no objection at all to the issue of a passport to Mrs. d'Aquino." But the Justice Department was soon to change its mind.

By strange coincidence, four days after Quinn sent off his letter to the Department of State, James F. O'Neill, commander of the American Legion, an organization with a long record of anti-Japanese sentiment, fired off a public statement asking that the Justice Department expedite the prosecution of "Tokyo Rose" in order to forestall her reported attempt to reestablish permanent residence in the United States. Just how the national commander of the American Legion managed such remarkable timing remains a mystery, but it is clear that the Legion had embarked on a campaign to bring "Tokyo Rose" to justice. Letters and resolutions of protest from local Legion branches began to trickle in to the Justice Department, and they continued to come in through the early months of 1948.

Fuel was added to the Legion's protests by continuing newspaper reports of Iva's desire to return to the United States. On Armistice Day, and the day after, newspapers across the country picked up a UP wire service story about a letter that Iva had written to Mark Streeter, a former Bunka Camp inmate living in Arizona. "Tokyo Rose," went the item, "is expecting a baby 'early next year'. . . . She said the expected baby is the principal reason for her desire to come to America. She wrote [to Streeter], 'I want my baby to be born in America. Japan is no country in which to have children.' "[13] The baby was due in January. Iva, remembering how her brother Fred had been denied American citizenship, desperately wanted her child to be born as a natural citizen in the United States.

The news item about Iva's expected baby did not rouse much public sympathy. If anything, it only served to spur on the witch hunt. A flurry of Legion resolutions poured in on Armistice Day, including a particularly vehement one from the Los Angeles chapter.

Another powerful patriotic organization joined the hue and cry a few days later. The Native Sons of the Golden West, a California organization that had supported anti-Oriental legislation since the turn of the century and had enthusiastically lobbied for the internment of the Japanese Americans in 1942, issued its own protest. Eldred Meyer, chairman of the organization's Grand Parlor Americanism Committee, dispatched a strong letter to James M. Carter, the U.S. attorney in Los Angeles:

> If [Iva Toguri] is the traitor which she is reported to be, she should not again be permitted the privileges that are granted to law-abiding American citizens.
>
> The evasion of our laws in this case, would be a dastardly slur upon the countless thousands of American women who stood faithfully by their men in service, who were defending the flag in the Southwest Pacific, while Tokyo Rose was pouring forth her venomous propaganda from her chosen place—Japan.[14]

Just to make sure the message got through, the committee sent off similar letters to the senatorial and congressional delegations from California, Secretary of State George C. Marshall, Under Secretary of State Dean Acheson, Attorney General Tom C. Clark, FBI Director J. Edgar Hoover, and Ugo Carusi, Immigration and Naturalization Service Commissioner.

On December 8 the Los Angeles City Council added its voice to the movement, passing a resolution:

> . . . That this Council does herewith vigorously oppose the return to this country of this person or any other person treasonably connected with the "Tokyo Rose" wartime propaganda broadcasts. . . .

Copies were sent to the Attorney General, the Secretary of Defense, the Secretary of State, and the California congressional delegations.

Doubtless the most influential figure to join the campaign against "Tokyo Rose" was Walter Winchell, the popular newspaper columnist and radio commentator. At the time the flamboyant Winchell was one of the best-known and most powerful figures in American journalism. An archetypical Hearst man, whose job was not to win Pulitzer Prizes but to "raise hell and sell newspapers," his syndicated columns are said to have reached seven million readers in the early 1940s.

His Sunday evening radio broadcasts reached an even wider audience—perhaps twenty million. With his hat pushed back and his collar loosened, he would fire out his famous greeting: "Good evening, Mr. and Mrs. America, and all the ships at sea." Then, punctuating himself with shouts of "Flash" and the dit-dah beeps of a telegraph signal, he would bombard his vast audience with tidbits of Hollywood and Park Avenue gossip. He was a sensationalist; his audience loved him. As a result he was an enormously powerful man who could influence public opinion with a single word.

Because of his power Winchell was a man politicians could ignore only at their peril. President Roosevelt made sure that Winchell stayed friendly by occasionally inviting him to the White House to ask his opinion on various questions. Harry Truman did not care to play that game. Shortly after Truman became President, some advisers persuaded him to get together with Winchell, but the forthright Midwesterner did not find

the columnist much to his liking, and afterward never paid much attention to him.

Walter Winchell got interested in the Tokyo Rose affair as the result
of a letter from the mother of a dead G.I. who wrote her own indignant
protest that the notorious Tokyo Rose was trying to get back into the
United States. The cause was ready-made for Winchell, who had been
outspoken in his attacks on the Nazis, the German-American Bund, the
isolationists in Congress, and other "enemies of democracy." He began
to chide the Truman administration for its failure to take any strong action on the case.

With Winchell's voice added to the protest raised by the powerful
American Legion, the Justice Department began to be very nervous
about its decision a year before not to prosecute Iva for treason. On December 4, 1947, U.S. Attorney James M. Carter met with Winchell in
his office at the Twentieth Century Fox Studios. With Carter was former U.S. Attorney Charles Carr, a friend of Winchell and the first public official to call for Iva's prosecution. Carter's mission was to smooth
Winchell's ruffled feathers and to explain that prosecuting Iva for treason would not be all that simple.

The interview did not get off to a good start. Winchell not only wanted the Justice Department to "do something about" people like Tokyo
Rose, he was also personally put out at Tom Clark. The source of his
pique was trivial. Several years before, Clark and Winchell had been together at a luncheon at Twentieth Century Fox. Winchell, probably
searching for a tidbit of Washington gossip, asked Clark whether he was
to be appointed Attorney General. According to Winchell, Clark "had
not given him a correct answer." A few days later news of Clark's ap-
pointment had been made public. Winchell was angry. As Carter reported to Clark, "He [Winchell] had been plugging you [Clark] for Attorney
General and intimated he had never received proper thanks."[15] Carr
piped in to assure Winchell that Clark had not known about the ap-
pointment when he had spoken to Winchell. This seemed to have some
calming effect, but hell hath no fury like a gossip columnist scorned, and
Winchell continued to complain about the Justice Department's handling of the Washington Sedition Case involving a group of wartime
pro-Nazi sympathizers, which had ended in a mistrial.

Carter persisted in his main mission: to persuade Winchell to modulate his campaign against Iva. He showed Winchell a press release the FBI had issued the day before, appealing for public help in a possible prosecution of "Tokyo Rose." It asked that anyone who had seen Iva broadcasting as "Tokyo Rose" or recognized her voice coming over the airwaves get in touch with the agency. It needed to find two witnesses to overt acts of treason in order to prosecute her. The press release also made clear that although the Justice Department had earlier concluded that Iva did not warrant prosecution and that she could be issued a passport, she was not to be permitted to return to the States.

Winchell read the release "with interest," according to Carter. He "stated he was glad to see that 'Tokyo Rose' was not to be allowed back into the United States; he intimated he was going to use the release, or part of it, on his Sunday broadcast. He commented that the release did not say that it had been brought about by his previous broadcasts." It was clear that the journalistic mind and the legalistic mind were not operating on the same wavelength, so Carter and Carr did their best to explain that a trial might not be around the corner. To quote from Carter's letter to Tom Clark:

(9) I repeated that I was not defending "Tokyo Rose" and wished him more power in his activities in exposing American citizens who engaged in harmful and unpatriotic conduct, at home and abroad, but stated that as a lawyer I was not going to recommend a prosecution unless we had some kind of a case against the defendant.

(10) Mr. Carr mentioned letters that he had received as United States Attorney from GIs all over the world, criticizing Mr. Carr for his announced intention of prosecuting "Tokyo Rose" and claiming that the "Tokyo Rose" broadcasts, instead of being morale breakers were morale builders. Winchell replied that these people were probably communists, but Mr. Carr continued with the argument and I think made some impression on Winchell.

(11) I explained to him the innocuous character of the "Orphan Ann" broadcasts, and offered to exhibit to him translations of the "Orphan Annie" broadcasts which were put over the air by Rose [sic] Toguri. He stated that he was familiar with the fact that many of them were innocuous.[16]

By this time Winchell appeared rather more friendly than he had been at first. As Carter left he suggested to Winchell that "a bad situation . . . would occur should the Government seek a prosecution without having a proper case, and the trial resulted in a dismissal or acquittal." Winchell agreed that this would be worse than having no prosecution at all. But Carter still felt it might be wise for Tom Clark to do what he could to keep Winchell under control: "I received . . . the impression that somewhere along the line his pride had been injured and I am of the opinion that you could go a very long way toward smoothing things out, should you have a personal chat with Mr. Winchell."[17]

Whether or not Clark ever had his chat with Winchell remains unclear. But even if he did, Winchell was not put off so easily by the niceties of legal argument. His campaign against Iva, alias Tokyo Rose, continued unabated. A little knowledge is a dangerous thing, and so is a crusading columnist in a wrong cause.

Dilemma at Justice

The Justice Department was in a delicate position, pressed by one of the country's most powerful columnists and by its most powerful patriotic organization. The pressure was all the more painful because 1948 was an election year and the President's popularity was at a low ebb and sinking. Attacks by Walter Winchell and the Legion were the last thing the administration needed, particularly if the issue in question was treason. In the deepening cold war atmosphere, members of Congress, especially the House Un-American Activities Committee, had already begun to criticize Truman for being soft on traitors, and the Republicans were beginning to take up the issue in preparation for the coming campaign. To be sure, most of the alleged "traitors" lurking in high places were "Communists" and "fellow travelers," but a traitor was still a traitor whether in the State Department making policy or applying to the State Department for a passport. The growing fear of treason was becoming so muddled that Winchell, by that peculiar suspension of logic pervasive at the time, had even been able to identify sympathizers of Tokyo Rose as "Communists."

Under these circumstances there were good reasons why Tom Clark, an old associate of Truman and one of his first cabinet appointees,* was ready to reopen consideration of the Tokyo Rose case. It was politically safe, and perhaps even made good sense politically, to take a strong stand against treason in this particular election year. Certainly it was more than just coincidence that in 1948, three years after the war had ended, the Justice Department began to move on a number of World War II treason cases: Best, Chandler, Kawakita, Gillars, Provoo, and others. There is a strong possibility that the Truman administration expected that these treason indictments would serve as examples of how the government intended to deal with "Un-American" elements. An attempt to impose a thorough-going loyalty program had already begun within the government, too.

There may have been other pressures on Clark from within the Justice Department bureaucracy itself. Some of this pressure may have come from Walter Winchell's good friend J. Edgar Hoover. Hoover and Winchell had known each other since the early 1930s when Winchell had chronicled in his columns the exploits of the G-men (a tag he popularized). Aside from FDR, the only public figure that ever escaped his censure was Hoover, who was careful to cultivate the relationship by providing Winchell with entrée to FBI information and occasionally assigning him FBI bodyguards. Both men knew that the relationship was mutually beneficial. Winchell got good scoops; Hoover got good publicity. It is therefore possible that there were unseen pressures put on the Attorney General by Winchell's powerful friend in the FBI.

In any event, the decision to reopen the Tokyo Rose case was certainly consistent with Tom Clark's other activities. Clark had been intimately involved in the relocation of West Coast Japanese Americans in 1942. As civilian coordinator for the Relocation Authority, Clark had traveled with General John L. DeWitt, who was in charge of the operation, to pick out sites for internment camps. To his credit Clark later (in 1966) admitted that the whole program had been a mistake. "I don't think that it served any useful purpose at all," he said. ". . . We picked them up

---

*Truman apparently regretted his choice, for he later said of Clark, "He was no damn good as Attorney General, and on the Supreme Court . . . it doesn't seem possible, but he's been even worse . . . it isn't so much that he's a *bad* man. It's just that he's such a dumb son of a bitch. He's about the dumbest man I think I've ever run across. And lots of times that's the case. Being dumb's about the worst thing when it comes to holding high office. . . .", from *Plain Speaking.*

and put them in concentration camps. That's the truth of the matter. . . . I am amazed the Supreme Court ever approved it." But in the immediate postwar period, while Attorney General, he took a hard line toward certain elements in the Japanese American community. He backed efforts to deport 200 to 300 Japanese Peruvians who had been brought to the States for internment during the war, and he also supported efforts to deport those Japanese Americans who had renounced their citizenship while interned. It is not surprising that he also decided to take a hard line against Iva.

Whatever the calculus of motives at work, it is clear the Justice Department had decided at the highest level to pursue Iva's case to indictment if it could. And even if it faltered, Walter Winchell was still there yapping at its heels, making sure his new campaign against one of the "enemies of democracy" would succeed.

Harry Brundidge Again

Public interest in the Tokyo Rose case mounted as Winchell continued his campaign. The case got more publicity when the Signal Corps newsreel Iva had made in October 1945 was shown around the country. Tokyo Rose was still a good story.

No one appreciated that better than Harry Brundidge. He had quit *Cosmopolitan* not long after his embarrassment over the case in the fall of 1945 and had joined the staff of the Nashville *Tennessean*. The renewed public attention to the case brought the old police reporter back on the scent. According to an account he wrote in May 1948, when he read the FBI press release appealing for witnesses in the Tokyo Rose case, he immediately fired off a long letter to his "friend," J. Edgar Hoover, offering his services to go to Japan and help find witnesses. He happened to be in Washington on business about a week after the press release appeared, and he put in a call to the FBI director. Hoover was "not in," so instead he had to talk with Special Agent Kline Weatherford.

It seems likely that Brundidge was already thinking that somehow or other he could bring "Tokyo Rose" to justice, as he had brought other evildoers to justice in the old days. But matters were not to be any simpler for him in 1948 than they had been in 1945, for Clark Lee was back in the act, too.

On January 8, 1948, Walter Winchell's column carried the following item:

Clark Lee (the INS correspondent) read the recent appeal by the Justice Department for information on the activities of Tokyo Rose. He considers it a "cynical evasion" on the part of Emperor-lovers and friends of the Zaibatsu in Washington. Lee says that nearly two years ago he turned over to FBI agents (in New York City) the original of an 18-page [actually seventeen pages] typewritten confession dictated to him by Tokyo Rose after he located her in Japan. Surely, he writes, this document must be available to the State Department and Attorney General Clark. Lee certifies that she named two witnesses against her, who would be easily available if they wanted to bring her to trial. One witness was Lt. Ted Ince of the U.S. Army. The other was Major Cousens of Australia, tried for treason in his country and mysteriously released without either conviction or acquittal. Lee also says that there are twenty-five others in Tokyo who could be witnesses. Yet the State Department claims there are none, ignoring the fact that the OWI made transcripts of her programs.[18]

The item was vintage Winchell, mixing garbled information with intimations of skulduggery in high places. Iva's 1945 statement to Lee and Brundidge had become a "confession"; Cousens had been "mysteriously released"; the OWI recordings demonstrating the innocuousness of Iva's broadcasts had become suppressed material evidence; and by implication the State Department and Attorney General Clark were "Emperor-lovers and friends of the Zaibatsu," covering up the Tokyo Rose case because they were pro-Japanese.

More to the point, Winchell reported that Brundidge lost Iva's "confession." Naturally Brundidge was upset to be skewered in public yet a second time for his handling of the Tokyo Rose case. Here is Brundidge's account of his reaction:

. . . Winchell reported that the 17-page confession obtained by Lee and me from Tokyo Rose had been stolen from me, and shamed me for the loss. . . . I wired Winchell from Memphis, Tenn., where I was investigating the Crump machine, that he was dead wrong—that the original was in my possession. The following Sunday Winchell admitted his mistake—and said it was a copy that had been stolen. There was no copy! We didn't have any carbon paper! I so informed Winchell, telling him that what had been stolen from me in the Imperial Hotel in Tokyo was

the contract I had entered into with "Rose." Winchell then demanded to
know why I hadn't turned it over to the FBI. . . . [Shortly afterward] I
handed the document [the "confession"] to Special Agents of the FBI.
Then I came in for more ribbing. The confession was unsigned. Naturally! It didn't even occur to us to have "Rose" sign because I had the signed
contract in which she set forth she was the "one and only Tokyo Rose."
Most of the essential facts in her confession were contained in the contract. By that time I was furious. I explained my feelings to Silliman Evans, my publisher. "Why don't you go to Japan and get Rose to sign it?"
[he said.][19]

There were good reasons why Brundidge became active in the Tokyo
Rose case again. His pride was at stake. He had beaten out the other reporters in finding "Tokyo Rose" in 1945 but had suffered only humili-
ation for his pains. He had been the laughingstock of the other correspondents when his editor had refused to pay for the story, and now he
was being roasted by the powerful Walter Winchell. He could retrieve
his pride, and his reputation as a reporter, if he became a key figure in
bringing Rose to trial—especially if he could get an exclusive inside story in the bargain. So he pushed ahead, determined to get a confession
from "Rose."

Brundidge later claimed that Tom Clark asked him to go to Tokyo to
get Iva to sign her 1945 "confession." In fact, he seems to have wangled
the trip by his own efforts. While he and his editor, Silliman Evans,
were visiting Clark to ask that they be shown the FBI file on a Memphis
candidate in the 1948 elections, the Tokyo Rose problem came up. Brundidge told Clark in the strongest terms that if he were sent to Tokyo he
would bring back Iva's signature and bring to a conclusion the Tokyo
Rose case. Clark, who was getting criticism about the case from all directions, appears to have given his consent, and soon Brundidge was on his
way.

On March 12, 1948, Harry Brundidge left for Tokyo by military airplane. With him was John B. Hogan, a former FBI man working as an
attorney in the Internal Security Division of the Justice Department, assigned to the task of gathering evidence for possible treason indictments
against Wallace Ince and David Provoo. Brundidge's expenses were
paid partly by the Justice Department and partly by his publisher. His
passport indicated that he was traveling on a special mission for the Jus-

tice Department, which had also informed GHQ he was working for them.

The plane stopped at Honolulu, where Brundidge and Hogan visited Clark Lee's house to pick up the autograph that Iva had given Lee ("To Clark Lee, who interviewed me at the Imperial Hotel on September 1. Iva Toguri 'Tokyo Rose' ").

When they arrived in Tokyo on March 22, the two men were put up at the Dai-ichi Hotel, reserved for high officials and important guests of the Occupation. Otherwise they did not receive a warm welcome. Indeed, according to Hogan's subsequent report, the attitude of the Civilian Intelligence Service of G-2, GHQ, was downright hostile, especially toward Brundidge. They remembered him very well.

On the afternoon of March 26, Iva was brought by an army driver to the Dai-ichi building, the gray fortresslike structure that housed the American Occupation GHQ. She looked tired, her face drawn and pale. She had been confined to bed since the beginning of the year. On January 5 Iva had gone to the hospital to deliver the baby she had so much wanted to be a natural American citizen. The child, a boy, had died half a day later. The shock had devastated Iva completely. "If my child had lived," Iva said recently, "my whole life would have been so much different."[20] Certainly it would have made it more difficult for the government to try the mother of a newborn child as the vicious propagandist Tokyo Rose. To make matters worse, Iva's physical recovery was poor. She came down with an inflammation of the joints. When she arrived at the Dai-ichi building, she was not only psychologically exhausted but still unsteady on her feet.

Brundidge and Hogan arrived a half-hour later. Brundidge started the conversation by saying, "You remember me, don't you?" Iva said that she did. Brundidge went on, "You applied to the Attorney of the United States, didn't you?" Iva said, "Yes, I did," and he said, "Do you want to return to the United States or stay in this hellhole for the rest of your life?" And Iva said, "Well, I made an application to return to the United States. I should like to return if I can." He said, "I am working with Mr. Hogan on your case. I am acting as an agent of the Attorney General's office. Today may decide whether you will be able to go home, back to the United States, or have to live in Japan forever."[21]

Hogan, who had been gazing out the window while listening to the conversation between Brundidge and Iva, now walked over and silently handed his briefcase to Brundidge. Iva related:

> Mr. Brundidge said, "You remember that story you gave us at the Imperial Hotel in September 1945?" And I said, "Yes, I remember." He said, "If you remember the interview, all you have to do is sign this story written by Clark Lee from the notes that he took in that room in 1945." He showed me the photostatic copy of this story that Clark Lee had written. He told me to read it. I read it, but the story was a complete story. Some of it [I] had never seen before. I told Mr. Brundidge that this was not the interview I gave to Clark Lee. I said, "Most of it is all made up." Mr. Hogan . . . told Mr. Brundidge to pull out the other copy . . . which was . . . a photostatic copy of notes by Clark Lee. I had never seen those notes. . . . Mr. Brundidge leaned over and said, "You remembered the interview?" He said, "Doesn't that look familiar?" I said, "Yes, it looks familiar, but I have not seen the copy in almost two and a half years because I did not see it at the time Clark Lee took the notes." . . . Mr. Hogan . . . told Mr. Brundidge, "Ask her if these are the notes of the interview." Mr. Brundidge spoke to me and I said, "Yes, they look a little familiar but there are a few mistakes in it." . . . Mr. Brundidge leaned over and told me I would be doing myself a good deal by signing the interview. "If it is the interview given to Clark Lee," he said, "it would aid you in getting back to the United States." And so I signed it.[22]

The irregularities of this encounter are manifest. At no point did Brundidge and Hogan advise Iva of her legal rights. She was not told that she had a right to counsel, that she could remain silent, that she had a right not to sign the "confession," nor that anything she said or signed might be used against her. On the contrary, Brundidge told her that signing the notes would be to her advantage and that it would help her return to the United States.

After Iva had signed the notes, Hogan said he would like to see the studios from which she had broadcast. When they arrived at the NHK building they found the studios on the first floor were locked. While Hogan went upstairs to find a janitor, Iva found herself alone with Brundidge. Suddenly he became quite friendly. You'll probably be indicted for treason, he confided, but they'll never hang a woman, so the worst that can happen is a short term in prison, and if things go well perhaps you'll go free. But either way, he said to Iva, you'll be going back to America.

According to Hogan's testimony, the entire meeting with Iva, including the trip to the NHK studios, lasted about forty or forty-five minutes. The meeting in the Dai-ichi building must have taken no more than half an hour. If this was the case, it is questionable whether Iva would have had enough time to read the seventeen pages of Lee's notes very thoroughly or thoughtfully before she signed them, especially in her weak and fatigued condition.

It seems likely that she signed the notes simply because she was told she would be able to return to the United States if she did. There was no way of telling how long it would take to return if she went through the regular bureaucratic channels. She gambled on Brundidge's half-promises, wanting to believe him even though she should have known he was not a man to be trusted. But whatever went through her mind, it is certain that she signed the notes—her "confession"—without fully realizing the significance of what she had done, and without any legal advice as to that significance.

Brundidge and Hogan were content with their day's work. They now had material evidence that might bring an indictment in the case. But there was other business to do. Brundidge remained in Japan to help line up witnesses for the grand jury—even witnesses who might be persuaded to stretch the facts a bit, or make them up out of whole cloth.

A Musical and An "Exclusive"

On April 14, about two or three weeks after Iva's reunion with Brundidge, an important new figure became involved in the Tokyo Rose case. It was Earl Carroll, the Broadway and Hollywood producer famous for his lavish musical revues—and for his spectacular liaisons with a series of beautiful show girls. Like Walter Winchell, Carroll was a flamboyant public figure, well known to the readers of the tabloid press.

Carroll was an old acquaintance of General MacArthur. He was in Tokyo on his way back from China to explore the possibility of making a movie set in occupied Japan. During a meeting with Major General

Charles A. Willoughby, GHQ: G-2, he asked to see Iva. Apparently he was thinking of doing a musical based on the Tokyo Rose story. Iva was invited down for another visit to GHQ, this time in Willoughby's offices.

> ... Mr. Carroll asked one question, "Did you ever call yourself, 'To-kyo Rose'?" I told him I never used the name. He told me that General Willoughby had talked with him [Carroll] and that the General told him that the "trial days are over" for me and as far as the General was concerned the case was closed. . . .
>
> Mr. Carroll asked me whether I had applied for a visa to return to the States. . . . I answered, "Yes," and . . . I was waiting for an answer from the State Department for clearance to return to the States. Mr. Carroll then told me that . . . Walter Winchell was the man who was holding up my clearance by "throwing mud at you" through his column. Carroll told me that he was leaving Japan that night, that if I wanted to write to Winchell giving him a general resume of the whole case, pointing out to Winchell that I never once called myself "Tokyo Rose," and to write about the POW who had written the scripts, helped to coach me, etc., he [Carroll] would see to it that the letter got to him [Winchell]. Carroll told me he was going to do everything possible for me to return to the States.[23]

It was an unexpected and pleasant turn of events. She even got an invitation to have lunch at the UP office with Carroll, UPI agency chief Earnest Hoberecht, and Shirley Yoshiko Yamaguchi, one of Japan's leading film actresses, who was to star in Carroll's film. She remembers how the two pet dogs Carroll had brought along on his trip kept leaping about the room.

That evening Iva gave Carroll a long letter she had written to Winchell. In it she explained that she had never used the name "Tokyo Rose," that her voice had been confused with other female announcers broadcasting from other Japanese propaganda stations, that her scripts had been written by the POWs, that she had never made any damaging remarks over the radio, and that she agreed to work with the POWs in order to help them out. She also tried to appeal to his sense of fairness:

> This case on "Tokyo Rose" is in its third year and it seems to be dragging on forever. . . . I was kept in prison in order to enable the various investigating bodies to get all the dope on "Tokyo Rose." Since my release I have been living as a housewife. I understand that during this period in-

vestigations have been carried on in my case and I am still sitting on the fence, not knowing on which side I am to fall.

All the rumpus about "Tokyo Rose" centers around one person, myself. I am sure there has been plenty of reasons for all the misunderstandings both by the press and the general public. I can't say I blame all the readers for forming their opinions. . . .

But please be kind enough to look into the matter more thoroughly and be generous enough to form your opinions again after investigating all the facts which I have presented above. . . .

The United States Justice Department, when releasing me from custody, stated that "due to lack of sufficient evidence" I was being released from Sugamo Prison, Tokyo.

. . . Since a person in the United States is "innocent until proven guilty," please give me the chance to clear up some of the misunderstanding through your kind offices.

. . . There were so many complicated cobwebs during the war years I was one who had to find a way to survive this war. I was one with United States citizenship in a foreign country and was one who was under close surveillance by the civilian and military police and although being cornered managed to come out alive. I was in a similar position as the prisoners of war and had little chance in choosing a way to survive.

I did not intend to cry on your shoulders. If I have given you this impression please forgive me. My only intention was to ask you to be generous enough to see both sides of the case and reform your opinions.[24]

Asking Walter Winchell to be generous or to see both sides of the question may have been like asking a hyena not to scavenge, but Iva had to grab at her chance.

On April 20, as soon as Carroll got back to the States, he sent Iva's letter with one of his own to Winchell. The two men had known each other since Prohibition days in New York, and had had an on-again, off-again relationship ever since. Winchell had come to Carroll's rescue in 1926 when Carroll had been arrested for throwing a wild opening night party complete with naked show girls cavorting in a champagne-filled bathtub. There had been a falling out in the early 1930s when Winchell had panned one of Carroll's shows and Carroll had walked up to him in public to tell him that he was not fit to associate with decent people—an opinion that was widely shared at the time, and later as well. The feud had persisted for several years, but by 1948 the two men were on speaking terms again.

About a month after she had sent off her letter with Carroll, Iva finally got a letter from Carroll together with a note he had received from Winchell. "When you write Miss Toguri [sic]," wrote Winchell, "please tell her that I have confidence in the administration of United States justice and she will get a fair trial in court." He added, "I may run part of her letter in some column and ask readers what they think."[25] Carroll expressed puzzlement about Winchell's reference to a fair trial, since he had understood from General Willoughby that Iva's trial days were over. He expected to go east in the first week of June, however, and he promised to have a "good talk" with Winchell if he met him in New York.

Iva, whose hopes had been raised by the intervention of an influential person like Carroll, was disappointed at Winchell's reaction. She could not help but feel uneasy. Still she had no choice but to wait, hoping that a direct talk between the two men would help. It was a long shot, but something might come of it.

Nothing ever did, for Carroll was never able to meet Winchell, and Iva was never to hear from him again. On the afternoon of June 17 a United DC-6 carrying Carroll and his party from Los Angeles to New York grazed a 60,000-volt powerline during an emergency landing and exploded in midair. The four crew members and the thirty-nine passengers were killed instantly, their mutilated bodies strewn over an acre of ground. The only thing left to identify Earl Carroll was his wallet.

Iva was shocked to hear the news. Now that Carroll was dead, there was no one else who might change Winchell's attitude. Her luck seemed to have taken a turn for the worse.

That was not all. Harry Brundidge, fresh from his triumphs in the cause of American justice, began an exclusive series on the Tokyo Rose case in the Nashville *Tennessean*. On Monday morning, May 2, a front-page headline in the *Tennessean* screamed: ARREST OF TOKYO ROSE NEARS: SHE SIGNS CONFESSION TO "SELL-OUT." The crusading crime reporter Harry Brundidge had finally come up with his "exclusive":

The *Nashville Tennessean* this morning can disclose that Attorney General Tom C. Clark is contemplating the arrest of Mrs. Iva Ikuko Toguri d'Aquino, frequently referred to as "Tokyo Rose."

. . . This writer went to Japan in March. While there he encountered John B. Hogan, special representative of the Attorney General. Hogan was seeking witnesses and evidence with treason cases. The writer's offer of assistance in the matter of "Tokyo Rose" was accepted. It was as a direct result of this cooperation that Attorney General Clark reopened the case.

Most of the new evidence, as well as the identity of new witnesses, resulting from the *Nashville Tennessean*'s participation in the matter, must remain secret at this time. However, the Attorney General now has in his possession:

A confession signed by "Tokyo Rose"

An important document, long missing, but recovered by this writer in Honolulu, in which Iva I. Toguri, in her own handwriting admits she was "Tokyo Rose."

The caption under Brundidge's picture at the beginning of the three-page article identified him as the man who "witnessed the vital signature to the confession." Once again, he was the chief character in his own news story.

Brundidge's "inside story" of the Tokyo Rose case continued in ten installments through the rest of May. The tone was sensational, and the content frequently strayed from the facts. It was now clear why Brundidge had offered his services to the Justice Department. He was after a chance to recover his pride and reputation, and to finish the "exclusive" story he had missed in September 1945.

The men in the Justice Department were not at all pleased with Brundidge's articles, which simply gave new impetus to the Tokyo Rose witch hunt. The Criminal Division was still considering the evidence in the case and had by no means decided to prosecute Iva yet. The publicity Brundidge was giving the case just meant extra complications. But the Justice Department officials also knew that Brundidge had to be handled as carefully as Winchell, although for different reasons. "I don't know what we can do to put a clamp on Harry's mouth or typewriter," wrote one Justice Department official, "but sure as we call him, he will blow it into a story thus giving him a leg to hang credence to the stuff." Attorney General Clark's subordinates persuaded him to get in touch with Silliman Evans, the publisher of the *Tennessean*, who was a friend of Clark. In a handwritten personal note dated June 3, Clark wrote: "The boys are a little disturbed on the Tokyo Rose matter. It would be helpful if no publicity came out until after action was taken. I will let you know. Thanks." But by that time Brundidge's exclusive had run its course, and the damage was already done.

"I Did Not Do Anything Treasonable"

The Justice Department made its decision in mid-August. On August 17 the *New York Times* reported:

"The Department of Justice chief asked the Army to arrest Iva Ikuko Toguri d'Aquino and transport her to San Francisco where a grand jury will be convened to determine if she should be tried [for treason].' A follow-up UP wire service dispatch from Tokyo reported Iva's reaction to the news:

> Pale and nervous, Mrs. d'Aquino said today that she was anxious for her treason trial because "this indefinite waiting is worse than physical torture."
> Interviewed in her shabby Japanese rooming house, the wartime broadcaster reiterated that she had been fully investigated by Allied occupation authorities and released for lack of evidence....
> "I would just as soon go through with it and have it over," she said. "I have been in the air for three years not knowing my fate."
> ... "I don't know what they have found now, but I'm certain I did not do anything treasonable," she said.[26]

The Justice Department had not discovered any new evidence, nor had it decided to arrest Iva for that reason. Iva's signed "confession" contained no information that the Justice Department did not have before. The simple fact of the matter is that the Justice Department had decided to arrest Iva because of the considerable public pressure that had been put on the department. The confession was merely an excuse.

The CIC arrested Iva on August 26 at her lodgings at Ikejiri in the suburbs of Tokyo. For the first time since the whole affair had begun, she was presented with a formal arrest warrant that charged her with "treasonable conduct against the United States Government during World War II." She was taken again to Sugamo prison, where the lights

Arriving in San Francisco for trial

in her cell were kept on day and night, apparently to make sure she did not commit suicide.

Iva must have felt that this was the year for her luck to run out. First the death of her long-awaited child, then the death of Earl Carroll who might have helped her, and now the arrest. But Iva's hopes had not run out, for she still welcomed the trial as an opportunity to bring all the facts out in the open. When she had told the press that she was certain she had not done anything treasonable, she was not trying to hide a guilty conscience but simply speaking her belief that she had done nothing wrong. Iva had no fear of a trial that might clear her name.

Nine days after her arrest, on September 3, with two MPs escorting her by either arm, she was hustled up the gangplank of the *General H. F. Hodges,* a transport carrying American troops returning to San Francisco. No one came to see her off. Filipe had visited Iva three times at Sugamo after her arrest, but he had not been told when she was to be sent back to the States. He learned about her departure from the newspaper—the day after she left.

There was a special reason why the Justice Department had decided to have Iva brought back by ship rather than by military aircraft, as originally planned. If an American residing overseas is to be tried for treason, the law requires that he be tried in a federal court of the district where he first sets foot on American soil. Had Iva traveled by plane, she would have first landed in Alaska or Hawaii, neither a desirable place for a trial from the government's point of view. Alaska was remote and inconvenient, and Hawaii had a large Japanese-American population. It would be far easier to get an indictment in California. For a while the government had considered Los Angeles, but in the end it was decided instead to bring her to San Francisco.

There were, however, some who doubted the wisdom of bringing Iva for trial to California, not so much for Iva's sake as for the sake of the Japanese Americans who had returned to the state from their wartime years of internment. In late August, before Iva had sailed, the California Federation for Civic Unity, a civil rights group, asked the Justice Department to reconsider its decision to try Iva on the West Coast. "The trial of 'Tokyo Rose' in San Francisco would, we feel, raise racial tensions and animosities at a time when it is most important to weld together as much as may be possible the different racial elements making up the American community."[27] The group suggested that the trial be held in the Midwest or in the East, where there were few Japanese Americans and less anti-Japanese hostility. But the Justice Department knew what it was doing. Iva came back by ship to San Francisco, a city with a long history of anti-Japanese exclusionist sentiment.

Wayne Collins Takes a Case

On the morning of September 25 the *General Hodges* sailed through the Golden Gate. Iva had wanted to come home in 1948, and now she was home—branded a traitor.

The city sparkled white and clean under the sun as the *General Hodges* put into the dock at Fort Mason. A crowd of several hundred stood waiting to greet the returning GIs. A different sort of welcoming party awaited Iva. Frederick Tillman, accompanied by several other federal officers, boarded ship to take her into custody. Iva had dressed as neatly as she could. She had lost so much weight from dysentery that she had to use a safety pin to keep her skirt from slipping off. A woman FBI employee who gave Iva a body search confiscated the pin (as well as Iva's bobby pins). It was against regulations, she said, for Iva might use the pins to commit suicide. Iva exploded. If she had wanted to commit suicide she would have done it in Japan, and if they took that pin away she would refuse to leave the ship on her own two feet. For once the FBI relented, and Iva got back her safety pin, but not her bobby pins.

Iva walked down the gangplank, her hair blowing loosely in the wind. The band played "California, Here I Come." As Iva was led to a waiting car through the crowd cheering the returning GIs, she was flooded for the first time with the realization that she was finally home, walking the soil of the country she had missed for seven long years, but walking it as an accused criminal, not a free person. Her head suddenly felt numb, as though she had been struck a blow.

Her first destination was the office of U.S. Commissioner Francis S. J. Fox, where she was to be formally arraigned. Some old familiar faces were waiting for her: her father Jun, who had come in from Chicago, and her sister June, married and living in Los Angeles. Jun looked older and smaller than he had when Iva last saw him, but he was shocked at the change in her. The daughter he remembered was plump and healthy-looking; the daughter standing before him was pale and thin. They hugged each other tightly, reunited at last. The newspaper reporters who had crowded into the room did not fail to note that there were no tears. (What was going on behind these "expressionless Oriental faces"?)

"Girl, I'm proud of you. You didn't change your stripes," said Jun. "A tiger can't change his stripes, but a person can so easily."[28] It was a simple greeting, but it meant much to Iva. When she heard her father's words, all her troubles seemed to melt away. Whatever else had happened, her family was going to stand behind her and support her. It was such a consolation. But at the time all she could reply was, "I'm tired."

Standing beside Jun was a small, wiry-looking man with short gray hair and bright sharp eyes peering out from under bushy black brows. He was Wayne M. Collins, the lawyer Jun had asked to defend Iva. Jun had hoped to get the best possible legal help for Iva. At first he had tried to secure the services of Jerry Giesler, the well-known Hollywood criminal lawyer who had made his reputation defending movie stars such as Charlie Chaplin and Errol Flynn. "If I have sharp legal teeth," Giesler once said, "it is because I cut them on gritty fare of cases no one else wanted. . . ." But defending a penniless Japanese American woman, pursued by a government that seemed hell-bent on convicting her of treason, was a bit too gritty even for Giesler. The feeling was shared by a number of other lawyers whom Jun approached—none wanted to handle a treason case, except for Wayne Collins.

The forty-nine-year-old Collins, Sacramento-born son of an Irish immigrant, had a reputation among his colleagues for being a champion of the underdog. He was especially well known among the Japanese American community after he served as defense counsel in the Korematsu case. Fred Korematsu, a *nisei* living in Oakland, had been arrested for refusing to go to an internment camp in 1942. His trial had become a test for the constitutionality of the whole relocation program, which was ultimately upheld. Collins had taken the case all the way up to the Supreme Court, against the advice of his colleagues, who warned him not to defend Korematsu given the temper of the times.

Collins continued his lonely efforts on behalf of the Japanese Americans after the war, too. When the federal government attempted to deport all those Japanese Americans who had renounced their citizenship while in the internment camps, Collins agreed to serve as counsel on their behalf. While in the relocation camps the Japanese American internees were given the choice of pledging their loyalty to the United States or of returning to Japan. Many chose to renounce their citizenship because they did not wish to remain in the camps for an indefinite period or were frightened at the thought of returning to a society that regarded them with such hostility. When the time came to be sent back to Japan, many "renunciants" wished to remain in the United States. The government refused to let them do so. Collins was reviled as a "mad man" for defending these "Jap traitors," but he ignored criticism even from friends and colleagues. As the sole lawyer for 5,000 "renunciants," he wrestled the government into an agreement to let them retain American citizenship.

Collins had also helped the Japanese settlers brought from Peru during the war for internment in the United States at the request of the American government. When the war ended, the Peruvians, who had confiscated their property and were glad to be rid of economic competition for their own laborers, refused to permit their return. Then the American government announced it was going to force the Japanese Peruvians to return to Japan on the incredible grounds that they had entered the United States illegally, without going through proper immigration procedures. As a result of this bureaucratic travesty, about 1,700 had to return to Japan, many of them born in Peru and unable to speak Japanese. The 365 who refused to go appealed to Collins for help. He worked on their behalf in legal actions that dragged on into the mid-1950s.

Despite his very considerable role in Japanese American history, and his very justifiable rage on their behalf, Wayne M. Collins was not on very good terms with the leaders of the Japanese American community. Like many men with a strong bent of idealism, Collins was not a man to compromise. He was stubborn, he was self-righteous, and he had a sharp tongue. He also had many enemies. One of his *bêtes noires* was the Japanese American Citizens League. Collins was particularly incensed that the organization actively endorsed the relocation policy in 1942. He made his anger known. He habitually expressed his contempt for the JACL calling them the "jackals."

It was natural that Wayne M. Collins became Iva's principal attorney. He was used to unpopular cases, and he was used to handling the plight of Japanese Americans hounded by their own government. When he heard that the Toguri family did not have enough funds to hire a lawyer for a long trial, he volunteered his services without fee. He even used some of his own resources to help defray the trial expenses. His sense of outrage at injustice was aroused, and he became a champion for Iva, as relentless as her pursuers.

This became clear enough on Collins's first day in her service.

On the afternoon of arraignment, Collins visited his new client at County Jail No. 3. It was the first time since her detainment in September 1945 that Iva had a lawyer. She had much to tell him. At 3:30 P.M. a prison matron suddenly interrupted their talk and told Iva she would have to change out of her prison garb. There had been a call from the U.S. marshal's office that a deputy marshal was coming to pick Iva up. Collins would have to leave right away. Something was fishy. The marshal's office was closed on Saturday, Collins protested, and besides no one had any right to remove Iva from the jail without being authorized to do so by judicial process. The courts were not open that day either, so no process could have been issued. Furthermore, no one had given Collins any notice. Removing her from jail was unauthorized and a violation of her rights. The matron impassively replied that she was merely following orders and would continue to do so.

Collins sprang into action. He phoned the marshal's office, then the U.S. attorney's office, then the offices of John B. Hogan and Special Assistant Attorney General Tom DeWolfe—no one answered. It was very suspicious. When the deputy marshal finally arrived, Collins discovered that FBI Special Agent John Eldon Dunn was waiting in the car below. Collins was furious. It was now clear that the government was trying to spirit Iva off for interrogation. To make sure they did not do so without counsel, he got into the car with Iva and the two federal men. When they arrived at the FBI offices, another FBI agent explained that Iva was in fact being brought there for questioning. Who ordered it? asked Collins. Who is going to question her? He was not permitted to say, replied the agent. Collins launched into a tirade: all this was highly irregular; it was a deliberate violation of the Fourth, Fifth, and Sixth Amendments; it was a violation of legal ethics and legal courtesy. The man left for a moment, then returned to say that FBI agents in the next room wanted to talk with Iva alone for about five minutes. Collins replied that his client would not go willingly but only under duress and protest, and that she would decline to answer any questions put to her.

Iva found Dunn and Frederick G. Tillman waiting for her. They seemed to want her to sign the statement she had earlier made to Tillman during her interrogation at Sugamo. She refused. Acting on Collins's advice she was trying to protect her rights as an American citizen. Since Collins was continuing to make loud and audible protests from the next room, the two FBI men decided to let Iva go after three minutes.

It was a small but important victory for Iva. For the first time since 1945 she had a lawyer, and one who not only stood up for her rights but who believed in her.

Collins, in need of help to prepare for such a major trial, eventually called in two other San Francisco lawyers with whom he had worked over the years: Theodore Tamba and George Olshausen. Both agreed to serve on the defense team without fee, even though it appeared that the trial would be long. Both, like Collins, were angered at the cavalier fashion in which the government had trampled on Iva's civil rights, and both saw a professional challenge in helping on a case that was bound to attract national attention.

Things were looking up again for Iva. She began to relax a bit. Her health also improved after doctors at the prison treated her dysentery. Jun came every day to visit, bringing things she liked to eat, and she began to settle into the prison routine. The only thing that still disturbed her was insomnia. County Jail No. 3 was a women's prison, and the prostitutes brought after roundup every night made so much noise that it was hard to sleep.

Indictment

On October 8, 1948, a federal grand jury charged Iva with committing eight overt acts of treason "with treasonable intent and for the purpose of, and with the intent in her to adhere and give aid and comfort to the

Imperial Japanese Government." The eight overt acts were as follows:

Overt Act I: That on a day between March 1, 1944, and May 1, 1944, the exact date being to the Grand Jurors unknown, said defendant, at Tokyo, Japan, in the offices of the Broadcasting Corporation of Japan, did discuss with another person the proposed participation of said defendant in a radio broadcasting program.

Overt Act II: That on a day between March 1, 1944, and June 1, 1944, the exact date being to the Grand Jurors unknown, said defendant, at Tokyo, Japan, in the offices of the Broadcasting Corporation of Japan, did discuss with employees of said corporation the nature and quality of a specific proposed radio broadcast.

Overt Act III: That on a day between March 1, 1944, and June 1, 1944, the exact date being to the Grand Jurors unknown, said defendant, at Tokyo, Japan, in a studio of the Broadcasting Corporation of Japan, did speak into a microphone regarding the introduction of a program dealing with a motion picture involving war.

Overt Act IV: That on a date between August 1, 1944, and December 1, 1944, the exact date being to the Grand Jurors unknown, said defendant, at Tokyo, Japan, did speak into a microphone in a studio of the Broadcasting Corporation of Japan referring to enemies of Japan.

Overt Act V: That on a day during October, 1944, the exact date being to the Grand Jurors unknown, said defendant, at Tokyo, Japan, in the offices of the Broadcasting Corporation of Japan, did prepare a script for subsequent radio broadcast concerning the loss of ships.

Overt Act VI: That on a day during October, 1944, the exact date being to the Grand Jurors unknown, said defendant, at Tokyo, Japan, in a broadcasting studio of the Broadcasting Corporation of Japan, did speak into a microphone concerning the loss of ships.

Overt Act VII: That on or about May 23, 1945, the exact date being to the Grand Jurors unknown, said defendant, at Tokyo, Japan, in the offices of the Broadcasting Corporation of Japan, did prepare a radio script for subsequent broadcast.

Overt Act VIII: That on a day between May 1, 1945, and July 31, 1945, the exact date being to the Grand Jurors unknown, said defendant, at Tokyo, Japan, did speak into a microphone in a studio of the Broadcasting Corporation of Japan, and did then and there engage in an entertainment dialogue with an employee of the Broadcasting Corporation of Japan for radio broadcast purposes.

Stanton Delaplane, covering the grand jury for the San Francisco *Chronicle,* took the charges to mean nothing more than that Iva had simply worked at NHK.[29] Compared to the indictments handed down in other World War II treason cases involving enemy propaganda broadcasts, the overt acts specified were rambling and general—no precise dates were given, no names were mentioned, no broadcasts or broadcast scripts were cited. Iva denied all of the charges to waiting reporters. "I do not and never have considered myself a traitor to the United States," she said.

The vote on Iva's indictment was a clear majority: twenty-one for indictment, only two against. The two dissenters were an employee of the University of California press, John Gildersleeve, and a radio engineer who had worked for OWI during the war. According to Gildersleeve, the indictment was reached rather easily by open balloting. But Gildersleeve also recalled recently that the government attorneys put tremendous pressure on the grand jurors. That particular grand jury, he said, would have indicted anyone the federal attorneys requested to be indicted.

Twelve witnesses had been called, eight from Japan (Major Tsuneishi, Kenkichi Oki, George Hideo Mitsushio, Hiromu Yagi, Kenichi and Mary Ishii, Emi Matsuda, and Yukio Ikeda) and four from the United States (Norman Reyes, Clark Lee, Harry Brundidge, and Frederick G. Tillman). Five or six witnesses appeared on the first two days of the deliberation. According to Gildersleeve, after a day's recess, Special Assistant Attorney General Tom DeWolfe told the jury, "I believe you have heard enough to convince you that she is guilty. We don't want to waste any more of your time." One juror asked, "How about the other Americans who broadcasted for Radio Tokyo during the war?" DeWolfe said that particular question was not under consideration and not within the jurisdiction of the grand jury. The others involved in the broadcasts could be dealt with at a later date, he said. Without further questions the vote was taken.[30]

DeWolfe apparently felt that the grand jury proceedings were a touch-and-go affair. On November 12 he wrote a personal memo to Ray Whearty, a Justice Department colleague: "I understood my instructions in the Toguri case. As it was two of the grand jurors voted against an indictment. It was necessary for me to practically make a Fourth of July speech in order to obtain an indictment." To Assistant Attorney General Alexander Campbell he wrote, "I think in retrospect that I personally presented the case against the d'Aquino woman . . . in a rather forceful manner. I told the grand talesmen that the case as to Colonel Ince, Mrs. d'Aquino's superior on Radio Tokyo, would be presented to a Federal grand jury here in the immediate future. . . . If the above action had not been taken by me, I believe that the grand jury would have returned a no true bill against Mrs. d'Aquino."[31]

In fact, from the beginning DeWolfe had not been enthusiastic about bringing an indictment against Iva. He was the sharpest and most agile of the attorneys who handled the World War II treason trials within the Internal Security Division of the Justice Department. His reputation within the department was very high. Earlier that year in Boston he had brought in convictions against two men involved in wartime propaganda broadcasts for the Nazis, Douglas Chandler and Robert Best. Both had gotten life sentences. But Iva's case was different. On May 25, 1948, when the Justice Department was still trying to make up its mind what to do about Iva's case, DeWolfe had written a long memo to Ray Whearty pointing out that there was not sufficient evidence to make a prima facie case against her. Indeed all the evidence seemed to point in the other direction. "There is no evidence upon which a reasonable mind might fairly conclude guilt beyond a reasonable doubt, and consequently a motion for a judgment of acquittal . . . would probably be granted by the court," he wrote. "The type and quantum of the proof available in the case against the subject is the direct antithesis of that available and utilized in the Boston litigation. . . ." It was not surprising that DeWolfe felt the need to make a "Fourth of July speech" to the grand jury a half-year later.

On October 11, Iva's request to be released on bail was denied on the grounds that treason was a capital offense and that the accused could not be extradited were she to flee the country. So while the defense and the prosecution began to prepare their cases, Iva passed her days in County Jail No. 3. The eight witnesses from Japan arrived home on October 24 after enjoying a two-day holiday in Honolulu. Oki and Mitsushio said they were glad to have had a chance to see family and old friends again.

The Trial of Axis Sally

Unlike other federal crimes, treason is defined in the Constitution itself. The treason clause had ancient precedents in fourteenth-century legislation aimed at protecting the English king against rebellious subjects. The Founding Fathers were equally concerned to protect their own fledgling government against internal revolt or dissension, but they also were aware of the need to protect the community against arbitrary uses of governmental powers. So the intent of the treason clause in the Constitution was to define the act as restrictively as possible, limiting the ability of judges to define or to create novel treasons by construction. Treason was defined under Article III, Section 3, as follows: "Treason against the United States shall consist only in levying war against them, or in adhering to their enemies, giving them aid or comfort."

Unlike other federal crimes, treason is not simply a legal question but a political one. Even a restrictive definition of treason could be interpreted and applied differently, depending on the period and the government in power. Treason is not like murder or arson, which can be defined in a way susceptible to more objective tests. Ultimately, treason is defined subjectively by those who hold power. Neither Aaron Burr nor Jefferson Davis was ever indicted or tried for treason, although some argued they should be, but John Brown was, albeit under provisions of the Virginia constitution that resembled those of the federal Constitution.

Twelve persons were indicted for treason as the result of activities during World War II. Seven had been involved in enemy propaganda radio broadcasts. Two of them—Iva (alias Tokyo Rose) and John David Provoo, a former prisoner at Bunka Camp—had worked for Radio Tokyo. The other five had worked for the Nazis: Robert Best (convicted, sentenced to life imprisonment); Douglas Chandler (convicted, sentenced to life imprisonment); Martin Monti (convicted, twenty-five years imprisonment); Herbert John Burgman (convicted, six to twenty years imprisonment); and Mildred Gillars (convicted, ten to thirty years imprisonment).*

Of all the indicted World War II traitors, the most famous beside Iva

*In 1947 a federal grand jury voted against an indictment of treason in the case of Edward Delaney, who had broadcast for the Germans until shortly after Pearl Harbor.

was Mildred Gillars, otherwise known as "Axis Sally." Gillars had been brought to the United States at about the same time as Iva—TWO SIRENS RETURN proclaimed the obvious headlines—and the press continued to compare the two women during their trials. But in fact the trial of Mildred Gillars, as well as her activities as "Axis Sally," were quite different from Iva's. A comparison is instructive. For the federal prosecutors, the "Axis Sally" case was an easy one while the "Tokyo Rose" case was hard.

Mildred Gillars, a large woman who was forty-eight years old at the time of her trial, was a native of Maine and a graduate of Hunter College. After several years of trying unsuccessfully to make a career as an actress, she had gone to study music in France in 1929. Five years later she arrived in Nazi Germany, two years after the Nazi takeover. In 1940 she had begun broadcasting over Radio Berlin. She had been a disc jockey like Iva, but her comments between records were laced with virulent anti-Semitism. "Damn Roosevelt! Damn Churchill! Damn all the Jews who have made this war possible!" went one of her broadcasts. "I love America, but I do not love Roosevelt and all his kike boyfriends." As a result, Axis Sally was the object of bitter GI hatred. At the end of the war Allied authorities arrested her, but soon afterward she was released.

In 1948, three years later, the Justice Department changed its mind and Gillars was brought back to the United States on August 21, about a month before Iva's arrival. Her trial for treason began in Washington on January 25, 1949.

The most telling evidence presented at Gillars's trial was OWI recordings that vividly demonstrated the nature and intent of her broadcast activities. One of the most dramatic prosecution exhibits was the recording of "Vision of an Invasion," a radio drama she broadcast in 1944 several weeks before D-Day. The program dramatized what might happen if the Allied forces crossed the Channel and invaded the Nazi-held continent. The plot involved the mother of an Ohio GI who sees her son in the midst of a dream; he tells her that he is already dead, killed when the Germans destroy his ship in mid-Channel; in the background could be heard the horrible shrieking and sobbing voices of other GIs. It was a bloodcurdling performance, and the prosecutors played the recording several times.

Equally effective was the testimony of a number of former POWs who appeared as witnesses at the trial. Gillars insisted she began her broadcasting so that she could help Allied POWs send recorded messages to their families back home. She had, in fact, visited a number of POW camps in Germany, France, and Holland to record messages. But all the POWs who appeared as witnesses at the trial said that she had approached them as a representative of the Red Cross, not as an employee of the German propaganda organization, and that she had promised their messages would be sent without any propaganda. When recordings of these POW message broadcasts were played, it became clear they were interwoven with propaganda from beginning to end.

The former POWs who appeared in court uniformly expressed their hatred for Mildred Gillars. One of them testified that when he had refused to cooperate and accused her of working for the Germans, she told him, "You'll regret this." Soon afterward he was sent to a concentration camp. Another said she had pulled the recording mike away and begun to scream abuse at him when he did not talk about his wonderful life as a POW. A third, who was a defense witness, suddenly turned in Gillars's direction and shouted, "She threatened us as she left, that American Citizen, that woman right there." The government prosecutors were so confident they had an ironclad case against Gillars that midway through the trial the government withdrew two charges of overt acts stated in the indictment on the grounds that the government did not wish to prolong the trial unnecessarily.

The last witness in the six-week trial was Mildred Gillars herself. She was on the witness stand for six days. On the first day she flatly denied that she was guilty of treason, amid dramatic and tearful protests that from beginning to end she had been under pressure by the Nazis. She repeatedly contended that she had been forced to broadcast by the Gestapo and that broadcasting had been the only way for her to make a living. In her heart of hearts, she insisted, she had always loved the United States. On the second day, however, her story changed rather abruptly. She suddenly became a romantic and tragic figure, betrayed by her womanly feelings. She had committed treason for her lover, her "man of destiny," Max Otto Koischewitz, a former professor at Hunter College who had been in charge of Radio Berlin broadcasts. In the final summation, the defense lawyers argued that Koischewitz had been a Svengali-like figure who turned Gillars into a puppet acting at his command.

The prosecution never conceded that Mildred Gillars was anything but a sadistic woman who had betrayed her country. On March 10, after seventeen hours and twenty minutes of deliberation, the jury returned a verdict of guilty on Overt Act X, which involved her broadcast "Vision of an Invasion." A week later she was sentenced to a term of ten to thirty years imprisonment.

The contrast between the Gillars case and Iva's is striking. First of all, Mildred Gillars was in fact the one and only "Axis Sally." She had used the name "Sally" during her broadcasts, and there were no other candidates for the title. Second, although Gillars first claimed that she had broadcast out of fear, she later admitted in open court that she committed treasonous acts for "her man of destiny." Third, it was fairly clear in Gillars's case that her intent had been to adhere to the enemy. Although she claimed to have broadcast only to make a living, when the Allied forces had entered Paris in August 1944 she had fled with the retreating German forces—and her beloved Max. Her salary as a broadcaster was 3,000 marks a month, second only to Koischewitz's and three times as much as other German employees at Radio Berlin. Finally, the government provided OWI recordings as concrete material evidence that Gillars had committed the overt act for which she was finally convicted.

On March 11, 1948, the day after her conviction, the *New York Times* editorialized:

> The case against Miss Gillars seemed complete. She had admitted making wartime broadcasts for the Nazis, in the course of which she did what she could to break the morale of American soldiers on the firing lines and of their relatives at home. If she had been successful the war would have lasted longer and more men would have died. It was a dirty business. . . . It is a story one would like to forget. But in returning this case to oblivion let us not minimize the crime of treason, which may cost lives, and more.

The editorial expressed the feelings of most Americans, who thought treason a more detestable crime than murder. By an act of betrayal one individual might cause the death of thousands and even shatter the foundations of a society. It was this public mood that ultimately made possible the power of a man like Joseph McCarthy. The fear that there were traitors in our midst had manifested itself in the prosecutions of Judith Coplon and Alger Hiss, both accused as agents of international Communism. The label of "traitor" touched a deep and sensitive nerve in the popular psyche. Even though the treason trials of "Axis Sally" and "Tokyo Rose" had nothing to do with the "Communist menace," the simple mention of the issue at stake, loyalty to the United States, was enough to excite emotion. By punishing "traitors" of whatever political stripe, the government could put the public on notice it was going to deal firmly and harshly with Communists and Communist sympathizers as well. Thus the treason trials of 1948 had the hidden political purpose of demonstrating public policy.

"Meatball" Kawakita

The trial of a Japanese American woman as the traitor Tokyo Rose possibly had other value as well. About the time that Iva returned to the United States, the treason trial of another Japanese American was coming to an end in Los Angeles. The defendant was twenty-seven-year-old Tomoya Kawakita, a native California *nisei* who had been stranded in Japan in 1941. Eventually he got himself a job as an interpreter at a POW camp. Although he had registered himself as a Japanese, automatically forfeiting his American citizenship by taking the POW camp job, he apparently had no difficulty getting back to the United States after the war.

His past caught up with him in 1947 while he was shopping in a Los Angeles department store. William L. Bruce, one of the POWs interned at his camp, happened to see him and immediately remembered him as "Meatball" Kawakita, one of the POW camp staff who had made life miserable for him. Bruce reported to the FBI, and Kawakita was arrested on suspicion of treason.

The Kawakita treason trial began in June 1948 in Los Angeles. A parade of former POW witnesses testified that Kawakita was unusually cruel, more cruel than any of the Japanese guards, and that it was routine for him to beat and kick the POWs. Doubtless their allegations were true. But one cannot help feeling that Kawakita was to some extent a scapegoat for all the mistreatment the POWs had received during the war, whether from him or others.

Kawakita was a scapegoat in another sense, too. During the war Japanese Americans had been interned because of a widespread public fear, shared by some public officials, that they were a potential fifth column of spies and saboteurs. In fact the Japanese Americans were not "dangerous elements," but turned out to be extremely cooperative toward the government, even as it was violating their fundamental civil rights. As Tom Clark later pointed out, there was never a single case of espionage or sabotage involving a Japanese American. By trying Kawakita—and later Iva—the government perhaps was putting the best face on its earlier action by demonstrating that there were in fact Japanese American traitors. The irony is, of course, that neither Iva nor Kawakita had been in the United States at the time they allegedly committed their treasonous acts.

Frustrations in Tokyo

On March 1, 1948, Iva's attorneys petitioned that forty-three persons (including General MacArthur and General Willoughby) be subpoenaed and brought at government expense from Tokyo, Hong Kong, and Australia to testify on her behalf. They asserted that these witnesses were absolutely necessary to Iva's defense and to assure that she received a fair trial. The petition was based on the Sixth Amendment ("In all criminal prosecutions the accused shall enjoy the right . . . to have compulsory process for obtaining witnesses in his favor").

Two weeks later the petition was denied on the grounds that Japan was a foreign country not under jurisdiction of American law. It was not possible to issue subpoenas for residents in a foreign country. Earlier, however, the government said it had been justified in arresting Iva without a warrant in 1945 because Japan was under the occupation of an American military force. Collins protested that the denial of the petition was "obvious sophistry. Refusal to bring defense witnesses from Japan was because the government did not want to, not because it could not."[32]

A precedent for bringing defense witnesses to the United States at government expense had already been established in the Gillars case. Five defense witnesses had been brought from Germany, a country as much under military occupation as Japan.

The government did agree to provide the defense with funds to take depositions from witnesses resident in Japan. It allowed only enough for one of Iva's lawyers to go, and none for an interpreter. The expenses for an interpreter had to be paid by Jun Toguri.

On March 25 attorney Theodore Tamba left for Tokyo with Tetsujiro Nakamura, a Sacramento-born *nisei* who had become acquainted with Wayne M. Collins at the time of the "renunciants" case. Nakamura had never been to Japan before, but his Japanese was fluent enough for him to serve as Tamba's interpreter.

According to Nakamura, after arriving in Tokyo he and Tamba found that most people they sought out as possible witnesses were uncooperative. Some even refused to meet or talk with them. Neither Tamba nor Nakamura knew his way around Tokyo, so they were unable to make much progress until Tamotsu Murayama, former staff member at Bunka Camp, came to their aid.

Murayama had become a reporter for the English-language *Japan Times*. Immediately after the war he had served as an informal liaison man between Prime Minister Kijuro Shidehara and General MacArthur. He was quite well connected at GHQ. Murayama, who had often been to the Overseas Bureau during the war, was sympathetic to Iva's plight and wanted to do what he could for her. It was largely through his persuasive efforts during visits to former *nisei* connected with the case that Tamba managed to get thirty-one depositions for the defense.

Why were so many of the former *nisei* connected with the case uncooperative? According to Wayne M. Collins it was a matter of government pressure. Scarcely had the defense lawyers submitted their petition to subpoena forty-three witnesses from Japan than the Justice Department sent off a teletype message to GHQ. "Thereupon," Collins later wrote, "FBI agent Fred Tillman, accompanied by one or two MPs, called upon a majority of the witnesses and coerced them to sign statements containing a multitude of falsities."[33] The MPs, of course, were in uniform and armed. The real or imagined sense of threat that many of the witnesses must have felt doubtless was one reason for some of the reluctance Tamba encountered in his search for defense depositions.

Another reason was that many former *nisei* were still capitalizing on their ability to speak English. They were no longer in the service of the Imperial government but had gone to work for the American occupation forces, who needed them as translators, interpreters, and censors. Some *nisei* used their connections or their positions at GHQ to lord it over the Japanese and even to line their pockets. These *nisei* did not want to attract the disapproving gaze of GHQ.

While in Tokyo, Tamba was accompanied by Noel Storey, a representative of the Attorney General who cross-examined the deposition witnesses. "Both of us reached the conclusion that we never had met persons who had such an aversion to the truth," wrote Tamba in 1954. ". . . They appeared to Mr. Storey and to me to be genuinely frightened of our troops in occupied Japan. A number of them had been led to believe that if they testified against Mrs. d'Aquino our government might react favorably to requests on their part to return to the United States as American citizens without being charged and put on trial for their own admitted treasonable utterances and conduct."[34]

At the time of the trial, Tamba also testified that potential witnesses had been contacted by the CIC. Indeed everyone he tried to talk to had already given statements either to the FBI or to the CIC. It was only natural that many were reluctant to cooperate with Tamba afterward.

GHQ was not particularly cooperative either. In February the Legal Section had grudgingly advised that Tamba and Nakamura be allowed to come to Japan, but only to prevent the defense from later claiming the government had obstructed their efforts to obtain a fair trial. But beyond that no help was forthcoming. In early May Collins registered a complaint to the court that the occupation authorities were being uncooperative, and that GHQ had classified as top secret the statements that Iva had made when she was questioned at Yokohama and Sugamo. The court replied that since Japan was under military law it could not compel the army to make these records available. However, GHQ had already handed all the related documents, including Iva's broadcast scripts, to the prosecutor, Tom DeWolfe, by way of FBI agent Tillman.

All these troubles—lack of cooperation from potential witnesses and from the occupation bureaucracy—so delayed Tamba's efforts that he and Nakamura had to stay on another month beyond the allotted forty-five days (only Tamba at government expense). Iva's trial, originally scheduled for May 16, had to be postponed.

The Witnesses Arrive

When Tamba arrived back in the States on June 7, he found that Collins had good news for him. Charles H. Cousens had agreed to come from Australia to serve as a witness on Iva's behalf. In the fall of 1948 Cousens had been astounded to read in the newspaper that Iva was going to be indicted and tried for treason as "Tokyo Rose." Shortly after the war he had heard that Iva had been accused of being Tokyo Rose, but he had not imagined that the affair would develop as it had. Since he had persuaded Iva to become an announcer in the first place, Cousens felt a sense of responsibility toward her, and he immediately contacted the American consulate in Sydney, asking that the Justice Department be informed that he wanted to appear as a defense witness. The State Department had notified the U.S. attorney in San Francisco of Cousens's offer in November, but Collins did not hear of it until nearly six months later.

Iva was delighted when Collins told her the news. They both agreed that her prospects looked brighter as a result. Cousens had created "Orphan Ann," and no one could explain better than he just what had gone on in the "Zero Hour" program. Kenneth Parkyns, another former Australian POW who had been held at Bunka Camp, had also volunteered to come from Sydney to testify on Iva's behalf, so Jun Toguri decided to put up the money needed to bring them both to the United States.

Cousens did not have an easy time of it after the war. In late August 1945 he and the other POWs from Bunka Camp were taken to Manila for questioning about their wartime broadcasting activities. Cousens got a thorough going-over by the American CIC as well as by the British and Australian intelligence authorities. The investigation of his activities continued even after he returned to Australia.

In July 1946 Cousens was formally accused of treason. The hearings on his case began on August 21 at the Central Police Court in Sydney. Cousens himself took the stand for five days. He testified that he had done his best to sabotage the broadcasts. Many of the monitored broadcasts attributed to him by the Australian listening service, he said, were in fact made by Kenichi Ishii, whose voice had been mistaken for Cousens's even by his own family.

In the course of his testimony he mentioned how he had met Iva at Radio Tokyo, how friendly she had been at the time, how she had told him that she had to report regularly to the Japanese police, and how she had retained her American citizenship. She was a "completely loyal American citizen," he said. He also described how she had become involved in the "Zero Hour" program.

> Cousens said he suggested that Toguri should take part in broadcasts to U.S. troops in the Pacific, mainly because of her extraordinarily rough voice and blunt manner. Her voice came through the microphone as he hoped it would, and he knew that if he could get away with it he would have an opportunity of presenting a comical program. After the show he noticed a heavy silence in the control room. He congratulated Miss Toguri and turned to Japanese officials and complained about the studio equipment.[35]

The charges against Cousens were dropped on November 7, 1946, and he went back to his old announcer's job at the Sydney radio station. He could have remained in comfortable obscurity, but when he heard of Iva's plight he knew that he ought to do what he could to help her.

Cousens and Kenneth Parkyns arrived in San Francisco about a week before Iva's trial was scheduled to begin. Afraid that the prosecution team might try to get to the two Australian witnesses first, Collins and Tamba had gone down to the airport to meet them. When the Australians failed to emerge from customs, Collins found out from a customs official that they had been met by FBI agents Dunn and Tillman. Collins was as angry as he had been when the FBI tried to question Iva after her arrival in San Francisco. He later protested that the FBI's action constituted an attempt to question defense witnesses unlawfully.

Iva had not seen Cousens since she had visited him in the hospital in 1944. When she met him again at the U.S. marshal's office in San Francisco, she broke down and wept, something she had not done when she had been reunited with her family ten months before. Time and time again she had asked that Cousens be brought to testify. He was the one person who could explain everything. Now, despite the government's refusal to subpoena foreign witnesses, he had come. She was encouraged by his words of reassurance that he understood her position all too well since he had been indicted for treason himself.

Filipe also came to be a witness for his wife's defense. Since he was a Portuguese national, not a Japanese citizen, GHQ expressed no objection to his leaving the country. Jun Toguri agreed to pay his passage and expenses. When Filipe had arrived in Seattle on June 4 he had been taken into custody for two days by immigration officials, who released him only when he stated that he would leave the country within six months and posted a bond guaranteeing his return to Japan. The government wanted to make sure that whatever the verdict at the trial, Filipe would not stay on in his wife's homeland.

The defense then had been able to assemble only three witnesses from overseas—Cousens, Parkyns, and Filipe. All of them had been subject to harassment when they arrived in the United States, and all had been brought at the expense of Jun Toguri, who had to borrow money to help his daughter.

The government brought nineteen witnesses from Japan to testify for the prosecution. They arrived in San Francisco by Pan American airliner on June 19. Since Japan was a foreign country, they had not been subpoenaed formally but "requested" to come by the Occupation GHQ. They fell into two groups. One group consisted of seven former *nisei* who had worked on Radio Tokyo propaganda broadcasts and had registered as Japanese citizens. They were in a vulnerable legal and psychological position. Some had come as the result of official arm-twisting. The other group was made up of twelve Japanese nationals, including some NHK technical staff workers unconnected with the propaganda broadcasts. Most had been tempted by the prospect of an expense-free trip to the United States at the courtesy of the American government.

But even those in the first group—the former *nisei*—could have refused to come. Others in the same position had done so, but some of those who came wanted the free ride, too. Oki and Mitsushio, who had come to testify at the grand jury proceedings, had even cooperated with Tillman in persuading others to come for the trial. Lily Ghevenian, a defense deposition witness, alleged that Oki had invited her to be a prosecution witness by asking her whether she would like a free trip to the United States.

None of the prosecution witnesses who came from Japan were particularly sympathetic toward Iva. Some thought she had brought on all her problems by identifying herself as "Tokyo Rose" to get a fat fee for her story. Even Kenkichi Oki, who told Filipe he regretted not suggesting his own wife as "Tokyo Rose," said to acquaintances that the affair was all Iva's own doing. Like Frederick Tillman, Oki seems to have thought Iva was a "stupid" woman.

There is no doubt that these former colleagues used Iva's troubles for their own advantage. The opportunity to enjoy American material comfort was beyond the dreams of most Japanese living under American occupation. As soon as they had settled down at the Hotel Whitcomb, many of the former *nisei* witnesses set off to visit friends or relatives they had not seen in many years. The Japanese nationals, some of whom had never been to the States before, went sightseeing.

There were financial advantages in being a government witness. At the Gillars trial witnesses had received fees of $5 a day ($3 for expenses and $2 witness fees). By contrast, at Iva's trial the government allowed $12 a day for domestic witnesses ($9 for expenses and $3 witness fee) and $10 a day for foreign witnesses. The government was willing to spend its money freely in its effort to bring in a conviction against Iva. Some of the witnesses from Japan moved into cheap boardinghouses so they could save part of the expense money. If a witness managed to save even $1 a day, he could save $30—over 10,000 yen—in a month. At a time when the average monthly salary of a recent Japanese university graduate was 2,200 yen, this was quite a substantial sum. Some witnesses even accumulated enough to go into business when they went home.

The proprietor of one large San Francisco Japanese grocery store recalls that one witness said it was possible to make good money by buying American goods to sell on the black market back in Japan. Saccharin was especially valuable, since it was easy to carry and fetched a good price in sugar-short Japan.

It is clear that the FBI and GHQ had twisted the arms of the former *nisei*, who could very well find themselves in the same position as Iva. But it is also clear that all the witnesses from Japan, including the former *nisei*, used the trip to America for personal advantage.

CHAPTER 5

The Trial of Tokyo Rose: The Prosecution

"As Exciting As a Spy Thriller"

The local newspapers began advertising the long-awaited treason trial—the first in the city's history—a week before it was to begin. The copy read like an announcement for a new movie hit. "This is the story of inside Japan during the war years and the Imperial Government's psychological warfare against America in the Pacific. As exciting as a spy thriller, as informative as history. Read the trial of Tokyo Rose daily in the *San Francisco Chronicle*."[1] The name of Iva Ikuko Toguri d'Aquino was not mentioned, nor that of Orphan Ann. There was no news value in either of them. But there was in the name of Tokyo Rose.

The trial attracted attention because of its expense. The government announced that the trial would last six to eight weeks, and that the prosecution would cost $500,000. In fact, however, the trial ran thirteen weeks and the government expenses ran over the anticipated amount, making it the most expensive trial in the history of federal courts to that time. (By contrast, the defense expenses were borne by the three defense lawyers, all working without fee, and by Jun Toguri, a small Chicago shopkeeper who had to borrow heavily to pay the other expenses.)

Despite the lurid advertising in the local press, the ten reporters on hand to cover the trial were sympathetic to the defense. Three of them worked for wire services, two for local Japanese American newspapers, and the rest for other Bay area papers. Nearly all had followed the case since the grand jury proceedings, and nearly all had been surprised at the vagueness of the indictment and at the dubious character of the grand jury witnesses. Their feelings of surprise and doubt grew as the "Tokyo Rose" trial progressed.

It began at 10:00 A.M. on July 5, the day after Iva's thirty-third birthday. The courtroom, decorated with the tasteless solemnity that official architects seem to feel upholds the dignity of the law, was dark and gloomy even at midday. It had to be lit by electric globes in the elaborately embellished ceiling. To one side of the room was a desk piled with recording equipment, connected to earphones on all the seats in the courtroom except for the spectators'. The dials and switches seemed out of place amid the vaguely Grecian figures lining the marble walls.

Silhouetted against a white, yellow, and green mosaic behind the bench was seventy-one-year-old Michael Roche, chief judge of the United States District Court of Northern California. Roche, the son of poor Irish immigrants, had put himself through college and become a lawyer. He had a deep patriotic faith in the country that had given him the opportunity to better his lot. As such he may not have been the most suitable judge to preside over a treason trial. He was a provincial man without much experience or much concern with the outside world. It was difficult for him to understand the background that had led to the trial, or the circumstances that had brought Iva to Japan.

To the left of the bench sat the prosecution lawyers. The Justice Department knew that it had a hard case on its hands, and it had taken care to pick a strong prosecution team. The government at first had intended to give the entire responsibility for the case to Frank J. Hennessey, a stern-looking San Franciscan, but as he later told AP reporter Katherine

Pinkham, after he had familiarized himself with the details of the case he recommended to Attorney General Tom C. Clark that the charges be dropped. His reasons were the same that DeWolfe had given in his memorandum of May 1948—the government did not have sufficient evidence to prosecute Iva.

The Justice Department decided to assign Tom DeWolfe to the trial. Hennessey remained the chief prosecutor in name; the real force in the prosecution team was DeWolfe, who had successfully prosecuted Douglas Chandler and Robert Best the previous year. DeWolfe had been scheduled to handle the Gillars trial, but since the Department anticipated that the "Tokyo Rose" trial was going to be the most difficult of all the World War II treason cases, DeWolfe was put to work on it instead. It seems likely that DeWolfe might have had mixed feelings about taking over the case. Although he had earlier doubts about Iva's indictability, DeWolfe was a good soldier who followed orders and did his job. The reporters who covered the trial had the distinct impression that he was under strong pressure from Washington to get "good results."

The other two members of the prosecution team were James Knapp and John Hogan, who had been Brundidge's traveling companion in 1948. Both men, as well as FBI agent John Eldon Dunn, had worked with DeWolfe on the Best and Chandler cases. The government obviously intended to field its winning team.

Sitting to their left were the three defense lawyers, Wayne M. Collins, Theodore Tamba, and George Olshausen, all local lawyers with little reputation outside San Francisco. They knew that national attention would be focused on the case, and that the trial was a once-in-a-lifetime opportunity. They wanted to win not for their own reputations but for the sake of "American justice," which had been ill served so far in the way the authorities had treated Iva.

In the midst of the three lawyers sat Iva, wearing an out-of-style plaid suit she had taken to Japan in 1941. Her shoulder-length hair was neatly bobbed and swept back by a band. Katherine Pinkham still remembers how impressed she was that Iva wore the same plaid suit every day from the beginning of the trial to the end. It looked as though Iva ironed her suit every day after the court session was over, for there was never a wrinkle in the skirt when she appeared in court the next morning.

Throughout the trial Iva, her face rather pale, usually sat scribbling penciled notes on a yellow legal-size pad on the table in front of her. Her rather solemn expression was a far cry from the image of sensual beauty the name "Tokyo Rose" conjured up. The newspapers described her variously as "unattractive," "undistinguished," "sharp-featured," "expressionless," and "drawn." It was a face, wrote the reporter for the *Pacific Citizen*, that in no way suggested the vivacious "Tokyo Rose" Iva was alleged to have been.

Behind Iva, sitting just an arm's reach away in the first row of the spectator seats, was her father, her sister June, her brother-in-law Hiroshi Hori, and his younger brother. All looked tense. Aside from them, however, there were few Japanese Americans in the courtroom. The Japanese American community in San Francisco tried to keep their distance from the whole affair, and few of them showed much sympathy toward the Toguris.

There were good reasons for this indifference. Only three or four years had passed since most Japanese Americans had left the relocation camps. Society still harbored feelings of hostility and prejudice toward them, and they were doing their best to be recognized as honest-to-goodness loyal Americans. Most had their hands full without trying to champion the cause of Iva Toguri. Besides, many Japanese Americans feared that the Tokyo Rose trial would only stir up anti-Japanese feelings again. A Japanese American like Iva, accused and probably guilty of treason, was a shame to the community, and some even refused to acknowledge that Iva was a Japanese American at all.

Since Wayne M. Collins had a running feud with the Japanese Americans Citizens League, it was not surprising that organization also kept its hand off the case completely. When the Toguri family tried desperately to raise money for the defense, they got not even a word of encouragement from the Japanese American community.

The jury was chosen on the first day of the trial from a panel of 110 persons. The selection took only two hours, an unusually short time for such a major case. Some had surmised that jury selection for a trial like this would take several days, perhaps even a week. All the jurors (as well as the two alternate jurors) were ordinary middle-class Americans: a glass company bookkeeper, a paper company executive, a paint company employee, a plasterer, an accountant, a retiree, five housewives, and an office secretary. Six were men and six were women. (On the third day of the trial the secretary had to be excused on account of sickness, and she was replaced by one of the alternate jurors, another housewife.) All of them were Caucasian.

In screening the prospective jurors, the defense team had tried to eliminate those who might have been prejudiced by a dislike of Japanese Americans, by Walter Winchell's broadcast comments, by loss of family or loved ones in the Pacific war, by prejudice against mixed marriage between races, or by a willingness to believe the government's witnesses in preference to the defense's. The government prosecutors seemed to have a simpler method of sifting jurors. They challenged six blacks and one Chinese American without any explanation—and with the assertion that no explanation was necessary.

The reason the prosecutors had maneuvered the selection of an all-white jury is quite clear. In the Kawakita trial a year before, the jury had included one black, one Japanese American, and one Jew and had taken long to reach a guilty verdict. The government prosecutors wanted to make sure this problem would not occur again.

The newspapers expressed surprise at the "all-white" character of the jury. Herb Caen of the San Francisco *Chronicle* observed that the "racial angle" was evident not only in the jury selection process.[2] The witnesses were segregated as well. The white witnesses were kept in one witness room, and those of color—Japanese, Filipino, or black—were kept in another.

The Trial Begins

The Tokyo Rose trial attracted as much public interest on the West Coast as the Hiss trial, which had opened about a month before in New York. The spectators' section was filled every day. People began to line up from around seven thirty in the morning, and sometimes there were as many as fifty or sixty people milling about during the day waiting for a vacant seat.

On the second day of the trial, the tall and balding DeWolfe made a ninety-minute opening statement. Although born on the West Coast, he had studied law at the University of Virginia, so there was just a trace of a southern accent in his voice. He spoke slowly and carefully, never raising his voice, and wasting no words in building the government's case.

He began by telling the jury it would be their responsibility to decide who was telling the truth: the plaintiff, the government of the United States, or the defendant, Mrs. d'Aquino, accused of the nefarious and hateful crime of treason, the only crime that the Founding Fathers had felt the need to define in the Constitution.

Iva, he said, had been born and raised in the United States, but she had "voluntarily" stayed in Japan, the country of her ancestors, after the attack on Pearl Harbor, and she had participated in Japanese propaganda broadcasts "without duress or compulsion." The government, he said, would "show that she liked the work, that she was glad to do it, that it was interesting and meant better pay and gave her excellent contacts . . . that she made these nefarious propagandistic broadcasts after it was clearly, fully, and completely explained to her and that she was aware of the purpose of the program and she voluntarily and wholeheartedly participated."

The government, he continued, would prove that the defendant was first used by Radio Tokyo as "listener bait," but that eventually "she told American troops that their wives and sweethearts were unfaithful, that they were out with shipyard workers with wallets bulging with money," and that she urged them "to lay down their arms, that the Japanese would never give up and had the will to win, and that there was no reason for Americans to stay there and be killed." The government would show that she tried to demoralize the American fighting men by reminding them of their girlfriends back home, that she called them "suckers" and "boneheads," and that she did all of this with malicious intent. All of these accusations, of course, centered on the so-called Tokyo Rose broadcasts.

DeWolfe had expressed quite different opinions a little over a year before. "The government's case must fail as a matter of law," he wrote in his May 25 memo, "because the testimony . . . will disclose that subject [Mrs. d'Aquino] did not adhere to the enemy or possess the requisite disloyal state of mind. There is no proof available that when subject committed said acts [of broadcasting] she intended to betray the United

States by means of said acts." The contrast between these views and those in his opening statement is almost shocking.

The prosecution began to build its case by making two main points. The first was that Iva was in fact an American citizen who had walked into trouble with her eyes wide open. The government introduced a series of documents to establish her citizenship: her Los Angeles birth certificate, her certificate of voting, the passport application she made in Japan, and the application for repatriation that she formally withdrew in September 1942 when she discovered she did not have money to board the second ship leaving Japan.

The defense, of course, contested the government's position on Iva's citizenship. Collins insisted that Iva was not an American citizen at all but a Portuguese national, registered as such from the time of her marriage to Filipe, and so recognized by the Portuguese consul in Tokyo. DeWolfe objected that Iva could not renounce her American citizenship simply by registering as the national of another country without making a formal renunciation of citizenship in proper legal fashion. He also argued that the American government ought to be the judge of whether Iva was a citizen or not, and that in any event she was not yet married at the time the alleged overt acts of treason were committed and was therefore unmistakably an American citizen then. The problem of Iva's citizenship would become a problem for prime consideration by the jury. If Collins's assertion was correct, then the American government had no right to try Iva, a Portuguese national, for treason; if it was not, then the trial was legitimate.

The second point was to prove that Iva herself admitted to being "Tokyo Rose." The first witness was called to the stand to make that point. Richard J. Eisenhart, who had been corporal of the guard at Yokohama prison when Iva was held there in the fall of 1945, testified that Iva had signed for him an old one-yen note with the autograph "Tokyo Rose." Eisenhart said that at the time he worked at the prison he had been an avid souvenir-hunter. He had thought he would like to have an autograph of the famous Tokyo Rose, but since he had no direct contact with her, he asked fellow guards to help him. He and his friends had gone to Iva's cell, and with his very own eyes, he said, he had seen her sign the note with the name "Tokyo Rose." She seemed to be delighted to give the autograph, he recalled.

According to Iva's later testimony the story was rather different. When Eisenhart had come to her cell with two other guards shortly after she was imprisoned, she had refused to give the autograph. Eisenhart had insisted. "Why not?" he asked. All he wanted was a souvenir to take back home. When Iva had continued to refuse, Eisenhart told her, "Well, you'll change your mind in two or three days."[3] About a week later he had come again, and, as he had predicted, Iva had changed her mind. She had hardly slept for the past six days. The guards had left the light on in her cell at night during the whole week.

The government presented other material exhibits—such as broadcast scripts Iva had autographed as "Tokyo Rose"—but the one-yen autograph seems to have made an impression on the jury.

Lieutenant Colonel Tsuneishi

Ex-Lieutenant Colonel Shigetsugu Tsuneishi of the Eighth Section, Second Division, Imperial Army General Staff, attracted considerable attention when he took the witness stand. His eyes were cold and narrow, his mouth turned down at the corners, and his five-foot, four-inch frame was straight and trim as a *kendo* expert, which he was. Every tough, taut inch of him reminded onlookers that he had been a professional officer in the Japanese Imperial army.

There was much curiosity about Tsuneishi, the former enemy propaganda boss, for other reasons as well. On July 7, the day before he appeared on the witness stand, Mark L. Streeter, a former inmate of Bunka Camp, had accused him of being "one of the worst war criminals" in Japan.

The fifty-year-old Streeter, who had come from Idaho to testify as a defense witness, had been surprised to see Tsuneishi's picture in the San Francisco *Chronicle*. He had thought that Tsuneishi had already been imprisoned for war crimes. Streeter, who said he had been beaten by Tsuneishi personally, demanded that Tsuneishi be arrested immediately as the man responsible for the "system of starvation and beatings" used to intimidate the prisoners at Bunka Camp. The authorities had ignored him, so Streeter had gone to the *Chronicle* instead.

Under direct examination Tsuneishi readily admitted that he had been in charge of wartime propaganda activities and that he had been the producer of "Zero Hour." When asked about the purpose of the program, he replied that it "was used to promote psychological warfare on the troops and cause them to become tired or disgusted with the war."[4] But under Wayne Collins's long and relentless cross-examination, the poker-faced Tsuneishi had to admit "Zero Hour" had not been very effective in that regard.

When Collins asked whether the broadcast had achieved its purpose, Tsuneishi replied: ". . . Lowering of the morale of the enemy was not entirely carried out because of the early conclusion of the war, but . . . the basis of propaganda is an appeal to the enemy, and from that angle, I consider that it was a success."[5] Collins kept pressing him. "Did the program provide entertainment?" he asked. Tsuneishi said that it had been an entertainment program. But, he continued, ". . . at that time Japan was suffering speedy defeat and it was satisfactory to me to produce any program appealing to GIs. . . . I figured we would wait until Japanese troops put up serious resistance and then the propaganda would be greatly increased. . . . It was unfortunate but the opportunity did not present itself to present the real, true propaganda program I wished to."[6]

All along Collins had insisted that "Zero Hour" was an entertainment program not at all harmful to GI morale and that Iva's broadcasts had been completely innocent. Now Tsuneishi, the producer of the program, had confirmed that. During the court recess, Hennessey, the chief government prosecutor, told reporters, who were already beginning to have doubts about whether the trial should take place, that the effectiveness of the propaganda did not mitigate the offense. Clearly he recognized that the defense had scored a point.

Collins scored a few other points with the close-mouthed Tsuneishi's testimony. One of the most important was that thirteen other women announcers had been employed by NHK. For the first time the jury heard the names of Ruth Hayakawa and June Suyama, as well as all the other women announcers, including "Mother" Topping, an elderly former missionary who tearfully appealed to Americans to stop fighting the Japanese. They were now aware that thirteen other women might fit the description of Tokyo Rose as well as Iva did.

Collins also tried to use Tsuneishi's testimony to establish that Iva had made propaganda broadcasts under duress without any treasonous intent. But when he asked Tsuneishi about the coercion applied to the POWs at Bunka Camp, which might have affected Iva's own state of mind, Tsuneishi's replies became guarded. As the man responsible for Bunka Camp, he was in danger of being charged with war crimes, so it is not surprising that his memory suddenly seemed to develop gaps.

He insisted that he had never threatened or ordered Cousens and the other POWs to broadcast. He repeatedly said he had "requested" them to participate in the broadcasts, and that in their "position as prisoners" they had agreed to do so. He also asserted that the POWs had been quite comfortable, treated almost like guests by the Japanese. Cousens and the other POWs were brought to Japan by airplane rather than by hospital ship, they had stayed in the Dai-ichi Hotel, they were given rations of meat and butter, they could go anywhere they wanted in civilian clothes without guards, and even after they had moved to Bunka Camp they commuted to the office every day in two Packard automobiles that Tsuneishi had managed to scrounge. (In fact, they were usually taken by truck.) Since he felt that broadcasts would not be effective if the prisoners were forced to make them against their will, he never threatened them, and he added that his personality would not permit him to tolerate barbarous acts such as beating prisoners.

When Collins pressed him for more details on how the prisoners were treated, Tsuneishi responded that he left details to his subordinates and that since the POWs were "lent" to NHK by the army, NHK took full charge of them. Again he responded with a great many "I don't know" answers.

Tsuneishi had the advantage of speaking through an interpreter. He had plenty of time to think about his answers. The prosecution frequently got him out of tight corners by objecting whenever the questioning turned toward the coercion of the POWs at Bunka Camp. The matter was unrelated to the trial, they insisted, and the coercion applied to the POWs had nothing to do with Iva. But Collins, who made the issue of duress one of the key points in the defense, did not give in so easily. When prosecution objections became repetitive, Collins would shift to another line of questioning for a while—and then suddenly bring the cross-examination back to Bunka Camp again. Judge Roche finally had to ask him when he was going to finish with Tsuneishi and warned he had been given ample time for the cross-examination. Indeed, Roche's warnings to Collins began to become more and more frequent as the trial wore on.

Tsuneishi's testimony was less than frank. In the spring of 1949 he had told Toshikatsu Kodaira that when the Australian investigators came to Japan to question him in connection with Major Cousens's treason trial, he had held back information. To protect his superiors (General Seizō Arisue and General Yatsugi Nagai) from prosecution as war criminals, Tsuneishi said, he did not tell the investigators that he had ordered Cousens to make propaganda broadcasts. The fact is that Tsuneishi himself had reason to worry that he might be accused of war crimes. He had been questioned closely by CIC more than twenty times on suspicion that he was a member of the Black Dragon Society, an ultranationalist group that was believed to have promoted Japanese aggression.

So despite his pangs of conscience about not telling the truth to the Australian investigators, Tsuneishi never said in court what every wartime Japanese easily knew to be the case—that in wartime Japan there was no way for Iva to have refused an army order to appear in a radio broadcast directly under the control of the army.

The closest Tsuneishi came to such a statement was during the cross-examination on July 14, which went as follows:

Q: Now, Colonel, if you gave orders through the civilian radio head of Radio Tokyo to a person on the "Zero Hour" and they disobeyed, they would be subject to punishment, wouldn't they?

A: Yes, I believe under some circumstances, that an employee who refused to obey would suffer the penalty of being discharged from Radio Tokyo.

Q: If the defendant had been discharged you would have conscripted her, wouldn't you? . . . Well, you did discuss conscripting her, didn't you?

A: I don't recall discussing such a matter.

Q: You know David Hyuga?

A: Yes.

Q: Didn't you tell him if she refused to participate in "Zero Hour" you would conscript her and put her under direct orders of the

army and if she then disobeyed she would be punished like a soldier in time of war?

A: This is a matter that happened considerable time ago and I don't
recall the details clearly, but I believe I had some sort of discus-
sion as follows: "Since the 'Zero Hour' was to be a propaganda
program concerning enemy troops it might be more desirable to
have her become an employee of the army and broadcast as such."
I recall having stated such a matter in a casual and informal conversation.

From Tsuneishi's testimony onward, Collins's tactics were clear. Until the time came for presenting the defense case, he would try to drag the
trial out, going into great detail in cross-examination, attempting to ex-
tract as much favorable testimony as possible for the defense, and wearing down the prosecution by attrition. Unfortunately these tactics proved
tiring not only to the prosecuting attorneys and the prosecution witnesses
but also to the judge and the jury. Prolonging the trial was especially
hard on Judge Roche, who was getting on in years and tired easily, and
who felt that every day the trial was prolonged unnecessarily was a
needless burden on the American taxpayers, who were ultimately footing
the bill.

Lee's Notes or Iva's Confession?

There was a stir of excitement in the courtroom when Clark Lee took
the witness stand on July 14. The forty-two-year-old former war correspondent had gained a bit of weight since the war, but he was still tall,
dark, and handsome. He was certainly the best-known witness at the trial, and he made a favorable impression on everyone in the court, including the jury.

DeWolfe questioned Lee very quickly, for only about half an hour.
He had Lee identify Iva's "confession" as well as the autograph she had
given him after the interview with him and Brundidge. A year earlier in
his May 25, 1948, memo, DeWolfe had expressed considerable doubt
about the usefulness of the "confession" as evidence:

The so-called "confession" or "admission against interest" given by
the subject to newspapermen Lee and Brundidge was given only after

those gentlemen offered subject $2000 for exclusive rights for subject's story.... Of course, Lee and Brundidge at the time were not acting under the authorization of the Department of Justice but were acting in their private capacity. Any inducements held out by a *private* person who is not occupying a position of *authority* to secure a confession do not *per se* render the same inadmissible.... However, the methods by which these newspapermen obtained the so-called "admission against interest" or "confession" from subject appear at least questionable and of doubtful propriety....[7]

Now, however, DeWolfe was presenting the "confession" as an important piece of material evidence.

In response to DeWolfe's questions about the interview, Lee testified that Iva had told him about the content of one propaganda broadcast.

She said that in the fall of '44, at the time that Japan claimed they had sunk a number of American ships off Formosa, a major came to her from Imperial headquarters and bluntly suggested that she broadcast as follows, "Orphans of the Pacific, you really are orphans now. How are you going to get home now that all of your ships are sunk."[8]

This testimony, of course, was intended to establish the charge in Overt Act VI.

The actual notes of Lee's interview were rather more terse and ambiguous than Lee's testimony. The relevant section read as follows:

Sometimes fighting news, admit defeat in typical German fashion, "well planned defeat," like seritorious [sic] advance to the rear, exaggerate your lossed [sic], minimize ours. Formosa claimed sunk American fleet. They sent major from GHQ who wanted to play up great victory wiping our u.s. fleet. i get inside news. and we add up ships claimed sunk and they wouldn't add. would be suicide say truth. after this time, last year we just mouth piece of GHQ. they'd bluntly suggest "you fellows all without ships. what are you going to do about getting home." "Orphans of the Pacific. You really are orphans."[9]

Clearly the nuances of the notes are rather different from Lee's testimony. For example, the typed notes nowhere indicate that the "major from Imperial headquarters" suggested that Iva broadcast the phrase about the "Orphans of the Pacific" or that these were words that Iva had broadcast. The "major" who came from the General Staff could have been no one but Tsuneishi, but in his own earlier testimony in court he said he had not once spoken directly to a subordinate staff person such as Iva. It seems unlikely that he would have ordered Iva directly to put the phrase into her broadcasts, as Lee's testimony suggested. The order might have been given to Oki or Mitsushio, or the phrase might have been included in another broadcast. If anything, the notes suggest that Iva secretly made fun of the news content that the General Staff insisted be used on "Zero Hour," since she had access to the Allied news reports from Filipe.

Lee did not have an easy time under cross-examination. Wayne Collins had brought to court a copy of *One Last Look Around,* a book Lee had published two years before about his postwar experiences in Japan and Asia. It included a chapter on the Tokyo Rose incident entitled "Her Neck in a Noose." The newsman was put in the awkward position of not being able to say in open court that in the book, as well as in the dispatches he had filed at the time, he had exaggerated to catch reader interest. Collins was fully aware of this and, using excerpts from the book, cross-examined Lee in great detail. Lee, who had earlier answered questions with assured responses such as "Absolutely" or "Certainly," gradually became vaguer and vaguer in his statements.

Collins got Lee to admit, as he had written in the book, that at the end of the war his old friend Colonel Fred P. Munson, an intelligence officer attached to G-2, GHQ, had told him that Tokyo Rose was a *nisei* girl from Canada. Since the defense kept insisting that there was more than one "Tokyo Rose," this was an important piece of testimony. Collins tried to pursue the identity of this Canadian "Tokyo Rose" further, but Judge Roche stopped him on the ground that he could not examine Lee on hearsay evidence. In response to cross-examination Lee also said that he had first heard the name Tokyo Rose in 1942, much before Iva had begun to make her broadcasts.

Collins suddenly changed his line of questioning. He asked Lee if he knew Hiromu Yagi, an employee of the Japan Travel Bureau who had testified at the grand jury proceedings. Then Collins asked a startling question: "Now, Mr. Lee, isn't it a fact that you and Mr. Brundidge requested me to go to the St. Francis Hotel on October 25 of 1948 because you wished to ascertain from me at that time whether or not I knew that Harry Brundidge had gone to Japan in 1948 and while in Japan advised Yagi to come before the Grand Jury and testify falsely in this case?"

This was a question that DeWolfe had feared even more than Lee did. Before Collins had even finished he leaped up to object. "You know that's nonsense!" he shouted.

"We'll demonstrate it in this court," replied Collins.

"No, you won't!" answered DeWolfe.

"I will."

"You're talking through your hat."

Judge Roche stopped the shouting match by sustaining DeWolfe's objection and told the jury,"You will disregard the question."

Lee was in a difficult position: if anyone was responsible for the Tokyo Rose trial, it was he, the man who had written the story that set off the Tokyo Rose furor in the first place. "If he had known the article he wrote could lead to the trial," commented Stanton Delaplane recently, "he would have written it much differently."[10] It was also Lee who was taking attacks that Collins really intended for Brundidge. On redirect examination DeWolfe tried to refurbish Lee's sullied honor by questioning him about his distinguished career as a journalist, but the prosecutor's anxieties about the damaged credibility of his witness were probably unfounded. The jury had been rather sympathetic to Lee during his harsh cross-examination by Collins, and it is even possible that Lee was the witness who had the most impact on the jury.

A Case of Perjury

Harry Brundidge, who had been subpoenaed as a prosecution witness, denied the story that he had persuaded his friend Hiromu Yagi to give false testimony at the grand jury hearing. "Utterly ridiculous," he said to reporters.[11] But strangely enough, despite these denials, Harry Brundidge, who should have been delighted to be on hand for the final chapter of the Tokyo Rose case, left San Francisco not long afterward. The man who claimed he got the goods on "Tokyo Rose" never appeared on the witness stand. DeWolfe recognized that it was too dangerous to put him there, for Wayne Collins had not been talking through his hat, and DeWolfe knew it.

On July 27, when FBI agent Frederick G. Tillman took the stand, Collins asked him point-blank: "Didn't you tell [Theodore] Tamba that Yagi had confessed he had been bribed to come to San Francisco in the fall of 1948 and testify falsely before the grand jury in this case?" DeWolfe shot up from his chair to object. Collins asked that the objection be overruled. "It goes to this question, if your Honor please," he said, "that here, if the answer be 'yes,' we have an open and notorious interference with the rights of the defendant, and in addition to that, we have what is an obstruction of justice in this proceeding."[12] Roche overruled DeWolfe's objection, so Tillman had to answer Collins's question. "Yes," he said simply.

There had been, it appeared, perjured testimony at the grand jury proceedings. This crucial point was never pursued in court, however. DeWolfe continued to raise objections, and Roche continued sustaining them, so Tillman's statement was left dangling. It need not be left dangling here.

Responsible officials in the Justice Department, from the Attorney General down, had become aware of Yagi's perjury soon after the grand jury had returned its indictment. On December 2, 1948, Assistant Attorney General (Criminal Division) Alexander M. Campbell had sent Tom Clark a long memo on the matter.

> The witness Yagi whom Harry Brundidge produced as a result of his trip to Japan last spring was, it now appears, guilty of perjury in his testimony before the grand jury in the Toguri case. He has finally confessed to a CIC officer in Japan that he falsely stated that another witness, whom he identified as a result of persuasion by Harry Brundidge, was present at the broadcast.

The other witness was Toshikatsu Kodaira, an AP reporter who had known Yagi since before the war.

The fullest description of the episode is to be found in Kodaira's deposition.[13] In April 1948, when Brundidge had arrived in Tokyo to get Iva to sign her "confession," Yagi had called Kodaira's office. "Toshi," he said, "don't you want a trip to the U.S.?" Kodaira, somewhat surprised, did not answer right away, but agreed to talk it over. When the two men met, Yagi explained to Kodaira that his old friend Harry Brundidge, at the request of the Justice Department, was in Tokyo looking for witnesses for the Tokyo Rose trial.

At ten o'clock the next morning, according to Kodaira's deposition, Kodaira went with Yagi to meet Brundidge at the Dai-ichi Hotel. Brundidge came downstairs with a great show of amiability to invite the two men up to his room. At the time the Dai-ichi Hotel was being used by the American occupation authorities and ordinary Japanese could not enter it freely unless accompanied by an American. In his room Brundidge broke out a bottle of whiskey. After Yagi and Kodaira each had about two drinks, Brundidge got down to business. According to Kodaira's deposition, Brundidge "suggested that 'you and Yagi just saw and heard Tokyo Rose broadcasting.' . . . He suggested, the date will be a little after the March bombing. . . . He also suggested that we had heard Tokyo Rose broadcasting, 'Soldiers, your wives are out with the war workers.' "

Thus, Kodaira's deposition makes it clear that Brundidge was attempting to obtain false testimony from both Yagi and Kodaira to incriminate Iva. As Kodaira left, Brundidge handed him the half-full whiskey bottle as a present.

Kodaira, who lived in the United States as a child, was tempted by the invitation to visit the country again, but when he met Brundidge at the hotel the next day, he refused the offer. Brundidge pressed him. He picked up a copy of Clark Lee's book and read Kodaira the passage where Iva had "admitted" to being Tokyo Rose. She says it herself, Brundidge told him. Besides, he continued, they will never hang a woman in the United States, and after the trial she will be able to live there permanently.

As they were leaving, Brundidge urged Kodaira to think it over again and gave him an old three-piece suit as another gift. The suit was pure wool, nearly impossible for a Japanese to purchase in 1948. Kodaira had his wife cut it down to fit him better, but he said that afterward he had felt obliged to send Brundidge an old hanging scroll as a return gift.

Finally the next day Kodaira told Brundidge that he would not testify against Iva at the grand jury. Brundidge made him promise not to tell anyone about the invitation.

On the way home Kodaira and Yagi stopped at a nearby coffee shop, where Kodaira scolded his friend. "Damn you," he said, "we didn't contact each other during the war, and it was almost impossible for outsiders to get into the Radio Tokyo building, much less the studio where the broadcasting was going on." He told Yagi how serious it was to perjure oneself in court. Yagi, who sat quietly listening, said he had decided not to go either.

Hogan knew that Brundidge had called potential witnesses to his hotel room. He had tried to tell Brundidge that it would be better to interview them properly in the G-2 office at GHQ, but Brundidge, who did not feel very comfortable there himself, had replied that potential witnesses would not be at ease if he did. Hogan said that he did not know how comfortable the talks had been, but it is nonetheless clear that he left part of the job of finding witnesses to Brundidge.

Yagi, contrary to his promise to Kodaira, did finally come to the grand jury hearing in San Francisco in the fall of 1948. According to Theodore Tamba's account in 1968:

> The substance of his [testimony] was that one day during the course of the war he was walking down a street in Tokyo near Radio Tokyo where he met a friend. He asked the friend if he could arrange for him to listen to a "propaganda broadcast" and was told that he could do so. His friend had led him into Radio Tokyo to a room where he said Mrs. d'Aquino made broadcasts of musical recordings. He said his friend opened the door and showed him into the monitor's room. That while there he saw Mrs. d'Aquino state in substance, "Soldiers and Sailors, your wives and sweethearts are enjoying themselves at home with war workers who are making big wages while you are fighting in the jungles, etc." [14]

Yagi did not tell the name of his "friend" to the grand jury because he said that friend was afraid of getting involved in the case.

Frederick Tillman was the first person to be suspicious of Yagi's vague testimony. After the grand jury, Yagi was questioned several times further on the matter, and after talking it over with Brundidge he finally revealed the name of his "friend" to be Kodaira. DeWolfe asked James

Wood, the CIC man who had accompanied the Japanese witnesses to
the grand jury, to talk to Kodaira in order to persuade him to stand as a
witness at the coming trial. When Wood visited Kodaira after returning
to Tokyo, Kodaira strongly denied that he had accompanied Yagi to listen to Iva's broadcast. Yagi's testimony was a lie, he said. Wood called
Yagi down to his office for questioning. Yagi at first stuck to his original
story and said that Kodaira was lying. But finally, on November 5, he
admitted his whole testimony had been a put-up job. The CIC agent reported:

> At approximately 1515 hours, questioning of Yagi continued. Yagi ap-
> peared more nervous than previously mentioned. When advised that it
> was the intent of the writer to confront Yagi with Kodaira in an effort to
> resolve the conflicting statements, Yagi begged the writer not to do so,
> stating, "I will tell you the truth this time." Yagi then advised, "My
> friend, Harry T. Brundidge, came to Japan in March or April 1948. He
> asked me to go to the United States of America as a witness against To-
> guri. I told him I never had seen Toguri broadcasting. He stated, 'If you
> tell the story to Mr. Hogan then you will make a trip to the United States
> and we will have a nice time together.' "

Yagi agreed to sign a sworn statement of what he had said. "I want to
tell the truth now even though it gets me in lots of trouble," he said.[15]

Aware of the seriousness of the matter, on January 5, 1949, Assistant
Attorney General Campbell confronted Brundidge at the Justice De-
partment. "Brundidge stated that he could give no suggestions as to why
Yagi had now changed his story and could give no suggestions to the De-
partment which may be helpful in clarifying the situation except that
[Yagi] may have been stricken with fear since his return to Japan."[16]
Brundidge also denied that he had persuaded Yagi to testify before the
grand jury.

Campbell sent orders to Frederick Tillman, who had left for Japan on
December 28, to investigate the matter. After questioning both Yagi and
Kodaira at some length, Tillman reported back that both men stood by
their statements that Brundidge had urged them to give false testimony.
Tillman also added that Theodore Tamba, who was in Tokyo at the
time gathering statements from deposition witnesses, had gotten wind of

their revelations, and that the defense team could be expected to cross-examine Brundidge on the matter if he took the stand as a government witness.

Harry Brundidge had caused the Justice Department headaches before, but this was too much. The department even considered the possibility of bringing charges against Brundidge himself, although that was a delicate matter. "In considering the possibility of instituting prosecution against Brundidge for subornation of perjury," wrote Assistant Attorney General Campbell to Tom Clark, "we believe that such action taken prior to the completion of litigation involving Iva Toguri d'Aquino *would completely destroy any chance of a conviction in her case.* [Italics added.] We further believe that it would be unwise to initiate such prosecution of Brundidge at any time because *the chance of convicting a white man upon the testimony of two Japanese, particularly in California, is very slight.* [Italics added.]"[17] So Harry Brundidge had escaped by the skin of his teeth, or the color of his skin, and the Justice Department officials decided to express ignorance if the defense touched on the perjury matter at the trial.

As Theodore Tamba later pointed out, it was not only shocking that Iva had been indicted in part as a result of Yagi's false testimony, but that the rulings of Judge Roche prevented public revelation of the nefarious activities of Harry Brundidge. The portions of Kodaira's deposition that touched on Yagi's perjury met with steady objections from Tom DeWolfe when the defense presented them in court. Since Judge Roche sustained them, the jury was unable to hear anything about this side of the prosecution case. Of Kodaira's 131 replies to questions, 103 were stricken from the record.

The big question is whether Brundidge tried to suborn other witnesses. Were there others who decided to accept Brundidge's suggestions about testifying against Iva to get a free trip to the States? After all, the pay was good, and the work, if dirty, was easy.

Two Critical Witnesses

Of all the witnesses from Japan, Kenkichi Oki and George Hideo Mitsushio, the two Overseas Bureau staff members in charge of "Zero

Hour," were indispensable for the prosecution. In order to obtain a conviction in a treason case, it was necessary that there be two witnesses to
each overt act. Oki and Mitsushio were brought to provide such testimony, and without it the government's case would collapse. Strangely,
DeWolfe did his best to get through the testimony with these most important witnesses as quickly as possible. They responded to his questions
like schoolboys performing for visiting relatives, parroting the same
words and phrases, as though they had been carefully rehearsed. Iva,
who usually sat with her eyes cast downward, was bolt upright as she
listened to their testimony, looking directly at both of them, as DeWolfe
led them through each overt act.

With respect to Overt Act I, Oki testified that he had been present at
the first meeting of the Front Line Section, around March 1, 1944, when
all the staff of "Zero Hour" had met together. At the meeting he said,
"Mr. Reyes, first of all, suggested he take over the hot jazz music and
juke box music, and then he also suggested that Miss Toguri take over
the sweet and soft music. Miss Toguri agreed to that and she said that
she would prepare her part of the program with sweet music."[18] Oki also
testified that Mitsushio was definitely present at this meeting. When
Mitsushio took the stand he gave essentially the same answers as Oki,
and testified that Oki had been present at the alleged meeting. The two
men corroborated each other very neatly.

But Norman Reyes later testified that such a meeting had taken place
at the earliest between August and December 1944, and that while Cousens and the other POWs were still working on the program, the Front
Line Section had not yet been formed. Iva testified that she first heard
the name of the Front Line Section at the end of December 1944, but
that she had no recollection of the meeting Oki and Mitsushio mentioned. Both Oki and Mitsushio agreed that Cousens and the other
POWs had left "Zero Hour" in December 1943, a date that was off by
six months. Even assuming that the alleged meeting occurred, it must
have taken place half a year later than they testified.

With respect to Overt Act II, Oki testified:

> Well, sometime between March and June of 1944 the Japanese Gen-
> eral Staff invited the members of the Front Line Section to see the movie

Gone With the Wind. After we had seen the movie, it gave myself, Mr. Mitsushio, and others an idea for our "Zero Hour" program, and about a week or ten days later, after seeing the movie, we had a program made with the recordings of the *Gone With the Wind* program. On the day we were to broadcast I brought in the prepared script and I gave it to Miss Toguri and asked her to read it over before the broadcast. After she read the script, she told me she was rather upset about it. She said she thought the program was rather silly and corny. I told her there was not much time to change the program now. She said she wanted to go back to her regular "Orphan Ann" program and the script was not up to the regular standard of the "Zero Hour" program.[19]

Mitsushio said that he had been present during the conversation and had heard all of it. Once again the two witnesses were in complete agreement.

Their testimony referred to an occasion when the "Zero Hour" had broadcast an abbreviated version of *Gone With the Wind,* using recordings made from the movie sound track. The Japanese army had seized the film from the defeated Allied forces when they captured Manila. The "Zero Hour" version used the voices of Clark Gable and Vivien Leigh, but the story was narrated by an announcer. The script that Iva was supposed to have criticized was written by Shinichi Oshidari.

The broadcast of *Gone With the Wind* could not have occurred in the spring of 1944: Oshidari had not yet joined the staff of "Zero Hour." Reyes remembered the broadcast as having taken place at the end of November 1944 when he had gotten married. According to the testimony of George Henshaw, a Bunka Camp prisoner who had kept a secret diary, a movie projection room was not set up at Bunka Camp until September 17, 1944. General Arisue and Major Tsuneishi had come from General Staff headquarters to see the film, and it was only around November that the staff of "Zero Hour" had seen it. Once again the dates put forward in the testimony of Oki and Mitsushio were about six months off.

With respect to Overt Act III, Oki testified that "after 6:00 P.M. Miss Toguri did her part on the 'Zero Hour' program. . . . She spoke into the microphone."[20] Oki testified that the sound track portions of *Gone With the Wind* used on the broadcast were from scenes "about the terroristic

phases of warfare." Mitsushio testified that they were "scenes of dis-
abled soldiers lying in the sun around the railway stations, scenes in the
hospitals where the wounded men were groaning. . . ."[21]

Norman Reyes later denied this testimony completely. "There was no
hospital scene," he said. "The sound track of the hospital scene from
Gone With the Wind as taken on the recordings was of too poor quality
to be used at all for our broadcast and it was rejected."[22] Iva testified that
the broadcast had never been made at all: ". . . In fact, about 6:30 they
had to throw the whole thing up, and Norman Reyes and I played records from 6:30 to 7:00 o'clock. . . . The sound tracks were bad, the script
was bad. It was confusion, commotion. No one knew how to write the
script, so they just tossed it all away."[23]

With respect to Overt Act IV, both Oki and Mitsushio testified as to
the content of a broadcast Iva had made sometime in November 1944.
They remembered the date because on that day the "Zero Hour" staff
had held a party for Mieko Furuya, who was to resign from her job at
Radio Tokyo on December 1, 1944, in order to prepare for her marriage
to Kenkichi Oki. The party lasted about an hour after the "Zero Hour"
broadcast, finished at seven o'clock, they said, and strangely, Iva, who
usually went straight home after her part of the program had finished,
stayed on to attend the party. According to Oki's testimony, he remembered that she said, "This is your favorite enemy, Orphan Ann," that
she referred to her listeners as "my boneheads of the South Pacific," and
that "she called the soldiers dopes."[24]

Iva contradicted this testimony by saying that, to the best of her memory, there had been no party for Mieko Furuya before she got married.
In fact, Iva did not know about the marriage and was quite surprised
when she heard about it afterward. Even more peculiar is Oki's and
Mitsushio's assertion that Mieko Furuya left the employ of Radio Tokyo on December 1, 1944. The personnel records preserved at NHK
show that she left the station on May 23, 1945. It seems strange that a
farewell party should have been held for her six months earlier in November.

With respect to Overt Act V, Mitsushio testified: "I said to Toguri I
had a release from the Imperial General Headquarters giving out results
of American ship losses on one of the Leyte Gulf battles, and I asked that

she allude to this announcement, make reference or allude to the losses of American ships in her part of the program. She said she would do so."[25] Oki testified that she had said on her broadcast, "Now you fellows have lost all your ships. Now you really are orphans of the Pacific. How do you think you will ever get home"—or words to that effect.[26] Both Oki and Mitsushio also testified that they had seen her typing these words in her script.

Norman Reyes testified that around June 1944 something might have been broadcast about the loss of American ships, but he was certain it had nothing to do with the battle of Leyte Gulf. However, he did not say that he had used it in Iva's script. Iva denied that she had ever written a script about the loss of American ships or that Mitsushio had told her to do so. "Mr. Mitsushio has never asked me to put anything in the broadcast," she said. "He had nothing to say to me about anything like that."[27]

But Iva did remember that in June or July 1944, after Cousens had left the station, she had come to the office and heard Reyes and Oki talking with someone from the General Staff about a sea battle off Formosa.

> Mr. Oki stated that there had been a battle off of Formosa, and Norman said, "What kind of a battle?" I believe they said it was a naval battle. I was on the other side of the room typing up the script. It was almost time to go on the air. Mr. Oki said, "Why don't we say something like this?" . . . and then he said something about mentioning the phrase, "Orphans of the Pacific." Something about, "All your ships are gone, how are you going to get home?" [Oki said] "Let's incorporate that into part of the script today."
>
> He was talking to Norman. He wasn't talking to me.[28]

The mention of the loss of ships in Clark Lee's interview notes referred to this occasion, and so probably did Reyes's testimony on the same point. It seems reasonable to conclude that the words broadcast were not in Iva's script but were spoken in some other part of the "Zero Hour" program, most likely as part of the news or news commentary.

"Orphans of the Pacific" and "your ships are gone" were phrases most frequently heard on the wartime broadcasts from Radio Tokyo, especially on the news and news commentary programs. From early in the war the expression "orphans of the Pacific" was used to refer to the Australian army, isolated and cut off from the other Allies. Monitors in Australia had heard part of a news broadcast in September 1942 that went: "Australia is really the orphan of the Pacific." So it would not have been unusual for similar phrases to have been used on the news portions of the "Zero Hour."

With respect to Overt Act VI, both Oki and Mitsushio testified that they had heard Iva speak into the microphone the words about the loss of ships, and both said that they had seen each other present on that occasion. Iva strongly and consistently denied she made such a broadcast. (Theodore Tamba, who interviewed Oki in Tokyo, testified later that Oki told him the broadcast about the ships sunk in the battle of Leyte had been made by one of the regular Overseas Bureau announcers.)

With respect to Overt Act VII, Oki testified that he remembered that on May 23, 1945, Kenichi Ishii, who had been conscripted into the army, had come to visit the station. "I remember that date very well," Oki said, "because that evening there was a great bombing raid on Tokyo by Allied enemy planes, and my house was just a few blocks away from where other houses were burning, and I stood on the roof of my house and watched the air raid for several hours." [29] The selection of the date is rather interesting in view of the fact that when Brundidge had tried to suborn Kodaira and Yagi he suggested they say they heard Iva broadcast "a little after the March bombing." It is also interesting that at the time Brundidge had asked Kodaira whether he knew Oki. Most interesting of all, May 23, 1945, was the day Mieko Furuya left NHK.

In any event, Oki testified that on the day in question he had seen Iva, after talking with Kenichi Ishii for a while, finish typing her script, walk downstairs to the studio, and broadcast while playing records. Mitsushio gave no testimony about Overt Act VII, but Kenichi Ishii corroborated Oki's testimony with his own. Strangely neither explained what the content of Iva's broadcast had been on that day.

With respect to Overt Act VIII, Mitsushio testified that he had made the following broadcast with Iva:

> She said, "How do you like my new hat?" I spoke to same microphone, "What hat?" She said, "You can't see it from there, it's on this side of my head." [30]

Oki testified that he had been with them in the studio at the time and that he had heard this conversation broadcast.

Iva testified that she had no recollection of broadcasting such a conversation, but DeWolfe produced as evidence a transcript of a recording made by Hawaiian monitors of a "Zero Hour" broadcast on June 20, 1945. It contained the following dialogue:

> Man: Thank you, Ann. Will be expecting you tomorrow night. Why, what is the hurry?
>
> Ann: Sorry, boss. I am in a hurry. I have got a heavy date waiting for me outside the studio.
>
> Man: Stepping out, are you? I should think you would wear a hat, at least, when you go out.
>
> Ann: I do have. It is on this side, see? Good night, fellows.

The government was unable to produce the recording of this conversation, which would have established whether the voice of "Ann" who broadcast it was the same voice as Iva's. The point was an important one, for Iva had not been the only woman announcer on "Zero Hour," and frequently others had broadcast in her place during her absences. The government insisted that Iva was the only one who broadcast using the name "Orphan Ann." But Iva said that she had the impression, as the result of seeing a "Zero Hour" script for the day during which she was absent from work, that other women announcers used the name, too.

It did not take long for those at the trial to realize that the content of the broadcasts specified in the "overt acts" was fairly trivial. The San Francisco *Chronicle* commented that much of the propaganda brought to light in Oki's and Mitsushio's testimony was "hokum" and "corn." It was also clear that aside from the testimony of Oki and Mitsushio, the government had no evidence to show that Iva had committed any of these acts. DeWolfe had his two key witnesses state ad nauseam that all NHK broadcast scripts and recordings had been burned at the end of the war. It is also clear from an examination of the statements Oki and Mitsushio made to the FBI before the grand jury proceeding that the overt acts specified in the indictment were drawn up on the basis of what the two men had told the agents questioning them.

It must be said, however, that those watching the trial did not have much sympathy or respect for the two key government witnesses.

The Sacramento-born Kenkichi Oki, the son of a Japanese American newspaper publisher and a former football end at New York University, had gone to Japan in 1939. After registering as a Japanese citizen, he went to work for the Overseas Bureau in 1940.

The forty-four-year-old, pudgy, bespectacled George Mitsushio had been born in San Francisco. His father had died when he was five and he moved with his remarried mother to the Fresno area. He had grown up bearing his stepfather's name—Nakamoto. After spending a year at Berkeley and another at Columbia University, he went to work for a Los Angeles Japanese American paper, the *Rafu Shimpo*. In 1940 he was one of the few *nisei* recruited by NHK to strengthen the Overseas Bureau staff. In April 1942, four months after the war broke out, Mitsushio had registered himself as a Japanese citizen.

Both Oki and Mitsushio, though born and reared in the United States, had participated voluntarily in the Radio Tokyo propaganda broadcasts. The only thing that stood between them and treason charges was the piece of paper on which they had registered as Japanese citizens. Although Iva, by virtue of her marriage, had been recognized by the Portuguese government as a Portuguese citizen, the United States government insisted that she was still an American because she had not formally renounced her citizenship. Hence the government was able to indict her for treason. Curiously, the same American government expressed no doubt that Oki and Mitsushio were Japanese citizens, even though neither had formally renounced his citizenship either. It is not difficult to see the illogic of the government's position.

A sympathetic observer might note that both Oki and Mitsushio in a sense were victims of prejudice against Japanese Americans. Although both had grown up as 100 percent Americans and graduated from American colleges, neither had been able to find a place in American society because employers were reluctant to put them in jobs for which they were qualified. There is no reason to believe that either was very glad about leaving his native land behind to go to Japan on the eve of war. But even if some in the courtroom understood this point, none showed any sympathy toward Oki and Mitsushio. To most observers they were simply turncoats who had sold out their country in order to make a living. After Oki and Mitsushio appeared on the witness stand, the reporters covering the trial began to express more and more sympathy for Iva. As one observed, there was irony in the fact that neither Oki nor Mitsushio was at all hesitant about helping pin the badge of treason on Iva, even though both had abandoned their own citizenship. Iva, a *nisei* like themselves, had been merely their subordinate. It was unpleasant for those in the court to watch this injustice unfold before their eyes. The prosecution was well aware of the situation, but it had to have the testimony of the two men as witnesses to the overt acts. Indeed, the government had been able to get this testimony from them precisely because Oki and Mitsushio knew their own position was so vulnerable.

The patriotic Judge Roche, it is said, even asked Hennessey where in the world he got witnesses like those two. After cross-examination began, Roche was generous in giving Collins time for questioning. He sustained few of DeWolfe's objections. It was almost as if he wanted to see Oki and Mitsushio punished a bit.

In his testimony Oki had recalled with great detail broadcasts that took place five or six years before, and he had been especially precise in his testimony about Overt Acts V and VI concerning Iva's alleged broadcast about the loss of American ships. So Collins began the cross-examination by drilling away at Oki's other recollections of the day. What had he had for breakfast? What had he had for dinner? What had he been wearing? What were the musical records used on the broadcast that day? What news was broadcast that day? Had it been cloudy? Had it been clear? Had it been raining? Had it been snowing? Oki, expressionless as usual but glistening with perspiration, had trouble answering any of these questions very clearly. Yet whenever Collins turned the questioning back to acts alleged in the indictment, Oki became very specific and positive in his answers. He could remember, he said, there had been a news announcement that day about the sinking of American war vessels at Leyte Gulf, that Iva had typed the item into her script, and that she had broadcast the phrase "Orphans of the Pacific, you are really orphans now, etc." But when it came to breakfast, all he could say was, "I probably had rice for breakfast, we usually did."

"So your recollection of what transpired that day," asked Collins sarcastically, "is reduced to the fact that you had rice for breakfast and that you read this one release from the Dai Hon Yei [Imperial General Headquarters] that day?"[31]

"That is correct," replied Oki lamely.

When Collins cross-examined Mitsushio, he got even tougher. It was clear that he wanted to show the jury that it was Mitsushio and Oki, both born and reared in the States, who should be sitting in the defendant's seat instead of Iva. A dramatic moment came when Collins asked Mitsushio if he had ever taken a pledge of allegiance to the flag.

"Yes," said Mitsushio, "in grammar school."

"Now, Mr. Nakamoto," asked Collins, "would you please recite that pledge you made in grammar school." (Throughout the trial Collins made a special point of calling Mitsushio by his stepfather's surname, which he had used when he was growing up in America.) DeWolfe sprang up as usual to voice an objection, but Roche overruled him.

His face red and perspiring, Mitsushio began to recite in a low voice, "I pledge allegiance to the flag of the United States of America, and to the republic for which it stands, one nation indivisible . . ." Then his memory, or his nerve, failed him. As the audience sat transfixed, Judge Roche in a small, dry voice finished for him—"with liberty and justice for all."

At the end of the cross-examination, Collins extracted from Mitsushio the admission that immediately after arriving in San Francisco he had been handed a copy of the indictment by the government prosecutors, and that he had met to talk with DeWolfe, the other prosecutors, and FBI man Frederick Tillman almost every day. "On the face of his letter-perfect, unchanging word structure," commented Stanton Delaplane, the *Chronicle* reporter, "it was a damaging admission."[32]

The other witnesses from Japan—Kenichi Ishii, Tsutomu Nii, Mary Higuchi, Hisashi Moriyama, Fred Harris Sugiyama, and Shinjirō Igarashi—who had been brought, like Oki and Mitsushio, to testify that they had seen Iva in the NHK studios broadcasting as "Orphan Ann," did not much help the government's case. Most of them were rather vague and haphazard in their answers on the witness stand. Among them, Igarashi, who testified about Iva's alleged broadcast "concerning the loss of ships," was egregiously inept. It became clear under Collins's cross-examination that his English was not good enough to understand the fast, slangy patter of the "Zero Hour." He finally had to admit that he could get the meaning in substance "but not in particular words."[33] He also testified that his only direct contact with Iva had been to say "Hello" to her once, but Iva herself said she did not know him at all. "I was surprised at these witnesses I'd never seen before, who came out and said they knew me," she later commented.

One government witness from Japan, David Seizo Hyuga, might have had an impact on the outcome of the trial. During the noon recess one day he had come up to speak with Iva's lawyers. "He told us," Theodore Tamba later reported, "that what Oki and Mitsushio had recited from the witness stand was pure nonsense, that the events narrated had never happened, and that their testimony was downright perjury. . . . He asked that certain questions be asked of him on cross-examination and that he was sure the ill-founded case against Tokyo Rose would collapse." But when the prosecutors found out that he had been seen talking to the defense attorneys, he was suddenly sent back to Japan.

"Honey Babies, I Hope I Dream of You Tonight"

The government had assembled a number of former GIs who claimed to have heard "Orphan Ann" broadcasts all over the Pacific. When the FBI had appealed for witnesses in December 1947, there had been replies from several hundred ex-GIs, and those who appeared as witnesses in San Francisco had been selected from among them.

The testimony of the ex-GIs was generally of three sorts. First, there were those who said that "Orphan Ann" reported troop movements on her broadcasts ("This is dedicated to the Jolly Rogers who are moving to Dobodura on December 21. She promised us a reception committee").[34] Second, there were those who reported hearing "Orphan Ann" make remarks about the unfaithfulness of wives and sweethearts at home ("Well, fellows, I have to be going now. I am going to get my love tonight. How about you?").[35] Third were those who testified that "Orphan Ann" made broadcasts in which she tried to make the GIs homesick by talking about ice cream and beefsteaks ("How would you like to go to the corner drugstore tonight and get an ice cream soda?").[36]

Collins did not have much difficulty in showing during cross-examination that the "Orphan Ann" programs the former GIs allegedly heard were in fact the "Tokyo Rose" broadcasts of rumor. In most cases, the times at which the ex-GI witnesses claimed they had heard "Orphan Ann" simply did not match the times at which the broadcasts were made.

The unreliability of their testimony is supported by a perusal of FBI reports of their interrogations before the trial. For example, one former army lieutenant testified that in August or September 1944 he had heard "Orphan Ann" broadcast a statement that went in substance: "The island of Saipan is mined with high explosive. You are given forty-eight hours to clear the island or you will be blown sky high."[37] The FBI report summarizing his interview in December 1947 states, "[He] is unable to recall whether the statement was made by the subject or by one of the commentators or newscasters who preceded her or followed her on the 'Zero Hour.' " The FBI report also noted, "Before going overseas, he had heard her referred to as 'Tokyo Rose,' but when he got to Saipan, he believed that she used the name of 'Little Orphan Annie,' but he is not too positive of this and admitted *that he possibly got the idea that this was her name from reading press releases which appeared in local newspapers during the past week.* [Italics added.]"[38] In other words, judging from his testimony at the trial, the witness's memory had gotten fresher, not dimmer, in the year and a half after he gave his statement to the FBI.

If some of the GI witnesses were clearly unreliable, others gave courtroom performances quite damaging to the defense. One of the latter was a former chief boatswain's mate who had been on a converted PT boat patrolling between the Gilbert Islands and Saipan. Around January 3, 1944, he claimed to have heard Orphan Ann broadcast the following statement: "Wake up, you boneheads. Go and see your commanding officer and demand to be sent home. Don't stay in that mosquito-infested jungle and let someone else run off with your girl friends."[39] The witness said he remembered that he heard "Zero Hour" between six and seven o'clock in the evening just after dinner was over and the men were resting. "Zero Hour" had, in fact, been broadcast between those hours, but that was Tokyo time. There was a three-hour time difference between Tokyo and the Gilbert Islands, where the program would have been heard from three to four o'clock in the afternoon, not between six and seven after dinner. If the witness had heard the broadcasts he alleged he heard, then it could not have been "Zero Hour." Apparently DeWolfe had not remembered the problem of differences between time zones.

The slip-up was enough to question his testimony, but in fact this witness made a very strong impression on both the judge and the jury. When Collins asked him in cross-examination how he was able to remember the date of the broadcast he heard so well, he pulled a piece of thin green paper from his pocket. It was a letter that he had written to his wife between January 2 and January 6, 1944. He started reading it. "We have a radio now and we get Tokyo best," went the letter. "They have an American-Japanese girl who has turned down the United States for Japan. They call her Tokyo Rose and does she razz us fellows out here in the Pacific, telling how well Japan is getting along and to hear her start out you would think she was broadcasting from the United States and sorry we were losing so many men and ships. It sure makes the fellows sore." The letter also carefully established the date. "Put down January 2 on the calendar and reminded me to tell you things sure happen fast out here. . . . I'm a little older today and maybe a little grayer. Babies, it is all bad."[40]

Around December 29, 1943, three or four days before he wrote the letter, the witness said that Tokyo Rose had made a broadcast about a Commander Perry, two or three hours after he had landed on Abamama, one of the Gilbert islands. "She said congratulations on your safe landing and called him by his own name," testified the witness. "And she said, 'But you'll be sorry if you don't leave soon now.' That's the reason I blotted out January 2. We were sorry. . . . On the night of January 2 we were taking on stores in the lagoon at Abamama. . . . The Japs come in, some high, and some at low altitudes. They hit us from both sides. We tried to get to the jungle. They killed two of my men and I don't know how many marines."[41]

One of the reporters covering the trial, Paine Knickerbocker, had heard a somewhat different story from this witness. Wayne Collins had got wind of it, and he asked if there really had been an attack such as he described. "Isn't it a fact . . . that there were no casualities at that time?" he asked.

"I beg your pardon," said the witness. "I ought to know. I helped bury them." When he had made a statement to an FBI agent on March 9, 1948, however, he had said that some marines and sailors stationed on the island had been killed, but made no mention of two of his own men being killed.

For effect, the prosecution had the witness read some portions of the letter that had nothing to do with the trial. It added a touch of homely authenticity to his testimony. Members of the jury smiled when he read, "Dear, you must buy up some liquor and hold it if you can. I haven't had a drink in a long time." By the time he got to the portion that read, "Honey babies, I hope I dream of you tonight as I think of you all day,"[42] the women in the jury box were dabbing at their cheeks with handkerchiefs. "The letter had everything," commented one newspaper. "The prosecutors couldn't have dreamed up a more effective one."[43]

At the end the witness testified that he had listened to "Zero Hour" not for entertainment but for another purpose. At the end of 1943, he said, there had been a message from naval intelligence that Orphan Ann and Tokyo Rose were the same person and the "Orphan Ann" broadcasts should be listened to with great care. "We were alerted to listen to her by Naval Intelligence because she told us what was going to happen that day and it did. I lost some men and that's why I remember it very well."[44] But when he had been interviewed by the FBI he had not mentioned this extremely important fact at all. Is it possible that he suddenly remembered it in court? Probably not, for in his statement he had said quite clearly, "The main reason I and my fellow shipmates listened to the program was to hear the recordings of popular music which music was not available to us at the time from any other source."[45]

Despite the unreliability of his testimony, which sounded more like a war story told in a bar than testimony under oath, this witness made a deep emotional impact on the jury—clearly an advantage for the prosecutors.

Katherine Pinkham, who covered the trial for Associated Press, says that some of the GI witnesses discredited their own testimony. One of them, when asked to be specific about what he had heard "Tokyo Rose" say on the air, volunteered, "Well, she comes on the air and says, 'This is Tokyo Rose,' and then she goes on to say. . . ." The reporters at the press table exchanged quick glances of disbelief. Afterward, outside the courtroom, some of the reporters twitted the federal agents about the quality of some of the witnesses they had collected. "You ought to have seen some of the ones we turned away," replied one of them.[46]

The recollections some of the ex-GIs had of the "Orphan Ann" broadcasts that they had heard five or six years before at the front lines or on shipboard in the Pacific certainly lacked a good deal of credibility. And the investigation file of the FBI reveals that many of them made no distinction between the "Tokyo Rose" rumors and the "Orphan Ann" broadcasts. A number of the prosecution witnesses from Japan—Hisashi Moriyama, Satoshi Nakamura, and others who had been on the "Zero Hour" staff—had no recollection of the thirty-three statements the ex-GI witnesses alleged they had heard on the "Orphan Ann" broadcasts. Later on, Cousens, Ince, and Reyes, who had written Iva's scripts for her, all vehemently denied that they knew anything of these statements. In other words, in contrast to the rather positive memories that some of the GI witnesses displayed, none of those who had been directly connected with "Zero Hour" and had seen and heard Iva in the studio remembered any of these alleged broadcasts having taken place. That included the witnesses who testified for the government, too.

Six Recordings

When the court was finally presented with material evidence of Iva's broadcasts, it was something of an anticlimax after the lurid testimony of some of the ex-GIs. There was nothing frightening or sinister about them at all. If anything, they were exactly the opposite in tone.

During the war American monitors at Hawaii and at Portland, Oregon, had made daily recordings of all the "Zero Hour" broadcasts and had preserved all of them. While Iva was in Sugamo she heard from a CIC investigator that about 340 recordings of the broadcasts remained. But in court the prosecution produced as evidence about forty of Iva's broadcast scripts (among them some that Iva herself had handed over) and only six recordings of "Zero Hour" broadcasts. None of the six had anything at all to do with the alleged broadcasts cited in the indictment. DeWolfe said the government was using the records merely to identify the defendant's voice. But while the GI witnesses, including those for the prosecution, admitted that the voice on the record seemed to be the one they had heard, there was no proof that the voice they heard was Iva's.

Most of the GIs who testified that the voice of Orphan Ann that they had heard in the Pacific was the voice on the recordings had been more vague when the FBI agents played the recordings for them six months or a year before. "It was like the voice on record number one, but different from the voice on record number two" or words to that effect was how most of them responded. In fact, it seems likely that there were at least two different "Orphan Ann" voices on the six recordings presented in court.

On July 30, the twentieth day of the trial, all those in court, except the spectators, were finally able to hear for themselves the recordings of the Orphan Ann broadcasts that had been made five years before. The voice of the "vicious propagandist," finally came through the earphones—and what a disappointment.

> Hello you fighting orphans in the Pacific. How's tricks? This is after her weekend Annie back on the air strictly under union hours. Reception O.K.? Well, it better be because this is all request night and I've got a pretty nice program for my favorite little family—the wandering boneheads of the Pacific Islands. The first request is made by none other than the Boss and guess what. He wants Bonnie Baker and "My Resistance Is Low." My what taste you have sir, she said [broadcast of August 14, 1944].

All the six records were about the same—a little patter and sassy quips by "Orphan Ann" interspersed among records of light or semiclassical music. The music on most of the records was soft and scratchy and rather hard to hear, but several of the jury members sat tapping the beat with their feet or fingers as they listened. They seemed to be enjoying it.

The records were not much different from the excerpts from radio scripts that had been introduced as evidence earlier. A few samples:

> This is your little playmate, Orphan Ann. And by the way, wasn't that a lousy program we had last night. It was almost bad enough to be BBC or its little sister ABC.

We're going to listen now to a superb presentation of melodies of Stephen Foster by the well-known wandering minstrels, the orphans of the South Pacific, assisted by Nat Shilkret and the Victor Salon group.

For years collectors have been touring the jungles and atolls of the South Pacific to collect those superb specimens of the celebrated featherless songster, the singing boneheads.

Now let's have more close harmony work from the New Guinea nightingales and other chapters of the Pacific Orphan Choir. It's dangerous enemy propaganda, so beware.

Greetings, everybody. How are my victims this evening? All ready for a vicious assault on your morale.

[Following the news section announced by Ince]: Thank you, thank you, thank you. Now let's have some real listening music. You can have your swing when I turn you over to "Zero Hour." [By this she meant Reyes's portion of the broadcast, the "original Zero Hour."] Right now my little orphans, do what mama tells you. Listen to this—Fritz Kreisler playing "Indian Love Call." [Recording of "Indian Love Call".] Boy, oh boy. It stirs memories, doesn't it? Or haven't you boneheads any memories either? You have? Well, here's music you need then, "In a Persian Market" played for you by the Boston Pops. Orphan to orphan—over.

And much, much more of the same.

The incredible thing is that these were the portions of the "Orphan Ann" broadcasts that the government had culled and carefully selected to establish the "malicious" and "treasonous" character of the broadcasts. Not one of the recordings or broadcast scripts presented as government evidence made any mention of unfaithful wives and sweethearts, sunken ships, or movements of Allied forces in the Pacific. Had someone perhaps carelessly lost the daily monitor recordings of the "Zero Hour" broadcasts, recordings that would have supported the testimony of Oki, Mitsushio, and others as to the overt acts? Or had Iva perhaps never made any such broadcasts? DeWolfe supplied the probable answer in his memo of May 25, 1948: "The scripts of her programs seem totally innocuous and might be said to have little, if any, entertainment value."

Compared to the recordings that were played at the Gillars trial, the "Orphan Ann" broadcasts seemed tame indeed and totally apolitical. The innocent bantering and humorous character of the broadcasts supported the testimony of Colonel Tsuneishi, the wartime army propaganda boss, that "it was unfortunate but the opportunity did not present itself to present the real, true propaganda program I wished to."[47] Stanton Delaplane observed, "On the face of it, none of the material [in the broadcasts] seemed particularly vicious. . . . [One] program could have been any disc jockey's with a touch of Japanese American accent."[48]

On August 12, after a four-day recess to allow Iva to recover from a recurrence of dysentery, the prosecution rested its case after forty-six of the seventy-one witnesses it had subpoenaed had been put on the stand and 500,000 words of testimony had been taken.* DeWolfe had decided that, on the basis of the testimony and material exhibits so far presented, the government had adequately demonstrated that Iva had betrayed the United States with "plan and intent."[49] He was satisfied too that he had produced the two necessary witnesses to each of the eight separate alleged acts of treason. Now it was the defense's turn.

---

*The government later put four more witnesses on the stand.

CHAPTER 6

The Trial of Tokyo Rose: The Defense

Major Cousens Explains

On August 13, in a forty-minute opening statement for the defense, Theodore Tamba pointed out that in order to establish treason it must be shown that the defendant not only had the will to commit the act but that by the commission of that act he intended to betray his country. The defense, he said, was going to show Iva lacked any treasonous intent and that she had broadcast under threat and duress.

The first defense witness was Charles H. Cousens, a man who could readily testify to the atmosphere of intimidation and coercion that surrounded those involved in the broadcasts. Tall and distinguished-looking, Cousens strode up to the witness stand with erect military bearing, exuding confidence as he sat down to face Collins's direct examination. "He was articulate and assured," recalled reporter Katherine Pinkham.

"It was easy to see how Iva would have been impressed and influenced by this urbane figure."[1]

In a clear, clipped English accent, with his famous announcer's voice, Cousens began telling what had happened when the Japanese decided to send him to Burma for hard labor for refusing to broadcast.

He was waiting on the dock at Singapore to be loaded with 3,000 other POWs on a ship bound for Sumatra and Burma. "We had been warned by other working parties," he recalled, "that a new battalion of Japanese had arrived that was much more brutal than their front-line troops. They were known as *kempei* or police battalion."

"And what did you see on the docks?" asked Collins.

Cousen's voice began to choke. "I saw the *kempei* murder two men. . . . It was night—electric lights overhead—and I was attracted to the scene by screams. I saw these naked Japanese beating a coolie near the guardroom. They wore only a kind of G-string. The word went around that he was starving and had tried to snatch a can of food. . . . Three Japanese threw him to the ground and put his head under a tap so that as he drew breath and screamed he drew water into his lungs. . . ."[2]

Collins asked Cousens what else he had seen.

"The *kempeitai* killed one of the Allied prisoners," said Cousens. "He was an Australian and they beat him to death." Suddenly his voice broke, and tears streamed down his face. He put his head in his hands and sank into the chair. Cruel memories that he had tried to put aside seemed to come flooding back to him. The audience in the courtroom was surprised at the sudden change in Cousen's demeanor. Some women jurors had wept over an earlier witness's maudlin letter to his wife; no one wept now except Iva. She had not once shown emotion since the trial began, but now she was pushing back the tears with a white handkerchief.

Cousens recovered his composure and continued telling how two Japanese had held the Australian soldier, accused of stealing a can of onions, while a third beat him with a solid wood Japanese fencing sword until the soldier could no longer get up.

The prosecution attorneys kept interrupting Cousens's testimony with objections that his experiences had nothing to do with the defendant and were therefore irrelevant. Collins and Olshausen replied that Cousens's experiences as a POW were directly related to duress put on the defendant, and that they contributed to the psychological intimidation she felt. "We told her men were being starved, beaten, and tortured," said Cousens, "that the Japanese had discarded every semblance of civilized behavior, if you can apply that word to war, sir—that you did what you were told to do or you died."

During his three days on the witness stand Cousens supported a number of other defense arguments: that Iva had participated in the "Zero Hour" broadcasts at his request and as a "soldier" under his command; that she had no choice but to obey orders from the Imperial army; that Iva's voice was a comical one, precisely suited to his purpose of keeping "Zero Hour" a purely entertainment program; that he had written all her scripts; that after he left the station she had merely copied and recopied his scripts over and over again; and finally he made the point that there were many double meanings hidden in the scripts.

Cousens also testified that he told Iva that the nuance of words could change greatly depending on how they were spoken. Prompted by Collins, he demonstrated to the court how he had coached Iva on the reading of a particular script, explaining as he went along how an announcer could make a "wipe" of what had been broadcast before by the way he broke into the broadcast. "If you have a commercial program," he explained, "and the commercial has just been read, if the next unit in the program jumps in fast you get entirely a wrong effect from what the sponsor wants, because the listener's attention is jerked away from what has just gone before and you get in effect a 'wipe.' . . . I explained to her many times to pick this up as soon as the Home Front news [portion of "Zero Hour"] was over, not just 'Thank you' and into the program, but 'Thank you, thank you, thank you, thank you,' and it was written in here [referring to the script] a multiplicity of times, to jump in and take that fast." In other words, by jumping in fast with a series of rapid-fire "thank yous," the news just broadcast could be "wiped" away.[3]

James Knapp rather than DeWolfe handled the cross-examination of Cousens. He wasted no time going into the attack, sarcastically and pointedly questioning Cousens's character and reliability. He did not touch at all on Iva or the broadcasts she had made, but rather asked

Cousens about his life as a POW, a matter which until now the prosecution had insisted was not relevant to the main issue in the trial. He introduced as material evidence a bill from the Dai-ichi Hotel to show that Cousens had stayed at the "No. 1 Hotel" (a direct translation of Dai-ichi Hotel) and that he had supped on a splendid menu of soup, curried rice, and coffee. He worked hard to destroy the image of Cousens as a persecuted POW and to suggest that he had had a fairly soft time of it. Knapp even brought up the story of Cousens's trip to the red-light district in Yokohama.*

"I Would Have Trusted Her With My Life"

In May 1948 Tom DeWolfe had speculated that Cousens, Reyes, and Ince would be the "three most important witnesses against the subject if an indictment should be returned against her by a grand jury."[4] In fact, both Ince and Reyes had testified at the grand jury, and the government had said that they were the most important witnesses there. But shortly before Iva's trial began, both men agreed to appear as defense witnesses. The two men must have yielded to Cousens's persuasions, but it took a certain amount of courage for them to change sides, since they put themselves in a dangerous position by testifying for the defense. Both of them, as POWs, had participated in enemy propaganda broadcasts. As DeWolfe had noted earlier, they were "just as much, or more culpable than [Iva]," and the government had even announced that Ince was under investigation for suspicion of treason.

The thirty-seven-year-old Wallace E. Ince appeared in court smartly turned out in military uniform, his tunic covered with ribbons. He was still in active service. In fact, he had been promoted to major at the end of the war, and at the time of the trial was stationed at the Presidio, the scenic garrison overlooking the Golden Gate and perhaps the most attractive military post in the United States. There were not a few who wondered how it was that Iva, a civilian, had been indicted for treason as

*The prosecution later tried the same approach with Ince. DeWolfe was well aware that before the war Ince had married a Filipino woman of Spanish extraction and had two children. Nevertheless, he asked Reyes whether he knew that Ince had married a Filipino woman while he was in Japan. His intent was apparently to give the impression that Ince, even though a POW, had married a woman of color. Ince's attorney objected to this strenuously.

the result of the wartime broadcasts, while Ince, a military man, had not only escaped indictment but had been promoted. (To be on the safe side, Ince had brought along his lawyer.)

Ince confirmed Cousens's testimony that until the end of the war Iva had done her best to smuggle food and medicine to the prisoners. He told the court that she had continued to give him things in the hallway or in the record library even after he had stopped working on "Zero Hour." He also said that Iva had frequently informed POWs about news from the Allied broadcasts, and that she was especially quick in letting him know about the recapture of the Philippines, where he had left his wife and children when war broke out.

Ince had a difficult time under cross-examination. The prosecutors tried to show that in a statement to the FBI before the trial, he had made comments clearly to the advantage of the prosecution. For example, when questioned about whether Cousens had put phrases with double meanings into the broadcast scripts, Ince had replied that to the best of his knowledge Cousens had never done so.

The prosecution also questioned Ince in some detail about his own broadcasts. Kazumaro ("Buddy") Uno had told Frederick Tillman that during the period when it was not very clear who was going to win the war, Ince had been quite cooperative with the Japanese authorities. The statement is implausible in view of the fact that of all the prisoners at Bunka Camp, the obstinate Ince seems to have been the one the guards enjoyed persecuting the most.

When Collins undertook to reexamine Ince he pursued the matter. "Were you ever beaten at Bunka?" asked Collins. "Yes," replied Ince, "by Lieutenant Hamamoto, Japanese Army." Then suddenly he put his hands to his face. For a moment no one in the court understood what had happened. When he raised his head again there were tears in his eyes. Until this moment Ince, in contrast to Cousens, whose testimony was dramatic and animated, had been a tight and terse witness, very much under control, volunteering nothing until asked, and speaking in a dry, flat voice. He had been expressionless, and he had been cool. The sudden change in him was even more stunning to the onlookers than Cousens's breakdown three days before. It was several moments before he could speak again.

"I beg the court's pardon for breaking down," he said. "It's not so easy to speak so matter-of-factly of death and brutality."[5] He was interrupted by an objection from James Knapp, who said he was not telling what had happened. The objection seemed to stiffen him again. "I am telling what happened," he replied. Collins asked him, "Was your life threatened?" "Yes," said Ince, and he began to mention some names— Lieutenant Hamamoto, Major Tsuneishi, Kazumaro Uno, Hishikari, Ikeda. . . . But before he could finish his answer Collins withdrew his question and said his reexamination was at an end.

The government had shown some consideration for Ince, who was still in active service, but it showed none for the next witness, Norman Reyes. He had come to the United States in 1947 with his mother, brother, and sister to study at Vanderbilt University, where he majored in English and worked at a local radio station as an announcer. The tall, slender Reyes was still as handsome as in the days when the typists at Radio Tokyo had been all aflutter over him.

Reyes began his testimony by telling what happened after he and Ince had been captured at Corregidor. At Santiago prison in Manila he had seen two of his friends killed by Japanese army men. He also told in a quiet voice about being given the choice of going to Tokyo or losing his head.

Cousens and Ince had dropped out of "Zero Hour" in the midst of the war, but Reyes had been with Iva on the program from her first broadcast until the end of the war. He said that after Cousens left the program, "I assumed full responsibility for her scripts."[6] He also said that occasionally the General Staff had given him news items which he was told to put into the broadcast scripts. "I inserted these," he said, "because she did not understand how to do it." But he made it clear that there had never been any sort of propaganda in any of Iva's broadcasts.

Reyes further testified that Iva had broadcast under duress, and that she had often expressed a desire to stop working at the station. "The talk I remember clearly was December 19, 1944, on my wife's birthday, at the house we were renting at [the] Meguro district," he said. "Iva and Filipe came. I feared many heavier raids to come to Tokyo and expressed the wish that my wife and I could move out, [and] also the wish that Iva could move out of Tokyo. . . . I also expressed the fact that this would naturally involve leaving the jobs at Radio Tokyo. Iva said to me that she would like to, but she was afraid to for fear of what the army would do to her."[7]

Both Cousens and Ince had been cross-examined by James Knapp, but when Reyes's turn came Tom DeWolfe took over again. He began with a rapid-fire series of questions: "You have told the truth?" "Do you understand the question?" "You have told nothing but the truth?" "Has everything you testified here been truthful?" "Everything, Norman, you are sure?" Then began a four-day cross-examination in which DeWolfe chipped away at Reyes's credibility bit by bit.

Before the trial began, Reyes had been subpoenaed by both the defense and the prosecution. He had been a witness at the grand jury and he had also given three lengthy statements to the FBI—one in Nashville in April 1948 and two in San Francisco at the time of the grand jury hearings. The government had been certain he would testify for the prosecution. But several days before the trial, on June 30, he met with the prosecutors at the San Francisco Federal Building and told them he would testify first as a witness for the defense. It is not hard to surmise DeWolfe's reaction to this news.

DeWolfe had been careful to address the other witnesses by their title and surname, "Mr. So-and-So," but from beginning to end he called Reyes "Norman," or simply "Reyes." Perhaps he was following southern custom. DeWolfe also kept coming back in his questioning to the fact that Reyes had a Filipino father, an American mother, and a Japanese American wife. He apparently wanted the jury to remember that Reyes was the product of a mixed marriage—a half-breed—and that he had made such a marriage himself. (The *Pacific Citizen* later commented on DeWolfe's tendency to show racial prejudice toward the nonwhite witnesses, and at no time was that tendency more apparent than in his cross-examination of Norman Reyes.)[8]

DeWolfe's main weapon was the three statements Reyes had earlier given to the FBI. He used them to the hilt to discredit Reyes's truthfulness as a witness. In one of his statements to the FBI, Reyes had said, "I can say that I know of no threats, duress or coercion that was exercised or directed to influence her either in control of her script or broadcasting activities. . . . I believe she joined Radio Tokyo because she was desirous of increasing her income and the idea of being a radio character was not repulsive to her. . . . I did not trust her, having gained the impression that she was pro-Japanese."[9] Yet when he had been under direct examination by Wayne Collins, Reyes had given a somewhat different evaluation of Iva. "I would have trusted her with my life," he had said. DeWolfe read both statements to the court in as loud and clear a voice as he could. "Which is the truth, Norman?" he asked.

Reyes remained surprisingly cool for two days as DeWolfe questioned him with almost sadistic glee. Finally on August 22 DeWolfe moved in for the kill. He tried to get Reyes to admit he had been lying in his statement to the FBI about broadcasting under duress. "Norman, you were never threatened with death or torture if you stopped work at Radio Tokyo, were you?"

"I was."

"Now we have this statement. 'I wish to state at this time that during my employment at Radio Tokyo I was never conscious of threats or death or torture if my radio activities stopped.' Then that statement was false, wasn't it?"

"Yes, sir."

"Then since you testified here this morning that everything you told the FBI was true, consequently that was a false statement, wasn't it?"

"Yes, without reading the statement."

"How many other lies have you told here, Reyes?"[10]

DeWolfe's tactics were clear. He was trying to suggest that if Reyes had lied once, he might have lied many other times too. And if he succeeded in creating the impression that Reyes had lied, then he could cast doubt on the testimony of Cousens and Ince as well.

Tetsujiro Nakamura, who had helped in the defense preparations, later recalled, "Reyes' statement to the FBI was a complete shock to Collins. I think if Collins had known that the government had in its hands a statement from Reyes that contradicted his testimony, he would never have put Reyes on the witness stand."[11] Apparently Reyes never explained to Collins what was in the statements he had given to the FBI. Reyes himself says he is still bothered about the damage his "naïveté" did to the defense case.

Reyes's testimony was not all detrimental, for in response to Collins's redirect examination he made clear what the FBI tactics were. He had given his statement to FBI agents in San Francisco after being grilled by them for four days. "The agents told me Ince and Cousens and the defendant aren't going to worry about you—you are in a highly questionable position," he testified. One of them had also told him, "If you want to go over to the other side, all right. I want you to know we had got a lot of stuff on you. I'll pass this on to my CIC friends in the Philippines and you won't like it a bit." Reyes said he had been extremely frightened. "I could see them building up overt acts and I thought if overt acts was all that was needed for a case of treason, I might be held as guilty as the defendant," he said.[12]

Every time Reyes answered a question the FBI agents would argue until his original words were altered into statements favorable to the prosecution. Some portions of his statement were suggested to him by the FBI agents themselves, he said, and others were made up because he could not remember exact times and dates. "Firstly, I was signing both of these things [the statements] to get rid of these people," he said. "I had had enough of it. I would sign anything to get out from under. Secondly, I was afraid. I was afraid of these two men, the atmosphere under which the questioning was conducted and of my own status."[13]

There can be little doubt that the FBI used Reyes's vulnerability to frighten him into giving a statement unfavorable to Iva. In their enthusiasm to build an airtight case against her, the FBI may have used the same type of "persuasion" on prosecution witnesses from Japan who were equally prosecutable. But Norman Reyes at least had had the courage to stand up and recant his statement publicly in court, even though it meant he might face charges of perjury. It was a brave act for a young man with his future ahead of him.

GIs for the Defense

The defense had assembled its own set of ex-GIs who claimed to have heard the "Orphan Ann" broadcasts in the Pacific. Some of them were former fans of "Ann" and had volunteered their services to the defense.

Orphan Ann had called them "boneheads," but all of them insisted they did not feel any malice or viciousness in the broadcasts. On the contrary, they had enjoyed listening to them.

Sam Stanley, a former baker in the Seabees who listened to her broadcasts nearly every day in the Admiralty Islands, said that the "Orphan Ann" program was so popular that the radio tent could not hold all the GIs who came to listen. Often there was a large crowd standing outside to hear the show, even when it was pouring rain. "The only thing I was concerned with was the music," he said. "I was hoping . . . like a lot of other people who hadn't heard her, that we would hear Tokyo Rose that was witty and smutty and entertaining and telling dirty stories, but we never heard any one of them."[14]

Robert Speed, an ex-marine lieutenant who had served on Saipan and Okinawa as an intelligence interpreter, testified he had started listening to Orphan Ann every night to learn about Japanese propaganda techniques. "I listened to 'Zero Hour' originally with this specific purpose in mind and did not find propaganda . . . so thereafter my chief purpose in listening to 'Zero Hour' was just entertainment."[15] He also testified that he had not heard of the naval intelligence circular mentioned earlier by the former boatswain's mate who testified for the prosecution.

A retired naval petty officer, James F. Whitten, testified that he had heard a broadcast similar to the one the former army lieutenant claimed to have heard on Saipan about the island being mined with high explosives, but that the broadcast had been about the island of Nonomea nine months before. "It [the warning] was commonly used in the Pacific,"[16] he said, but he had never heard anything like it on Radio Tokyo broadcasts.

Among the former GI witnesses who spoke for the defense, perhaps the most important was Kamini Kant Gupta, an American citizen of Indian (South Asian Indian, not American Indian) heritage, who had been a warrant officer in the judge advocate's office stationed in Alaska. Gupta testified that a confidential Alaskan command bulletin had been issued to staff officers stating in substance that the Orphan Ann broadcasts were a strong factor in building up troop morale in the Alaskan district. The main drift of all this testimony, of course, was to suggest that the Orphan Ann broadcasts, far from being malicious programs intended to demoralize the Allied troops, in fact bolstered morale, and that the American army had recognized that. The American navy had done the same thing when it issued its tongue-in-cheek citation to Tokyo Rose at the end of the war. Because of DeWolfe's repeated and heated objections, however, Gupta never gave this testimony in his own words, merely replying "That's right," when Collins inserted the statement in one of his questions.

DeWolfe's reaction to these GI witnesses is worth noting. Under cross-examination he questioned them not only about the "Zero Hour" broadcasts but also about their attitudes toward the government of the United States. It was clear that he intended to raise the question of why men who had fought for their country refused to cooperate with its law enforcement officers and instead supported the cause of a Japanese American woman indicted for treason against it. All of these witnesses, of course, had received visits from the FBI when their names appeared on the list of defense witnesses. Indeed, all the defense witnesses experienced government harassment in some way or other.

One other important defense witness was Ruth Yoneko Kanzaki (née Matsunaga), the young woman who had accompanied Iva and Chieko Ito on their walks during the early days of the war. In May 1944, when the Japanese government had decided to recruit students into war service, she had been assigned to work in the mornings as a war plant worker and in the afternoon as an English-language announcer on the "German Hour." The program was under the control of the German embassy, which paid her 200 yen per month.

As Ruth Kanzaki told her story in court, parallels between her role on the "German Hour" and Iva's on "Zero Hour" became obvious. She was a disc jockey and she often played the same records as those on "Zero Hour," the NHK record library being limited in its holdings. But in one respect her job was quite different. Scripts for the program were written by Reginald Hollingsworth, who had earlier made German propaganda broadcasts from Shanghai, and who may have been either an Englishman or a German named Wollbauer working under an alias. Consequently, her patter between records, far from being innocuous, was filled with propaganda.

When Ruth Kanzaki went to work on the "German Hour," it was

broadcast from around one thirty in the afternoon from Studio No. 4, just after the POW program "Humanity Calls." Before that, however, it had come on the air at five thirty, just before "Zero Hour," and the announcer had been a Miss Kramer, an Australian who later married Hollingsworth. Like "Zero Hour" it was beamed toward the South Pacific, so both Ruth Kanzaki and Miss Kramer were as strong Tokyo Rose candidates as Iva, and perhaps even stronger.

Manila Rose

Nineteen of the depositions that Theodore Tamba had taken in Tokyo were read in court. Since most were short, and since DeWolfe frequently rose to make objections to some portions, not much of what was in them reached the ears of the jury. Because the government had refused to let these witnesses come from Japan, the defense had no other way of getting their testimony at all.

The two most important pieces of testimony that emerged from the depositions were those of Ruth Hayakawa, who had worked as Iva's substitute on the Sunday version of "Zero Hour," and Lily Ghevenian, who had often typed Iva's scripts. Ruth Hayakawa said quite simply, "I have not heard her [Iva] broadcast anything detrimental to America."[17] Lily Ghevenian said she had never typed anything in Iva's scripts about unfaithful wives and sweethearts, the loss of American ships, or the movement of Allied troops.

The most interesting deposition, however, was made by Ken Murayama, a New York *nisei* who had been a Domei News Agency reporter during the war. Murayama did not know Iva directly, but while stationed at the Domei office in Manila he had been connected with the Japanese army-sponsored propaganda broadcasts there. He had written scripts for Myrtle Lipton, otherwise known as "Manila Rose."

Throughout the trial the defense had maintained that the so-called Tokyo Rose broadcasts were not the same as the "Orphan Ann" broadcasts, and that the "Tokyo Rose" broadcasts were other programs originating from Radio Tokyo, including the "German Hour," or from one of the many other Japanese army-controlled stations in Asia. When the American Division staff members had first heard of "Tokyo Rose" in the spring of 1944, for example, a number of them had wondered whether it might not be a broadcast from the South Pacific or Southeast Asia region. One such broadcast was Myrtle Lipton's.

Murayama testified in his deposition that the scripts he wrote for her "were designed to create a sense of homesickness among troops in the Southwest Pacific. Their tone was one of trying to make the soldiers recall certain good times they might have had when they were back in the United States. . . . We had stories of girls having dates with men at home, while possibly their sweethearts and husbands might be fighting in the Southwest Pacific area. . . . "[18] Such broadcasts were precisely the sort attributed to "Tokyo Rose."

Murayama also testified that Myrtle Lipton had a very sexy broadcasting voice, like a torch singer. "It was quite low-pitched, husky. The sort of voice that would carry well and was in keeping with the general tenor of the program itself."[19] Murayama's brief deposition went no further than suggesting that Myrtle Lipton's "Manila Rose" broadcasts were close in character to the "Tokyo Rose" broadcasts of rumor. It may be that they hold the key to the origins of the "Tokyo Rose" rumors.

When *Yank* magazine reporters went to interview the famous "Manila Rose" in the suburbs of liberated Manila in June 1945, they described her as being "about five feet four, an American mestiza (half-breed) with dark brown eyes, black hair, . . . the kind of complexion generally described as golden brown . . . [and] starlet's legs to go with all the rest of it."[20] Like nearly everyone who knew Myrtle Lipton, the *Yank* reporters found themselves much taken by her physical charms.

Myrtle Lipton had been born and raised in Manila. According to *Yank*, after briefly attending a girls' college, she had followed an American military unit to Shanghai, where she had spent a year "seeing the town," she said. In March 1944, she told the *Yank* reporters, she heard from a Japanese "friend" working at Radio Manila that the Japanese army was looking for a woman with an American accent to make propaganda broadcasts to the South Pacific. She visited the studio, auditioned, and got the job. Her new boss, a civilian Information Bureau employee named Omura, was apparently attracted as much by Myrtle's good looks as by her voice.[21]

According to the deposition of Kazumaro Uno, Myrtle's program,

"Melody Lane," was broadcast between 5:30 and 6:00 P.M. (Manila time) on two bands to the New Guinea area. The structure of the program was much like the Orphan Ann portions of "Zero Hour." Myrtle played seven or eight records, all pre-1941, and introduced them with a little easy patter. According to Uno, Omura apparently told Myrtle "to listen to Tokyo Rose and model her program accordingly" since, he said, Tokyo Rose's technique "so appealed to the Americans." By Tokyo Rose, Omura seems to have been referring to a program that was broadcast from Radio Tokyo, although whether it was "Zero Hour" or the "German Hour" or something else is not at all clear.

Buddy Uno, who had been transferred from Bunka Camp to Manila, also began to write "Melody Lane" scripts. When Theodore Tamba took his deposition, Uno became quite animated as he talked about Myrtle. "I thought her program was wonderful," Uno said. "It carried a punch; it was sexy; she had everything in it. She had her heart and soul in the program. She had a perfect flow of English language, which would appeal to soldiers. . . . She painted horrible pictures of jungles, dropping bombs, and foxholes. Then she described the 'good old days' back home, saying things like 'what a pity fellows have to die in the jungle without even knowing what you are fighting for.' But she put it over in a language that was good to listen to."[22]

Her records were also different from those played on "Zero Hour." "The 'Zero Hour' program usually was either 'hot,' lively, and on Sundays they reverted to playing classical music," said Uno. "Down in Manila, however, the idea was to make the boys recall the 'good old days'— make them homesick, so the music they played was not only popular, fast music but also slow music, but seldom classical, even on Sundays."

From the time of the battle of Leyte Gulf at the end of October 1944, Uno stated, Myrtle Lipton stopped doing a solo broadcast and became part of an hour-long broadcast that included news reports and other segments as well. She was still a disc jockey, ad-libbing most of the patter between records. It was about this time, said Uno that Myrtle played the "Notre Dame Fight Song." The General Staff in Tokyo complained that this was not likely to demoralize the GIs; Omura, who had to take responsibility for the gaffe, was sent off to Java and Buddy Uno took his place.

There is no question that under the direction of Uno, who had often watched and heard "Zero Hour," the "Manila Rose" broadcasts came to resemble "Zero Hour" in style. But unlike Cousens, who had done his best to maintain "Zero Hour" as pure entertainment, Uno had no reason to hesitate writing propaganda into Lipton's scripts.

In 1945 Myrtle told the *Yank* reporters, "I'm not pro-Jap. I'm not pro-American, either. I'm pro-Filipino."[23] Whatever her true loyalties, Myrtle did not have an easy time of it. Other Filipinos ostracized her because she worked for the Japanese, and the Japanese did not trust her because she was an American mixed blood. She thought about quitting her job several times, but she said that the Japanese had reminded her that that was a good way to lose her neck. According to the deposition, she began to drink heavily.

"Sometimes she would come to the station at the last minute pretty well under the weather," recalled Uno. "She would say, 'I can take care of myself, and Ken . . . would hand her the script and she would squat down by the mike and give off pretty much like a professional announcer, and all of a sudden she would lose control of herself and all of a sudden she was reading something that was plain imagination, but it did not worry me because anything she did was very effective."[24]

Uno's deposition gave the most complete description of Myrtle Lipton's activities, but Collins did not use it in court because in the cross-examination section the government attorney pointed out that Uno had mixed up Iva's broadcasts and Myrtle Lipton's in his statement to FBI agent Tillman. It is unfortunate that the defense did not go deeply into the "Manila Rose" broadcasts, since Myrtle Lipton was the strongest candidate for the title of "Tokyo Rose." There was also a strong possibility that her broadcasts were confused with Iva's.

The story of Myrtle Lipton does not end there, according to Nicholas Alaga, a San Francisco attorney who had gone to Manila in 1945 as an FBI representative along with Frederick Tillman, attached to Eighth Army G-2. His main job was to investigate Filipinos alleged to have collaborated with the Japanese. One day he got a call from a CIC officer who asked him to meet a woman suspected of treason.

"When I walked into the interrogation room," said Alaga recently, "there was a lovely young woman sitting surrounded by a CIC colonel, a

major, and a lieutenant. The interrogation seemed to have gotten along
pretty well, and everybody seemed to be having a good time. But when I
walked in the fun seemed to quiet down a bit. I felt as though I was in-
truding on something."

The colonel sat across the table, saying almost nothing. The lieutenant
was questioning the women, and the major was sitting on the desk taking
down her answers. The young woman, who turned out to be Myrtle
Lipton, was answering their questions calmly. She was beautiful,
thought Alaga, and seemed quite aware of that herself. After the interrogation had gone on a little longer, the lieutenant turned to Alaga and
said, "Nick, is there anything you want to ask?"

"Then I remembered the name Lipton had appeared on a list of Filipino collaborators that I had gotten, and I asked her two or three questions about her broadcasts. The questions really didn't amount to anything, but Lipton all of a sudden got tense and looked offended, and
started to stutter and cry."[25] Alaga was completely surprised. After
someone brought a glass of water, Myrtle calmed down, but when Alaga
asked her two or three more questions, she began to cry again. The colonel turned to Alaga ill-humoredly and said, "She's tired from being
questioned all day, so why don't we take this up some other time." Alaga
agreed and left.

Alaga heard nothing more from the CIC about Myrtle Lipton. About
six or eight weeks later he came across a file with her name on it in the
CIC record room. He discovered it contained an interrogation report
about twelve pages long. The date was the day he had sat in on the CIC
interrogation. Written on the reports were words to the effect that "FBI
liaison agent Nicholas Alaga agreed further investigation not required."
The Lipton case had been closed—with Alaga's unknowing approval.

FBI investigating agents operate under regulations that do not permit
them to give their own conclusions about a case. They are merely supposed to report the facts they uncover in an investigation. Alaga, astounded at seeing his name on Lipton's file, immediately sent off a report to FBI
Director J. Edgar Hoover, but he never got a reply. He says he has no
idea whether Hoover ever made a complaint to Eighth Army G-2.

Just what happened to Myrtle Lipton after that remains a mystery.
According to one rumor she died shortly thereafter; another rumor indi-

cated the story of her death was concocted to make sure she did not get arrested for treason, and that in fact she had married an American officer and gone to live in the United States. In response to a recent inquiry, the National Archives in Washington said there was no file on Myrtle Lipton in the records of the Eighth Army Counter-Intelligence Corps.

Her story is a very strange one indeed.

"The Truth Would Win, I Thought"

"Iva, take the stand, please," said Wayne Collins in a quiet voice on the forty-sixth day of the trial. It was 2:15 on the afternoon of September 7.

With her head slightly tilted to one side, Iva stood up. She walked to the witness chair with a jerky, flat-footed stride and raised her right hand to be sworn in.

Judge Roche, who the day before had celebrated his fourteenth year on the bench, swiveled his chair around to stare with evident interest at the "notorious defendant." An American flag behind her, she was sitting slightly forward in the witness chair. In the first row of the spectators' benches sat Jun with his head bowed, June looking slightly away, and Filipe with his eyes directly on his wife.

"I thought about it this way," Iva said recently. "If I got on the witness stand and told only the truth, then the truth would win, I thought. My family was very worried when I took the witness stand. But I wasn't all that worried. I did not feel the least bit as though I had betrayed America. If I had felt that way, I wouldn't have stood up in court. I would have run away to Lisbon. I had the chance to do so."[26] Shortly before she had been rearrested in 1948, the Portuguese consul had urged Iva to escape to Portugal, and had even arranged a ticket by way of Macao. If the American government was putting that much effort into the case, he thought, the prospects that Iva would win were slim indeed. But Iva had turned down his offer. She never doubted that if she told the truth in a free court, people would understand what she had done and why.

Jun, however, was deeply worried whether his daughter's true feeling would get through to the jury members. He thought the outcome depended on how well the jury understood Iva's position in Japan during

Taking an oath at the trial

the war. As it turned out, Iva had little chance to explain it. Whenever Collins tried to get Iva to do so, the government attorneys leaped up with objections. Judge Roche, apparently feeling that the background of the case was irrelevant, sustained them, so Iva's experiences with the *kempeitai* and the secret police, the condition of the prisoners at Bunka Camp, her efforts to smuggle in food and other supplies to the POWs— all these mitigating circumstances were not fully explored in her testimony. Neither were the circumstances surrounding her year-long incarceration at Sugamo Prison.

If the pale and haggard-looking Iva was nervous, it did not show in her voice. Loudly and clearly she identified herself as Iva Ikuko Toguri d'Aquino, and gave her address in Tokyo. The courtroom listened carefully to the famous voice so much discussed during the preceding weeks, the voice that the prosecution had claimed was "soft and appealing" and that the defense had insisted was "like a hacksaw." Every newspaper had a different word to describe it in their reports of the day. For the San Francisco *Chronicle* it was "a hard voice, slightly accented"; for the *Pacific Citizen* it was "harsh" and "jerky." No one called it "soft and appealing." Many spectators, including some reporters, doubted Iva's was the voice of Tokyo Rose, who had lured and charmed the GIs, and many were quite disappointed to hear what it sounded like.

The court had already listened to pieces of Iva's story, time and again, from other witnesses. Now she was telling it herself from the beginning. She talked about her family, her schooling, her life growing up. When, smiling slightly, she mentioned that her mother spoke English with a broken accent, her sister June wept softly and her father Jun wiped at his nose with his handkerchief.

Iva continued her story eagerly that day and the next, her words bubbling out almost as if she could not control them, even before Collins finished his questions. She told of her departure for Japan, of how she had tried in vain to return to the United States, of her shock at the news of Pearl Harbor, of how she had been harassed by the *kempeitai* and the secret police, of how she had tried to get on the repatriation ships, and of her whole experience in Japan until the time she had gone to work as an announcer at NHK.

But on the third day Iva faltered. She seemed a different person. Even her voice had changed. No longer firm and emphatic, it fell to a bare whisper, then lapsed into a stammer. She gripped a handkerchief in her hand, from time to time twisting it nervously. Obviously trying to control her emotions, she frequently dabbed at her eyes to push back tears. Observers wondered what had come over her since she had left the court the day before. Was the fatigue of the long trial beginning to weigh on her? Was she apprehensive about the approaching cross-examination? Was it because Collins had stopped leading her along chronologically but had begun to hop, skip, and jump about with his questions, as if trying to cram everything into them?

Collins's questions had reached a critical issue: whether Iva had broadcast under duress. He asked if she ever had fears about what would happen to her if she quit "Zero Hour." Yes, answered Iva, she had. About September 1944, she testified, Seizo Hyuga had come to "get a verbal statement from me stating that I would cooperate with the army. He said he had gotten the verbal agreement from Mieko Furuya and Ken Oki and the rest of the members of 'Zero Hour.' He said he was acting on orders from Major Tsuneishi. . . . He said I was the last one he needed to get an oral agreement from."[27]

Hyuga told her he wanted a direct answer. " . . . I told him to tell Major Tsuneishi that he could never get an oral agreement from me. I told him I would quit that day and suffer the consequences." Hyuga advised her, "It could be easier for you [if you made the verbal agreement] because things are going to tighten up."

"I told him I was only on the 'Zero Hour' for one purpose," testified Iva. "I told [him] I was going to stick by the POWs until the house collapsed."

Iva got no further. Was she perhaps remembering how trapped she felt at the time? Or could she not bear the irony of sitting in the witness chair accused as a traitor even though she had worked so hard to help the POWs? Tears began to well up in her eyes. After hesitating silently for a moment or two, she bit her lip, looked up, and continued.

"He said, 'What do you want me to tell Tsuneishi,' and I told him to 'tell him what you like to tell him. Tell him that I would quit today.' And Mr. Hyuga said, 'Well, I can't tell him that.' " Afterward Hyuga managed to smooth things over so Iva was not disciplined for her refusal.

Iva continued her testimony, telling how she had tried her best to avoid cooperating with the Japanese army in any way throughout the war. Despite being requested to do so several times, she had never bought any Japanese war bonds; she had refused to give to the Japanese Red Cross; she contributed nothing when the government started a drive to collect old clothing, precious metals, and jewelry. Instead, she had bartered some of her old clothes for food to give to the POWs. Using the excuse that she did not understand Japanese, she had also not taken part in air raid drills.

Collins then read one by one the statements that the ex-GI prosecution witnesses claimed to have heard on the Orphan Ann broadcasts. Answering with "No" or "Never" in a strong voice, she denied emphatically having said any of them on her broadcasts. She also insisted she had never made any broadcasts at all about Imperial headquarters announcements, about philandering wives and sweethearts, about 4-Fs, about the names of individual islands, about dancing in the moonlight, or anything similar. Her voice was strong once again, easy to hear even in the corner of the courtroom. When Collins then read off the broadcasts alleged in the eight overt acts named in the indictment, she answered again with the same strong voice. She was especially firm in denying Overt Acts V and VI.[28]

"Mrs. d'Aquino, did you from March 1 of 1943 to August 15 of 1945 or at any time whatever adhere to our enemies, the Imperial Japanese Government?"

"Never."

"Did you at any time whatever intend to give such adherence?"

"Never."

"Did you at any time whatever give any aid to the enemies of the United States or to any of those enemies?"

"Never."

"Did you at any time intend to give any aid to those enemies of the United States or to any of those enemies?"

"Never."

"Did you . . . at any time whatever give any comfort to those enemies of the United States?"

"Never."

"Did you . . . do anything whatever with intent to undermine or lower American or Allied military morale?"

"Never."

"Did you . . . do anything with intent to create nostalgia in the minds of the American or Allied armed forces?"

"Never."

"Did you do any act whatsoever with the intention of betraying the United States?"

"Never."

"Did you at any time whatsoever commit treason against the United States?"

"Never."

At the end Iva's voice was quivering with emotion. The four days of direct examination were at an end. Collins, with his head slightly bowed, turned and said to prosecutor Tom DeWolfe, "Your witness." The cross-examination was now to begin. It was to last four days.

DeWolfe began by raising the problem of Iva's citizenship. "Now, Mrs. d'Aquino, when you were young you were registered as a Japanese national?" "You told the people on Radio Tokyo you were an American citizen, didn't you?" "After a marriage you told your friend Chieko Ito you were still an American citizen?" "You told the Japanese police you would not change your citizenship, that you couldn't change it with a little piece of paper?" "And since your marriage you represented yourself as a Portuguese citizen?" "But in 1947 you said you were not a Portuguese citizen?" "You did not state in 1947 that you were not a Portuguese citizen, did you?" "Are my questions too difficult for you? How much schooling have you had?"

Skillfully he had led her toward a contradiction. On May 26, 1947, when Iva had applied for repatriation to the United States she had signed an affidavit that she had not become a Portuguese citizen. On May 4, 1949, just before the trial, she had filed a petition for release stating that she was a Portuguese national. "When you wanted to come back to the United States you swore you were not a Portuguese citizen," said DeWolfe. "When you signed an affidavit for release here, you said you were. Which is true?"

Iva, in contrast to Norman Reyes, did not fall into the trap DeWolfe laid for her. She answered simply—and honestly. "I do not know myself. From the legal standpoint of law I do not." She had been confused and she admitted it. "They are both true at the time. They were both signed at separate times. I had no legal counsel when I signed at the United States consulate. . . . I later found out by virtue of registration I had become a naturalized citizen. I did not know [that] at the time I signed the application for a United States passport."[29] The first round was a stalemate.

A key point in Iva's defense had been that she acted under threat and duress, so DeWolfe moved on to that. "You were not forced by physical force, Mrs. d'Aquino, to go on the air and broadcast, were you?" Not forced, replied Iva, just fearful. "And you were never jailed by the Japanese police authorities?" No. "And, of course, you were never personally assaulted or beaten or whipped or suffered any physical as contradistinguished from mental torture, were you?" No, said Iva, there had never been any physical force.

DeWolfe had made his point. Whatever sense of threat or fear Iva may have felt, whatever psychological duress she may have experienced, was beside the point. Duress, coercion, and threat were physical acts as far as the prosecution was concerned, and DeWolfe had gotten Iva to admit she had been only under mental pressure. It was an honest admission, but damaging to Iva's case.

DeWolfe moved on to the "confession," Lee's typed interview notes, which DeWolfe himself had said the year before would not stand up as evidence in court. Were the notes correct? he asked. Iva denied that the statement was an accurate reflection of what she had said at the time. ". . . Some of the things that were in that statement," she said, "[were] descriptions of things that Mr. Clark Lee phrased himself."[30] But DeWolfe kept pressing the point, trying to get Iva to admit that the notes were a "confession" and that she had signed them in the presence of Brundidge and Hogan a year and a half before. Iva stuck to her guns.

As the cross-examination went into its second day Iva's fatigued eyes revealed the strain of five days on the witness stand and her lack of sleep. The crowd of spectators had grown. Every seat in the courtroom was filled, and there was a long line in the corridor outside waiting to see DeWolfe break Iva on the witness stand. Iva was willing to answer

"Yes" or "No" to his questions, but she wanted always to qualify or explain. DeWolfe would not let her. Iva, increasingly irritated, began to give snappish answers instead of slow, careful ones. But she held to her story as DeWolfe kept running her over it again and again, trying to trip her into contradictions, wearing away at her nerves and her strength. The courtroom was warm from a mid-September heat wave, and reporters noticed that even Judge Roche, who was tired himself from the long weeks of the trial, was beginning to nod at his seat on the bench.

Iva bore up under DeWolfe's skillful and sarcastic grilling with grit, never tearful, determined not to lose her nerve. She made no concessions, no admissions of guilt, and kept insisting on her innocence under DeWolfe's browbeating. She admitted that she thought the voice on the six government recordings was her own, but she denied once again that she had made any of the broadcasts alleged in the eight overt acts or any of the statements the former GIs alleged they had heard on the Orphan Ann broadcasts. Finally, on the morning of September 15, DeWolfe brought it to an end.

The rest of Iva's testimony came with a final redirect examination by Collins, who turned once more to the question of Iva's citizenship. He had tried to quash the indictment by insisting Iva was a Portuguese national, but he knew how Iva really felt. "Mrs. d'Aquino," he asked quietly, "do you still want to be a citizen of the United States?"

Iva took a deep breath. "Yes," she said, stumbling slightly, "I always—that is why I made those applications to find out whether I could claim United States citizenship." She continued, "But unfortunately I still don't know what my citizenship status is."[31]

Then, after seven days of testimony, she stepped down from the stand, returned weakly to her seat at the defendant's table, and sat with her head in her hands. She closed her eyes and pressed her fingers into her temples.

The Jury Decides

On September 19, during the twelfth week of the trial, the testimony finally ended. The prosecution had called fifty witnesses to the stand and the defense forty-five, among them nineteen deposition witnesses who were not present in court and whose statements had to be read by Iva's lawyers. Nearly one million words of testimony had been given. The cost of the trial to the government had climbed beyond the $500,000 originally anticipated. On September 20 the final arguments for both sides began.

U.S. Attorney Frank J. Hennessey, the chief prosecutor, led off with a two-hour presentation in which he emphatically insisted that Iva was indeed an American citizen recognized as such by the United States government, and that the government would not concede that she had broadcast under duress or that she and the POWs had attempted to sabotage the enemy's propaganda broadcasts.

In the course of his statement, however, he made the following remarkable comment: "I don't think the element of who is Tokyo Rose is of any importance in this case. Apparently it was simply a name given facetiously by the GIs [to] some woman announcer of Radio Tokyo." He continued, "We are more concerned in this case with 'Orphan Annie' than Tokyo Rose . . . . Mrs. d'Aquino was the only person who used the name Orphan Ann." If Hennessey had made such a statement at the beginning of the trial it would have made sense, but at this point it was pure sophistry.

The government knew better than anyone else that this was the "trial of Tokyo Rose." "Orphan Ann" and "Iva Toguri" were obscure names and no one would care if neither came to trial, but the government had been pushed to making an indictment because the defendant was the infamous "Tokyo Rose." Otherwise the government would not have been able to spend the taxpayers' money. At the beginning the government labored long and hard to prove that Iva admitted to being "Tokyo Rose"; it had attempted to attribute remarks made on the "Tokyo Rose" broadcasts to Iva; and it had brought before the court a whole string of witnesses who testified to having heard "Tokyo Rose" broadcasts. From beginning to end, the government kept bringing up the name "Tokyo Rose" over and over again. The reporters who covered the trial from beginning to end had called it the "Tokyo Rose trial" in their stories, the headlines had shouted the name "TOKYO ROSE" as the trial wore on. But since the defense had made clear, perhaps too clear, that Iva was not the only candidate for the title of "Tokyo Rose," the prosecution had changed its story, insisting the trial had nothing to do with Tokyo Rose and that it was concerned only with Orphan Ann. If that was not sophistry, what was it?

During the next two days George Olshausen presented a six-hour defense summation in a quiet, almost scholarly fashion. The government, he argued, had put forth three main assertions to establish treason in the case: Iva was a citizen of the United States; she committed one or more overt acts of treason by rendering aid and comfort to the enemy; and in the commission of these acts there was intent to betray the United States. "The government's case will not hold water," he said, "if there is reasonable doubt on any one of these three points."

Olshausen quoted from the trial transcripts, pointing out contradictions in the testimony of prosecution witnesses and singling out for special attention Oki and Mitsushio, who had testified to witnessing the eight overt acts. He also noted the frailty of the testimony given by former GIs for the prosecution. "They don't remember clearly in their own minds what they heard by radio and what they heard by rumor." The only reason the government had needed their testimony was that it had no material evidence, scripts or recordings, that Iva had said anything treasonable.

"This really isn't a treason trial at all," he said in conclusion. "It's a story of intrigue like the kind you see in the movies but hardly ever in real life." Iva was not the villainess but the heroine. "In effect, she had really been working behind the enemy lines." He flashed a brief look at Iva, then turned back toward the jury. "I think she served the United States very well, and all she got for her trouble was a year in jail. The least—and the most—we can do at this time is to acquit her."

Iva had watched with fascination while the gangling Olshausen made his summation, but she nervously lowered her eyes and picked up her pencil again when DeWolfe rose to make his final statement. In contrast to Olshausen, who was cool, dry, and scholarly in his presentation, DeWolfe was tough, emotional, and histrionic, carefully choosing his words and cadences. Perhaps he was making another "Fourth of July" speech.

DeWolfe pulled no punches. He called Iva "a smart plumber and clever," "a woman quite ambitious to better herself, even though it be by working for the land of the enemy," "a betrayer of her native land and a betrayer of her government in time of need," "a female Nipponese turn-coat and a female Benedict Arnold." With heavy sarcasm he attacked the defense contention that Iva's motive had been to help the POWs. "The defendant says she was one of our little soldiers—our little Nell—working behind the enemy lines," he said. "This is, to the government, a very odious comparison, when you think of our young men and women who were risking their lives fighting the government which paid her, the woman they knew as Tokyo Rose." The trial, he said, "should serve as a warning to others" that "they cannot in an hour of great peril . . . adhere to the enemy with impunity," a message with considerable political meaning in 1949.

On September 26 Judge Roche gave his final instructions to the jury. He began by saying that the jury had to decide whether Iva had been a citizen during the period specified in the indictment. Under American law citizenship in more than one nation at the same time was not recognized, he said, and a citizen of the United States owes allegiance to the United States "until, by an open and distinct act, he renounces it, forswears it, and becomes the citizen or subject of another government." Hence, despite her marriage to a Portuguese national, unless the jury found that Iva did in fact renounce and abandon her citizenship, they should regard her as owing allegiance to the United States.

If the jury found that Iva was an American citizen, continued Roche, then they had to consider a second problem—whether she had adhered to the enemies of the United States with the intent to give aid and comfort to the enemies of the United States. "The element of intent," he said, "is an essential element of every crime." He told the jury that "intent and motive should never be confused." He gave an example:

> Let me illustrate. I belong to a benevolent society—one that feeds the poor. The organization is badly in need of an automobile to make deliveries of food. This circumstance moves me, induces me to steal an automobile from my neighbor. My motive is a laudable one, but my intent is an entirely different matter. I intend to steal, commit larceny, and it is no defense at all to a charge of larceny that my motive was praiseworthy.

By implication, it was no excuse if Iva had made treasonous broadcasts simply to aid the POWs.

He then went on to explain another key point. "Adherence to the enemy may consist in nothing more than a disloyal state of mind and heart—an intent to betray one's country," he said. "But adherence to the enemy in thought, in intellectual or emotional sympathy, without more, does not constitute the crime of treason. The crime is not complete unless one or more acts—overt acts of treason—be committed." For that reason Roche said that while the jury should give full consideration to the testimony of the ex-GI witnesses, the statements given to the FBI, and other evidence, they should pay special attention to the testimony of Oki and Mitsushio, who alleged they had seen Iva commit the overt acts.

He added that actions giving aid and comfort to the enemy were distinct from the effects of these actions. "It is not necessary that one single soldier, sailor, or marine be affected in any manner whatsoever by enemy propaganda or by anything said or done by the defendant" to establish treason. It was "immaterial that the enemy mission as a whole, which the defendant assisted, if she did assist, did not achieve its purpose." In other words, it made no difference whether the GIs had enjoyed Iva's broadcasts or whether they had been made homesick by them. The effect of the broadcasts was not at issue.

Roche's longest and most detailed instruction dealt with the problem of duress or coercion: "In order to excuse a criminal act on the ground of coercion, compulsion, or necessity, one must have acted under the apprehension of immediate and impending death or serious and immediate bodily harm. Fear of injury to one's property or of remote bodily harm do not excuse an offense. That one committed a crime merely because he or she is ordered to do so by some superior authority in itself is no defense, for there is nothing in the mere relationship of the parties that justifies or excuses obedience to such commands. . . . The fact that the defendant may have been required to report to the Japanese police concerning her activities is not sufficient. Nor is it sufficient that she was under the surveillance of the *kempeitai*. If you find that she, in fact, was under such surveillance, it is not sufficient that the defendant thought that she might be sent to a concentration or internment camp or that she might be deprived of her food ration card. Neither is it sufficient that threats were made to other persons and that she knew of such threats if you find, in fact, such threats were made to her knowledge."

When Judge Roche had ended, Iva sat slumped in her chair, looking as shocked as if she had been struck in the face. The judge's instructions had undercut all the key points of the defense: that she was a Portuguese citizen not an American, that she had helped the POWs sabotage the broadcasts, and most important of all that she had acted under coercion and threat. She sat motionless, her back hunched, her lips closed tightly, her fingers clenched. Herbert Cole, the court bailiff, walked over to tell her that reporters were waiting outside the courtroom to take some pictures. Iva started to rise from her chair, sat back, tried again, and shook her head at Cole.

Five minutes later she set her jaw and stood up. As Cole supported her elbow, she walked with jerky little strides out the courtroom door into a shower of popping flashbulbs, then went downstairs to wait for the verdict in the bailiff's office.

About one hundred spectators and many reporters were waiting, too, staring at the high courtroom ceiling, wandering in the corridors, or talking in low nervous voices on the marble steps of the stairwell.

At 2:41 in the afternoon John Mann, the short, gentle bookkeeper who had been chosen jury foreman, requested copies of the judge's instructions and the entire transcript of the trial. The instructions were handed over, but the jury was told it would not be able to get the transcripts unless it asked for the testimony of a specific witness. Every time the jury reassembled in the courtroom, Iva had to be present. Each time she appeared she seemed a little more depressed. Wayne Collins had told her that if the jury reached its verdict quickly, the chances were good she would be acquitted, but if they dragged on the prospects for Iva were not so good.

Time passed slowly. The majority of the spectators who stayed on had been regulars since the first day of the trial. Most of them thought Iva would be acquitted, and a few even said so. One woman walked up to Theodore Tamba and said, "How can she stand it? My heart goes out to her." [32] Another had a cup of hot coffee sent down to Iva in the bailiff's office where Herbert Cole sat playing cards with her, using paper clips for stakes.

As the sky grew dark, the halls inside the Federal Building grew dimmer and dimmer, with only a few lights turned on at the end of the corridors. At six-thirty the jury filed out for dinner. They sat chatting good-humoredly at the meal, evidently happy that the verdict was near and that soon they would be able to go home to their families. At eight o'clock they went back to work. Wayne Collins and the other two defense attorneys paced the hallways, growing more and more anxious as time wore on. At eleven o'clock the jury emerged once again into the courtroom. John Mann, the foreman, told Judge Roche that they were going to quit for the day. One of the spectators, a middle-aged black woman, said to no one in particular as she left the courtroom, "I'm going to pray for her tonight."[33]

At nine o'clock on the morning of September 27 the jury went into deliberation again. At 11:42 they asked for transcripts of testimony from Clark Lee, Kenkichi Oki, and George Mitsushio concerning Overt Acts V and VI, the alleged broadcasts made about the loss of American ships during the battle of Leyte Gulf. That was a clear sign the jury had satisfied themselves as to Iva's nationality—she was American, not Portuguese as her lawyers contended—and had now turned to the question of whether or not she had given aid and comfort to the enemy. Iva, who entered the courtroom unsteadily, sat staring without expression at the jury. Then the jury asked for Material Exhibit No. 15, the typed notes of Lee's interview, Iva's alleged "confession."

By that evening the jurors were beginning to show signs of fatigue. In contrast to the gaiety and cordial conversation at the dinner table the day before, they looked rather glum and sour as they ate their meal. The reason became clear after they went back into deliberation.

At 10:04 P.M. they filed into the courtroom again. John Mann stood up and said to the judge, "We cannot reach a unanimous verdict." Wayne Collins's eyes lit up for a moment—it was a hung jury, good news for the defense. Collins was about to request that the jury be released from duty. That would mean that the defense had won, for some of the prosecution team had indicated they would probably not take the case to court again if there were a hung jury.

But Judge Roche was not going to let the trial end so simply. "This is an important case," he told the jurors. "The trial has been long and expensive to both the prosecution and the defense. If you should fail to agree on a verdict, the case is left open and undecided. Like all cases it must be disposed of sometime. There appears no reason to believe that another trial would not be equally long and expensive to both sides. . . ." Any future jury, he continued, would be selected in the same fashion as they had, and there was no reason to believe that they would be any "more intelligent, more impartial, or more competent" to decide the case than the present jury, nor was there any reason to believe that either side could produce "more or clearer evidence." He told the jurors to sleep on it for a night and to try to reach a decision again on the following day.

The judge was telling the jurors how much money the trial was costing the taxpayers. Wayne Collins and the other defense lawyers were at a loss for words. The reporters silently looked at one another. At ten thirty the jurors left for their hotel.

On September 28 the jury put in another long day. At 5:25 P.M. they came out to ask for the depositions given by Ruth Hayakawa, Lily Ghevenian, and others. Judge Roche suggested they knock off deliberations and spend the evening relaxing at their hotel. Even though weariness was etched in their faces, a few jurors shook their head violently to show they did not want to do so. One asked that they be allowed to talk it over among themselves. Five minutes later they sent out a note to Judge Roche saying they would continue. By about 8:00 P.M. they had changed their minds, however. As they trooped off to their hotel, they said little to one another, all of them looking quite out of sorts. Anyone could see that the deliberations had reached another impasse.

On September 29 at 5:38 P.M., as yet another long day was nearing its end, the jury once again appeared in the courtroom. They asked for clarification of the phrase "related events" in a portion of Roche's instruction that went "Overt acts of an apparently incriminating nature, when judged in the light of *related events* [italics added], may turn out to be acts which were not of aid and comfort to the enemy." Roche gave them no direct reply. He simply cautioned the jury not to single out any portion of his instructions for special attention, but to give uniform attention to all the instructions. "It is time to go to dinner," he continued. "I have a desire to go to dinner, and I hope the jury has." He suggested that they stop working for the day. They did not.

At 6:04, half an hour later, the jury filed back in again. The courtroom had emptied of all but about forty diehards. Most of the reporters
were still sitting in the back row of the courtroom. By an informal vote
they had already decided the verdict for themselves—nine to one for acquittal, the only dissenter being Frances Ogara of the San Francisco *Examiner*. The reporters, like the other spectators, thought the jury had
simply come out to say that they would go to dinner.

Suddenly, and unexpectedly, Judge Roche asked, "Has the jury arrived at a verdict?"

"We have, Your Honor," replied John Mann. He handed the jury's
findings to the court clerk, James Welch, who immediately passed them
on to Judge Roche. Without a word Roche handed them back. In a voice
that reached every corner of the silent room, Welch read, "Guilty."

The Witch Hunt Ends

The announcement of the verdict was greeted by an audible gasp of
surprise from the spectators. Several women began to weep. "How could
they do it?" cried Mrs. McNamara, an alternate juror.[34] Iva's father, sister, and husband sat still in their chairs.

After seventy-eight hours and twenty minutes of deliberation, the jury
had reached the verdict that Iva was guilty of having committed Overt
Act VI, the broadcast allegedly made after the American victory at Leyte
Gulf: "Orphans of the Pacific, you are really orphans now. How will
you get home now that your ships are sunk."

Despite all the evidence of perjury at the grand jury hearing and all
the irregularities that surrounded the gathering of the prosecution's evidence, the jury still had decided Iva was guilty. They had not heard a
single recording to prove with certainty that she had made the broadcast
alleged in the indictment, so they must have believed Clark Lee's 1945
interview notes, the recollections of the GIs who could not distinguish
between what they heard on the radio and what they heard by the grape-
vine, and above all, the sometimes vague but always well-rehearsed testimony of Oki and Mitsushio. Iva's belief that "the truth will win" was
miserably shattered.

Judge Roche thanked the jury and announced he would pronounce
sentence a week later, on October 6.

Wayne Collins, surprised and shaken, said the verdict was "guilty without proof." He told reporters, "She [Iva] just can't believe it."

Tom DeWolfe, to no one's great surprise, pronounced satisfaction with the verdict. "The United States feels that the verdict was a just one and one which was rendered after patient and persevering deliberation," he said.[35]

Frank J. Hennessey announced the verdict meant that Iva, as a convicted traitor, would automatically lose her citizenship and become a legally stateless person. It was one of the neater ironies in the law of treason. The American government had accepted her as one of its own citizens in order to indict and convict her, and having succeeded in both, it was going to take her citizenship away.

With a weary face John Mann, the jury foreman, said that the jurors had agreed among themselves not to talk about how they arrived at their verdict, but when he heard that the reporters at the trial had voted nine to one for acquittal, he said, "You were not far from it." One reporter asked him, "Did you at any time consider her not guilty?" Replied Mann, "If it had been possible under the judge's instructions, we would have done it."[36] Judge Roche's instructions, he revealed, had had an important influence on the final decision.

According to later accounts, on the first ballot taken on the first day the jurors had voted ten to two to acquit Iva. All the jurors agreed that Iva had done much to help the POWs, that she had retained her citizenship, and that she had tried to return to the United States after war broke out. But in subsequent deliberations they had focused on the issue of intent: whether Iva had made her broadcasts with the intention of betraying the United States and whether she had the "intent of heart and mind" to betray. On this issue the jury was evenly split. A series of votes were taken, all of them six to six.

On the second day there was a shift in ballots in favor of conviction. At 10:00 P.M. that evening the vote was stuck at nine to three, and so the jury decided to report their inability to come to a unanimous verdict. They hoped there could be a retrial, only to hear from Judge Roche that he would not rule a hung jury and that the trial was costing the taxpayers a lot of money.

At the beginning the jurors had agreed to leave emotion out of their considerations, but as the hours dragged on emotions became more and more important. The two jurors who originally voted for conviction began to work on the others' feelings. How might it feel, they asked, to be off on a tiny island thousands of miles in the Pacific and hear a radio broadcast that your ships had been sunk? First one, then two more, of the six who had voted to acquit on Monday deserted camp, until only John Mann, the foreman; Flora Covell, a dentist's wife; and Earl Duckett, a San Francisco plasterer, were left.

The jurors were exhausted. The trial had been too long. They all wanted to get home as soon as they could. The supporters of a guilty verdict made no bones about using those feelings to put pressure on the three who were holding out for acquittal. Tempers rose, and an atmosphere of animosity began to infect the jury voting. John Mann later told reporter Katherine Pinkham that ultimately the resistance of the three jurors holding out for acquittal was broken by the growing, and very distressful, feeling that they were perhaps giving aid and comfort to a traitor.

As a last effort Mann decided to get clarification of instructions from the judge, hoping somehow to persuade the other jurors for acquittal. He was astounded at Roche's reply—or rather lack of one. With that, Mann and his two allies lost their resolve to hold out against the other nine jurors, and a few minutes after they returned to the jury room, all twelve had unanimously agreed on a verdict of guilty.

The verdict was a shock to a majority of the reporters who covered the trial from the beginning. They felt that Iva, who had tried so hard to maintain her citizenship throughout the war, was not a traitor but a patriot. When they heard that she was to become a stateless person as a result of her conviction, they were even more shocked.

On October 6 Judge Roche pronounced sentence—ten years imprisonment and a fine of $10,000. It was far harsher than most people had expected. Iva listened impassively. It was hard to imagine that at lunch that day she had wept uncontrollably, unable to touch her food. Her father stared at the floor as he listened to the sentence. John Mann, who had hardly been able to sleep since he had voted "guilty" the week before, was surprised at how severe it was.

After the sentencing was over, Wayne Collins made a statement for Iva. "Her own conscience is clear," he announced. "She is sorry because

With defense counsel Wayne M. Collins and reporters after the sentence on October 6, 1949

she wishes she could say the Government's witnesses' consciences were also clear." [37]

Wayne Collins himself announced that the judge's instructions had prejudiced the jury and that he intended to file an appeal right away. The Alameda *Times Standard,* a Bay area newspaper, agreed with him. A few days before, on October 1, it carried an editorial attacking the judge's prejudicial handling in the case. "The judge, speaking with the awesome dignity of the law behind him, did in effect bribe the jurors to arrive at a verdict which they would not, if left to their own devices, honestly have come to. . . . By pointing out to the jury that the trial had cost so much money he almost certainly made the jurors feel that they would let the government and the people of the country down if they did not reach a verdict." [38]

There seems little doubt that Roche had not been completely neutral in the case. Indeed there is evidence that he had a rather strong bias toward belief in Iva's guilt. Katherine Pinkham, who knew him quite well, remembers two occasions on which he expressed this bias. "Twice he made surprising, off-the-cuff comments to me," she recalled. "Once was between acts in a community theater lobby while the trial was still in progress. He spoke of his son's war service, of the trial, and then remarked he was surprised that neither his son nor his fellow servicemen friends who had been stationed in the Pacific seemed to hold any resentment against Tokyo Rose. They 'just laughed' about her. 'I can't understand it,' he said. The second comment came in his chambers some time after the trial. . . . He turned to me, dropped his voice to a confidential tone, and said, 'You know, I always thought there was something peculiar about that girl's going to Japan when she did. I always thought she might have been up to something.' " [39] Katherine Pinkham also says that Roche told her when he saw the former PT boat chief boatswain's mate take out the letter to his wife, he had become certain that Iva was guilty.

The reporters who covered the trial had criticism not only for the judge but for the defense lawyers as well. Some of them, especially the women reporters, said that it would have been better for the defense to make a more emotional assault on the jury. This was a trial in which the emotions of the jurors were critical. But from beginning to end Iva had never dropped her guard in front of the jurors. Instead of trying to sway their sympathies with histrionics, she remained composed. Her lawyers were also reluctant to use dramatic tactics to press home their case. They simply seemed to feel, as Iva did herself, that a just cause could not lose.

But from the beginning the odds were against the defense. As Stanton Delaplane says, the trial was "a kind of show piece for the American people."[40] At a time when popular feelings still ran strong against Japan and the Japanese, Iva, as the hated Tokyo Rose, probably would have been found guilty on whatever evidence the prosecution put forward. As the *Pacific Citizen* pointed out, Judge Roche's harsh sentence "was punishing a legend rather than the human being who stood in the dock of justice."[41] The trial had been the trial of Tokyo Rose, not of Iva Toguri, no matter what the prosecution had said. Had it not been for the legend, the trial might never have taken place at all.

To put the matter plainly, the Tokyo Rose trial was apparently a frame-up. The Justice Department, for its own political purposes, capitulated to a popular craving for revenge against the Japanese that had been blown into hysterical proportions by sensationalist journalists such as Walter Winchell and Harry Brundidge. Iva was the object of this frame-up because the unfortunate label of Tokyo Rose had stuck to her. She was a victim of lingering wartime sentiments and the victim of American racism.

She also suffered the tragedy of being a *nisei*. During the war these Americans who looked like Japanese were treated as foreigners by their own government, and those stranded in Japan met with equal suspicion from the Japanese, who distrusted them as aliens, perhaps even spies. Iva had clung tenaciously to the conviction that she was an American and that she would remain so forever, but she could not escape her status as *nisei*, carrying the burden of two homelands, both of which rejected her.

When pleading for a reduction of her sentence, Wayne Collins pointed out that if there was a guilty party it was the United States government. The State Department had not granted her a passport in 1941 and it had left her stranded on enemy territory. "It can be truly said that the United States government abandoned and betrayed her rights, but she did not abandon the United States."[42]

Epilogue

Iva boarded the train at Oakland on November 15. Her trip across the United States would take her to the Federal Reformatory for Women at Alderson, West Virginia. Her father and her sister June had come to see her off, but her husband had not. About a month before, Filipe's permission to remain in the country had expired and he had boarded a ship home for Japan. At Hawaii, for reasons that are not clear, an immigration official boarded the ship and had him sign a document affirming that he would never set foot on American soil again. The government's appetite had not been sated by putting Iva in prison; it destroyed her marriage, too. Iva and Filipe, both Catholics, remained husband and wife, but they never saw each other again.

Most of the Japanese prosecution witnesses went to New York, where they were to be witnesses in the treason trial of John David Provoo, a former POW at Bunka Camp. The government, hoping to save on expenses, had arranged to hold Provoo's trial before they returned to Japan. The trip was quite pleasant, an opportunity for sightseeing in New York. Ruth Hayakawa, who came to join the other witnesses against Provoo, later said that it was just like a high school excursion.

Provoo, who went in and out of mental hospitals several times, did not finally come to trial until three years later. In February 1953 he was found guilty of four overt acts of treason and sentenced to life imprisonment and a $10,000 fine. Provoo appealed, and in August 1954 a Federal Appeals Court overturned his conviction and sentence on the ground that the government had illegally tried him in New York instead of Maryland and that it had made wrongful insinuations before the jury about his sexual preferences. The government decided to try him a second time, but in February 1955 a federal judge ruled that Provoo could not have a fair trial at that late date and that he had been "denied the right of speedy trial within the meaning of the Sixth Amendment." Provoo, now a free man, told the press that he would like to sign up for another stint in the army and that he was going to see what he could do about clearing up his undesirable discharge.

Iva, whose rights under the Sixth Amendment had likewise been violated, still remained in prison in 1955. The several appeals she filed were all denied. The Ninth Circuit Court of Appeals, and later the Supreme Court, ruled that her original conviction had been proper.

At the time of the trial the newspapers had predicted Iva would be free on parole in three and a half years. In fact she had to wait until January 28, 1956, six years and two months after her term began.

The prison years had been quiet and had passed faster than Iva had expected. A model prisoner, she served as an assistant in the prison infirmary. She was sustained by the hope that Tokyo Rose would be forgotten by the time she got out and she would be able finally to go home to live quietly in Chicago and help her father run the now flourishing family store. Once again Iva was wrong.

Tokyo Rose had not died; she had merely gone into hibernation. As Iva prepared to leave prison, Tokyo Rose awoke and began to flaunt her dubious charm once again. Iva could not shake free of her.

On January 5, when the prison authorities announced that Iva was to be released later that month, the newspapers once again fell under the sway of Tokyo Rose's mysterious spell. It was not "Iva" or "Orphan Ann" who was getting out of jail, but the "wartime radio siren Tokyo Rose," clothed in Iva's form. Even the sobersided *New York Times* dredged up old clichés about her "seductive female voice."[1]

As the day for Iva's release approached, the press began laying the groundwork for coverage. The only telephone close to the prison was in a nearby farmhouse. A United Press reporter, surmising that Iva would be released early in the morning, rented one of the bedrooms. An International News Service reporter, arriving on the scene late, had to settle for the kitchen, where to his great delight he found the telephone. The next morning he did not let any of the other reporters use it.

The prison authorities picked the unusually early hour of 6:15 A.M. to release Iva, but their efforts, like those of the authorities at Sugamo nine years before, were to no avail. The inevitable crowd of reporters was standing outside waiting for her first comments. "All I ask is a 50–50 chance to get back on my feet,"[2] she said briskly, and then quickly climbed into a car with her family—Jun, brother Fred, and sister Inez—to set off for Chicago. The headlines read: "TOKYO ROSE QUITS JAIL: SHOWS NO REPENTANCE."[3] The Tokyo Rose witch hunt had not ended, it seemed.

On January 27, the day before Iva's release, the United States Immigration and Naturalization Service in Washington announced that since Iva had become a stateless person as a result of her conviction for treason, the government intended to deport her as an undesirable alien. The deportation notice was handed to her officially the next day when she walked out of prison. She had been freed only to find herself once more confronted with the problem of her citizenship.

The newspapers speculated that if deported, Iva would go to Japan to live with her husband. But after Iva had settled down at her father's house in Chicago the next day, she released a statement that she was going to fight deportation "every step of the way" in order to remain in the United States as an American. She had been convicted of treason because she was a citizen, and she would do her best to keep that citizenship. She was stubborn, and she was angry.

On March 13, 1956, the Chicago branch office of the Immigration Service issued a formal order for Iva to leave the country within thirty days or face deportation proceedings. In San Francisco Wayne Collins, with considerable justice, called the move "cruel and needless." "They know she is not legally subject to deportation," he said, "but they still insist in persecuting this harmless little typist."[4] He said he would use every possible means to fight the order. In April, Iva, who had been forbidden by the immigration authorities to travel more than fifty miles from

Chicago, received permission to travel to San Francisco to live in her attorney's house while she contested the deportation. The matter was not settled until two years later, when the government announced on July 10, 1958, it was canceling deportation proceedings. A recent Supreme Court decision had been interpreted to mean that Iva had not lost her citizenship before conviction, and hence was not deportable. This did not mean that Iva had her citizenship restored. She was still a stateless person.

The government's pursuit of Iva, or rather of Tokyo Rose, continued. In 1968, since Iva had not yet paid her fine, the government seized an insurance policy with a cash value of $4,745 that Jun had taken out for her. A demand for the rest came in 1971, and it was paid in 1972. The government's memory was long.

So was the public's. People still remembered "Tokyo Rose," the UCLA graduate who went to work for the wartime enemy Japanese and stabbed her country in the back. Iva could not escape her calamitous nickname. Whenever an article would appear somewhere about Tokyo Rose or the Tokyo Rose case, letters would start pouring in, filled with hate, calling her a "treacherous Jap" or accusing her for the wartime death of someone's son or brother or husband.

In her post-prison years Iva did not get much comfort from anyone, least of all the Japanese American community, who thought of the Tokyo Rose affair as a blot on the wartime achievements of the *nisei.* For the most part the attitude of the Japanese American community was hostile toward her. In February 1956, shortly after she was released from prison, *Newsweek* magazine carried a letter from one of its readers, Lincoln Yamamoto, which read in part: "I think it was prejudice and miscarriage of justice that Tokyo Rose . . . was convicted of treason. Was MacArthur guilty of treason for fighting for his country? Why then was Mrs. Iva d'Aquino guilty of treason for doing her duty to hers? It's our custom to consider ourselves citizens of Japan, regardless of where we were born, and our first allegiance is to Japan. We *nisei* are proud of Mrs. d'Aquino, and we're going to give her a heroine's welcome."[5]

Iva would have been the first to disagree with the letter, which was a bit off the mark in several ways, but more interesting is the passionate flood of response it provoked from other Japanese American Citizens

Leagues all over the country. The letter from Lincoln Yamamoto is "a blot on the name of the *nisei* Japanese American,"[6] said a letter from Cincinnati; the opinions of Lincoln Yamamoto "do not represent those of anyone other than Lincoln,"[7] said a letter from Sacramento; we have "operated on the principle that we are Americans and that our first and only loyalty is the United States of America,"[8] said the national director of the JACL in San Francisco.

But times change, and feelings change with them. At the beginning of 1974 the Japanese American Citizens League took a new interest in the trial of Iva d'Aquino. Some of its members had come to the conclusion that the trial had been unfair and that it had taken place in an atmosphere of public hysteria. The JACL sent a formal letter of apology to the Toguri family, which it had ignored and refused to help over the years, and the organization began a movement to right the wrong that had been done to Iva twenty-five years before.

What had happened to change their minds? Two things, probably. One was that the American people, after learning that their government on countless occasions from the U-2 incident to Watergate had lied to them as a matter of deliberate policy, no longer had the same simple and naïve trust in their government as in the immediate postwar years when the tides of national pride had run high. The other was that in the twenty-five years since the trial the Japanese American community had not only established itself in a confidently comfortable place in American society, but members of the third and fourth generation, like their peers in the black and the Mexican American community, were beginning to discover the history of injustice that had been inflicted on their grandparents and parents.

In 1975 Dr. Clifford I. Uyeda, a retired San Francisco pediatrician, organized a JACL committee to campaign for a presidential pardon for Iva. Petitions had been forwarded to Washington before, once to President Eisenhower in 1954 and once to President Johnson in 1968, but neither was answered. The new campaign, backed by the entire JACL national organization, was far more effective. Working in an atmosphere no longer clouded by postwar anti-Japanese sentiments, it managed to generate widespread support for the pardon effort. A number of prominent Japanese American politicians—Governor George Ariyoshi of Hawaii, Representative Spark Matsunaga of Hawaii, and senatorial candidate S. I. Hayakawa of California—endorsed the pardon movement. So did many non-Japanese American individuals and organizations, from the Washington *Star* to the Willard Anderson VFW Post 2471 in The Dalles, Oregon.

The campaign immediately attracted the attention of the press, susceptible as ever to the seductive charms of Tokyo Rose. But the headlines and stories had a different twist from those at the time of the trial. Nearly all the press notices called for forgiveness, not revenge. Indeed, the journalists seemed to be as busy proclaiming Iva's innocence as they had been two and a half decades before proclaiming her guilt.

In late March 1976, Ronald Yates, Far Eastern correspondent for the Chicago *Tribune,* published a story based on interviews with several key prosecution witnesses at the trial, including Kenkichi Oki and George Hideo Mitsushio, both businessmen comfortably living in Tokyo. The story made clear what Iva had known all along: the testimony the government used to establish the commission of the eight overt acts was perjured. The government should have known that this testimony was untrue, and indeed some persons connected with the prosecution may have had knowledge that the testimony was untrue. In any event it was the government that pressured the witnesses to give testimony harmful to Iva.

According to one of them: "We had no choice. U.S. Occupation police came and told me I had no choice but to testify against Iva, or else. Then, after I was flown to San Francisco for the trial along with the other government witnesses, we were told what to say and what not to say two hours every morning for a month before the trial started."[9] Other witnesses told of FBI harassment and threats if witnesses did not "do what we were told." "The postwar sentiment against Japanese and against Americans of Japanese descent was tremendous," said one. "We were told that if we didn't cooperate, Uncle Sam might arrange a trial for us too. All of us could see how easy it was for a mammoth country like the United States to crucify a Japanese American—all we had to do was to look at Iva." One of the key witnesses commented that Iva never made a treasonable broadcast in her life. "She got a raw deal—she was railroaded into jail."

Obliquely, of course, these former prosecution witnesses were as eager to provide excuses for their perjury as they were to protest the injustice to Iva. They gave the impression that they had had no choice under pressure from the FBI and the prosecution. But was that really the case? Frederick Tillman, now retired and living in California, recently scoffed at their revelations. "Do you believe somebody who said that he had told a lie nearly thirty years ago?"[10] He neither confirmed nor denied what they claimed.

Ruth Hayakawa, in commenting on the admissions of the prosecution witnesses, called them a cowardly evasion. She too had been a candidate for the title of Tokyo Rose, and had been under pressure to testify against Iva, but she had not done so. There was, of course, plenty of opportunity for prosecution witnesses like Oki and Mitsushio to refuse to give false testimony. Norman Reyes, for example, had been under heavy pressure from his FBI interrogators, but he had chosen to recount his FBI deposition even though it meant that he might be branded a liar in open court. He recently said the hurt he received at the time of the trial has still not healed. What is more, after the trial was over, one of his FBI interrogators came to visit him once for no apparent reason, probably for psychological harassment.

The American authorities, of course, used the vulnerability of some prosecution witnesses to "persuade" them to testify falsely against Iva. But it offends the ear to hear any admitted perjurer try to excuse himself on the grounds of FBI or other government pressure when his perjury sent a person to jail and ruined the rest of her life. If either of the key witnesses had been willing to stand up in court and tell the truth, Iva would have escaped a trial that railroaded her to prison.

In an interview with a Chicago *Tribune* reporter, one of Iva's former accusers said, "I've heard Iva is very bitter about our testimony. I understand her bitterness and I feel she has a right to feel that way. I just wish I had the opportunity to talk with Iva and tell her why we had to do it." One wonders how Iva, her life ruined by that testimony, might respond to that. Perhaps she might say, as she did recently, "My life has been very lonely. They robbed me of the most important part of it."[11]

"I can't really say that I am not bitter," she also said, "but I haven't been carrying on an active vendetta. You just can't live that way. You can either sit in a room and feel sorry for yourself or you can go outside and look ahead. I've tried to look ahead." She says she tries to forget the past and live with an eye to the future, trying to make a new life for herself while she forgets the old one. Indeed she looks to the future with a determination that seems hard to believe.

Still, it is possible to see scars the past has left on Iva. She has said herself that after the trial was over the only people that she trusted in the world were her father and her three defense lawyers; all but one are dead. Her father, Jun, whom she so loved and respected, died at the age of ninety in 1972, the same year that the Japanese government awarded him a medal for his service to the Japanese American community during the war, and for service as the first president of the Chicago Japanese American Association. Theodore Tamba died of a heart attack in 1973. Wayne M. Collins died suddenly a year later, in 1974, on an airplane between Honolulu and San Francisco returning home from a trip to Hong Kong. He was seventy-four years old. George Olshausen lives in Yugoslavia, where he has been for some years writing a history of economic slavery in the United States.

"I believe in what I did," said Iva recently. "I have no regrets, and I don't hate anyone for what happened."[12] Iva is a strong woman. But somewhere in her past she lost something, and even though she tries hard not to see it, there is a big empty space in her life. She was not really able to place her trust in other people, and that made her life a lonely one. After her release from prison she was no longer the happy-go-lucky person she had once been. What kept her going was the hope that someday she might regain her full rights as an American citizen, rights enjoyed by three other women who had been on the Radio Tokyo propaganda broadcasts—Mieko Furuya Oki, Katherine Morooka Reyes, and Ruth Hayakawa, all of whom obtained American citizenship in the 1950s.

The fastest way for Iva to regain her citizenship rights was through a presidential pardon. In November 1976, after the national election was over and the efforts of the JACL committee had succeeded in creating a favorable public mood, her lawyer, Wayne Collins, who had taken over his father's law practice and most famous client, forwarded a pardon petition to Washington. In contrast to earlier attempts at a pardon, the new

Talking with the author

petition had the support of a national political figure, Senator-elect S. I. Hayakawa, the controversial ex-president of San Francisco State University. Hayakawa had been one of the early supporters of the JACL campaign to right the wrong done to Iva. In March 1976 he had given support to the pardon movement in his newspaper column. On a visit to the White House in early December he discussed the case with President Ford. About a week later FBI agents were checking out character references on Iva, apparently with instructions to complete their investigation by mid-December. It seemed a hopeful sign. Perhaps the President was planning a special Christmas present for Iva.

Christmas came and went, and so did New Year's, without a pardon forthcoming. The optimism of the JACL committee members wavered. In early January Hayakawa paid another visit to the White House, where he talked with the President once again. But the suspense dragged on until the very end. On the morning of January 19, the day before he was to leave office, President Ford was saying goodbye to a group of leading Republicans, among them Hayakawa. He told Hayakawa that he had signed the pardon, and a few hours later the Department of Justice made an official announcement that Iva Toguri d'Aquino had been granted a full and unconditional pardon. She could reclaim her rights as a full citizen. "After all these years," she said, "it's hard for me to believe that the pardon is really true." But it was true, and the news was happy for her and her supporters. It even rekindled some of her old sparkle.

Yet now that the cheering is over, the word "pardon" does not go down well, especially in light of the evidence from official files of governmental abuse of power. The presidential pardon was a decent act, and a proper one, but it does not erase the stain of injustice. In a telephone conversation in the spring of 1976, former FBI agent Frederick G. Tillman remarked, "I am all for a pardon. She took her punishment. It's O.K. to pardon her now."[13] I wondered then, and I wonder still: Who should have asked for a pardon?

Notes

CHAPTER ONE: THE SEARCH FOR TOKYO ROSE

1. Nashville *Tennessean,* May 2, 1948.
2. Clark Lee, *One Last Look Around,* Duell, Sloan and Pearce, 1947, p. 4–5.
3. Ibid., p. 6.
4. Ibid., p. 9.
5. *Yank,* October 19, 1945.
6. *New York Times,* March 27, 1944.
7. *New York Times,* May 24, 1944.
8. San Francisco *Chronicle,* September 8, 1945.
9. *New York Times,* August 8, 1945.
10. Kenkichi Oki, testimony, July 18, 1949.
11. *New York Times,* September 1, 1945.
12. Nashville *Tennessean,* May 12, 1948.
13. Clark Lee, testimony, July 14, 1949.
14. Leslie Nakashima, deposition, September 1, 1949.
15. Ibid.
16. Clark Lee, testimony, July 14, 1949.
17. Los Angeles *Examiner,* September 1, 1945.
18. *New York Times,* August 8, 1945.

19. *Yank,* October 19, 1945.
20. Clark Lee, *One Last Look Around,* p. 110.
21. Ibid., p. 107.
22. Iva Toguri d'Aquino, interview, January 13, 1976.
23. Iva Toguri d'Aquino, testimony, September 9, 1949.
24. Clark Lee, *One Last Look Around,* p. 86.
25. *Yank,* October 19, 1949.
26. Ruth Hayakawa, interview, March 20, 1976.
27. Iva Toguri d'Aquino, testimony, September 9, 1949.
28. Nashville *Tennessean,* May 2, 1948.
29. *Yank,* October 19, 1949.
30. Filipe d'Aquino, testimony, September 6, 1949.
31. Iva Toguri d'Aquino, testimony, September 9, 1949.
32. Ibid.
33. Filipe d'Aquino, testimony, September 6, 1949.
34. Iva Toguri d'Aquino, testimony, September 9, 1949.
35. Los Angeles *Examiner,* September 14, 1945.
36. Filipe d'Aquino, testimony, September 6, 1949.
37. Los Angeles *Examiner,* September 14, 1945;
    New York Times, September 12, 1945.

CHAPTER TWO: FROM L.A. TO RADIO TOKYO

1. Iva Toguri d'Aquino, statement issued through attorney Wayne M. Collins, September 1948.
2. Ibid.
3. Dwight Ryerson, interview, March 22, 1976.
4. Joe Gorman, interview, March 21, 1976.
5. Iva's statement, September 1948.
6. Ibid.
7. Iva Toguri d'Aquino, letter to family, October 13, 1941.
8. Ibid.
9. Ibid.
10. Iva Toguri d'Aquino, testimony, September 7, 1949.
11. Iva's statement, September 1948.
12. Iva Toguri d'Aquino, testimony, September 7, 1949.
13. Ibid.
14. Ibid.
15. Chieko Ito, testimony, August 31, 1949.

16. Iva Toguri d'Aquino, testimony, September 7, 1949.

17. Ibid.

18. Iva's statement, September 1948.

CHAPTER THREE: "ZERO HOUR"

1. L. D. Meo, *Japan's Radio War on Australia,* Melbourne University Press, 1968, p. 43.

2. Iva Toguri d'Aquino, testimony, September 8, 1949.

3. Ibid.

4. Charles H. Cousens, testimony, August 15, 1949.

5. Norman Reyes, testimony, August 22, 1949.

6. Charles H. Cousens, testimony, August 15, 1949.

7. Akira Namikawa, unused deposition.

8. Peter de Mendelssohn, *Japan's Political Warfare,* George Allen and Unwin, 1944, p. 39.

9. Wallace Ince, testimony, August 18, 1949; Norman Reyes, testimony, August 22, 1949. Tsuneishi also mentioned the occasion in his testimony.

10. *New York Times,* June 29, 1943.

11. Charles H. Cousens, testimony, August 15, 1949.

12. Ibid.

13. Ibid.

14. Iva Toguri d'Aquino, testimony, September 8, 1949.

15. Ibid.

16. Charles H. Cousens, testimony, August 15, 1949.

17. Kazumaro Uno, unused deposition.

18. Charles H. Cousens, testimony, August 15, 1949.

19. Iva Toguri d'Aquino, testimony, September 8, 1949.

20. Charles H. Cousens, testimony, August 15, 1949.

21. Shigetsugu Tsuneishi, testimony, July 12, 1949.

22. Nicholas Schenck, deposition, August 25, 1949.

23. Iva Toguri d'Aquino, testimony, September 8, 1949.

24. Ibid.

25. Lars Pedersen Tillitse, testimony, September 2, 1949.

26. Ruth Hayakawa, deposition, August 24, 1949.

27. Iva Toguri d'Aquino, testimony, September 8, 1949.

CHAPTER FOUR:
THE TOKYO ROSE WITCH HUNT

1. Frederick G. Tillman, testimony, July 26, 1949.
2. Ibid.
3. Iva Toguri d'Aquino, testimony, September 9, 1949.
4. Frederick G. Tillman, testimony, July 26, 1949.
5. Iva Toguri d'Aquino, testimony, September 9, 1949.
6. Deputy Chief of Staff, memo, April 29, 1946.
7. Legal Section, memo, April 17, 1946.
8. San Francisco *Chronicle,* May 6, 1946.
9. Mark Gayn, *Japan Diary,* William Sloane, 1948, pp. 186–187.
10. Caudle memo to Clark, September 24, 1946.
11. *Common Ground,* September 1948.
12. Frederick G. Tillman, interview, April 20, 1976.
13. *Stars and Stripes,* November 11, 1947.
14. Meyer letter to Carter, November 13, 1947.
15. Carter letter to Clark, December 5, 1947.
16. Ibid.
17. Ibid.
18. Los Angeles *Herald Express,* January 8, 1948.
19. Nashville *Tennessean,* May 2, 1948.
20. Iva Toguri d'Aquino, interview, May 11, 1976.
21. Iva Toguri d'Aquino, testimony, September 12, 1949.
22. Ibid.
23. Iva Toguri d'Aquino memo to Wayne M. Collins during trial.
24. Iva Toguri d'Aquino letter to Winchell, April 14, 1948.
25. Winchell letter to Carroll, May 27, 1948.
26. *New York Times,* August 17, 1948.
27. Isaac Pacht letter to Clark, August 25, 1948.
28. Iva Toguri d'Aquino, interview, April 1, 1976.
29. San Francisco *Chronicle,* October 9, 1948.
30. John Gildersleeve, interview, April 1976.
31. DeWolfe letter to Campbell, November 12, 1948.
32. Wayne M. Collins, statement in support of appeal.
33. Wayne M. Collins, statement in support of presidential pardon petition, November 4, 1968.
34. Theodore Tamba, statement in support of presidential pardon, June 7, 1954.
35. *Argus,* August 26, 1946.

CHAPTER FIVE:

THE TRIAL OF TOKYO ROSE: THE PROSECUTION

1. San Francisco *Chronicle,* July 4, 1949.
2. San Francisco *Chronicle,* August 2, 1949.
3. Iva Toguri d'Aquino, testimony, September 9, 1949.
4. Shigetsugu Tsuneishi, testimony, July 11, 1949.
5. Ibid., July 12, 1949.
6. Ibid.
7. DeWolfe memo to Whearty, May 25, 1948.
8. Clark Lee, testimony, July 14, 1949.
9. Clark Lee, typed notes, September 1, 1945.
10. Stanton Delaplane, interview, February 7, 1976.
11. San Francisco *Chronicle,* July 15, 1949.
12. Wayne M. Collins, statement to judge, July 27, 1949.
13. Toshikatsu Kodaira, deposition, September 1, 1949.
14. Theodore Tamba, statement in support of presidential pardon, October 24, 1968.
15. Campbell memo to Clark, December 2, 1948.
16. Ibid., January 5, 1949.
17. Ibid., June 8, 1949.
18. Kenkichi Oki, testimony, July 18, 1949.
19. Ibid.
20. Ibid.
21. George Hideo Mitsushio, testimony, July 20, 1949.
22. Norman Reyes, testimony, August 19, 1949.
23. Iva Toguri d'Aquino, testimony, September 9, 1949.
24. Kenkichi Oki, testimony, July 18, 1949.
25. George Hideo Mitsushio, testimony, July 20, 1949.
26. Kenkichi Oki, testimony, July 18, 1949.
27. Iva Toguri d'Aquino, testimony, September 14, 1949.
28. Ibid.
29. Kenkichi Oki, testimony, July 18, 1949.
30. George Hideo Mitsushio, testimony, July 20, 1949.
31. Wayne M. Collins, cross-examination, July 19, 1949.
32. San Francisco *Chronicle,* July 22, 1949.
33. Shinjirō Igarashi, testimony, August 10, 1949.
34. Charles Hall, testimony, August 12, 1949.
35. Jules Sutter, Jr., testimony, August 2, 1949.

36. Ted Sherdeman, testimony, August 1, 1949.
37. Jules Sutter, Jr., testimony, August 2, 1949.
38. Jules Sutter, Jr., statement to FBI, September 1, 1949.
39. Marshall Hoot, testimony, August 2, 1949.
40. Ibid.
41. Ibid.
42. Ibid.
43. San Francisco *Examiner,* August 4, 1949.
44. Marshall Hoot, testimony, August 3, 1949.
45. Marshall Hoot, statement to FBI, March 9, 1949.
46. Pinkham statement in support of presidential pardon, not sent.
47. Shigetsugu Tsuneishi, testimony, July 12, 1949.
48. San Francisco *Chronicle,* August 2, 1949.
49. DeWolfe, July 5, 1949.

CHAPTER SIX:
THE TRIAL OF TOKYO ROSE: THE DEFENSE

1. Katherine Pinkham, interview, August 2, 1975.
2. Charles H. Cousens, testimony, August 15, 1949.
3. Ibid., August 16, 1949.
4. DeWolfe memo to Whearty, May 25, 1948.
5. Wallace E. Ince, testimony, August 18, 1949.
6. Norman Reyes, testimony, August 19, 1949.
7. Ibid.
8. *Pacific Citizen,* September 17, 1949.
9. Norman Reyes, statement to FBI, October 5, 1948.
10. Norman Reyes, testimony, August 22, 1949.
11. Tetsujiro Nakumura, interview, August 27, 1975.
12. Norman Reyes, testimony, August 23, 1949.
13. Ibid.
14. Sam Stanley, testimony, August 30, 1949.
15. Robert Speed, testimony, August 30, 1949.
16. James Whitten, testimony, August 29, 1949.
17. Ruth Hayakawa, deposition, August 24, 1949.
18. Tamotsu Murayama, deposition, September 6, 1949.
19. Ibid.
20. *Yank,* June 29, 1945.

21. Ibid.

22. Kazumaro Uno, deposition, not used.

23. *Yank,* June 29, 1945.

24. Kazumaro Uno, deposition, not used.

25. Nicholas Alaga, interview, January 15, 1977.

26. Iva Toguri d'Aquino, interview, May 20, 1976.

27. Iva Toguri d'Aquino, testimony, September 9, 1949.

28. Ibid., September 12, 1949; Iva Toguri d'Aquino, interview, May 20, 1976.

29. Iva Toguri d'Aquino, testimony, September 12, 1949.

30. Ibid.

31. Ibid., September 15, 1949.

32. San Francisco *Chronicle,* September 27, 1949.

33. Ibid.

34. Ibid., September 30, 1949.

35. Ibid.

36. Ibid.

37. Ibid., October 7, 1949.

38. Alameda *Times Standard,* October 1, 1949.

39. Katherine Pinkham, interview, February 12, 1976.

40. Stanton Delaplane, interview, February 7, 1976.

41. *Pacific Citizen,* October 8, 1949.

42. Collins, appeal for light sentence.

EPILOGUE

1. *New York Times,* January 8, 1956.

2. *New York Times,* January 29, 1956.

3. Ibid.

4. San Francisco *Chronicle,* March 14, 1956.

5. *Newsweek,* February 20, 1956.

6. Ibid., March 5, 1956.

7. Ibid.

8. Ibid.

9. Chicago *Tribune,* March 22, 1976.

10. Frederick G. Tillman, interview, April 20, 1976.

11. Iva Toguri d'Aquino, interview, May 20, 1976.

12. Ibid.

13. Frederick G. Tillman, interview, April 20, 1976.

Index